The First World War

SEMINAR STUDIES   IN HISTORY

The First World War

Second edition

STUART ROBSON

PEARSON
Longman

Harlow, England • London • New York • Boston • San Francisco • Toronto
Sydney • Tokyo • Singapore • Hong Kong • Seoul • Taipei • New Delhi
Cape Town • Madrid • Mexico City • Amsterdam • Munich • Paris • Milan

PEARSON EDUCATION LIMITED
Edinburgh Gate
Harlow CM20 2JE
United Kingdom
Tel: +44 (0)1279 623623
Fax: +44 (0)1279 431059
Website: www.pearsoned.co.uk

First edition published in Great Britain in 1998

© Pearson Education Limited 2007

The right of Stuart Robson to be identified as author of this work has been
asserted by him in accordance with the Copyright, Designs and Patents Act 1988.

ISBN: 978-1-4058-2471-2

British Library Cataloguing in Publication Data
A CIP catalogue record for this book can be obtained from the British Library

Library of Congress Cataloging in Publication Data
Robson, Stuart.
    The First World War / Stuart Robson. — 2nd ed.
        p. cm. — (Seminar studies in history)
    Includes bibliographical references and index.
    ISBN 978-1-4058-2471-2 (pbk.)
    1. World War, 1914–1918.   I. Title.

D521.R585 2007
940.3—dc22
                                    2006051548

10   9   8   7   6   5   4   3   2   1
10   09   08   07

Set by 35 in 10/12.5pt Sabon
Printed and Bound in Malaysia (CTP-VVP)

The Publisher's policy is to use paper manufactured from sustainable forests.

CONTENTS

Introduction to the Series   vii
List of Maps and Plates   viii
Acknowledgements   ix
Chronology   x

PART ONE: BACKGROUND   1

1. WAR KNOWN AND WAR IMAGINED   3
   The Civilian View of War   3
   The Professional View of War   5
   War Plans   6
   The Naval Race   9

PART TWO: LIMITED WAR, 1914–15   11

2. 1914: OOPS! THE PLANS FAIL   13
   The Battles of the Frontiers   13
   The British Expeditionary Force (BEF) up to Mons   15
   The End of the Schlieffen Plan   16
   The Marne   17
   First Ypres   19
   Eastern Front: Tannenberg to Lemberg   20

3. TAKING STOCK   23
   The Soldiers   23
   The Politicians   24
   Civilians and the Suspension of Partisan Politics   25
   War Aims   27

4. THE WAR IN 1915: BADLY PLANNED DISASTERS   29
   Russian Poland, Second Ypres   29
   The Trench System and the Code of the Front   30
   Neuve Chapelle, Champagne, Artois and Loos   34
   Gallipoli   37

5. THE HOME FRONTS   40
   Britain: DORA and Conscription   40
   Propaganda and Censorship   42
   War Economies   44
   Germany, War Aims and War Means: Submarines   45

PART THREE: TOTAL WAR   49

6. 1916: ATTRITION AND THE WELL-PLANNED DISASTERS   51
    Jutland   51
    Verdun   52
    The Somme   61

7. ORGANIZING FOR VICTORY   68
    Ludendorff Takes Charge in Germany   68
    Unlimited Submarine Warfare   69
    Offering Peace   69
    Lloyd George Knocks Out Peace   70
    The Russian Revolutions   71
    The Fall of Bethmann Hollweg: July 1917   72

8. TECHNOLOGY AND TACTICS   73
    A Technological Solution? The Air War and Tanks   73
    A Tactical Solution?   77

9. 1917: 'MERE UNSPEAKABLE SUFFERING'   79
    The Nivelle Offensive and the Mutiny: April to June, 1917   80
    Third Ypres (Passchendaele)   82

PART FOUR: 'GOING ON OR GOING UNDER'   89

10. THE BITTER END: 1918   91
    Ludendorff Rolls the Iron Dice in the West   91
    The Spring Offensive: Winning the Way to Defeat   93
    The Allies Counter-Attack   95
    The Collapse of Ludendorff   95

PART FIVE: ASSESSMENT   101

    Numbers   103
    So what?   103

PART SIX: DOCUMENTS   113

    Glossary   137
    Who's Who   141
    Primary Sources, Websites and Further Reading   147
    Index   163

INTRODUCTION TO THE SERIES

History is a narrative constructed by historians from traces left by the past. Historical enquiry is often driven by contemporary issues and, in consequence, historical narratives are constantly revisited and reshaped. *Seminar Studies in History* was designed to bridge the gap between current research and the broad, popular general surveys that often date rapidly.

The volumes in the series are written by historians who are not only familiar with the latest research in, and current debates about, their topic, but also have contributed to that research and the debates. The books are intended to provide the reader with a clear introduction to a major topic in history. They give a narrative and analysis of events and highlight contemporary controversies. They include the kinds of tools generally omitted from specialist monographs – chronologies and a glossary – as well as that essential tool, an up-to-date bibliography. They conclude with a selection of documents – some traces of the past illustrative of events described, which also serve as the historian's raw materials.

LIST OF MAPS AND PLATES

MAPS

1. German invasion of Belgium and France 1914: up to the Marne   15
2. Eastern Front   21
3. Western Front, 1915   35
4. Gallipoli   38
5. Verdun, 1916   55

PLATES

1. Postcard: 'Born to Command. With the shortage of qualified   26
   officers during the war, Emma's natural leadership abilities
   were finally recognised'
2. Famous cartoon by Bruce Bairnsfather: 'Well, if you knows   33
   of a better 'ole, go to it'
3. Women of the Land Army in Britain   43
4. Troops of the Canadian Machine Gun Company holding the   86
   line in shellholes near Passchendaele, November 1917
5. 'For What?' by Fred Varley   104

ACKNOWLEDGEMENTS

The Publishers would like to thank the following for permission to reproduce copyright material:

Plate 4 courtesy of the Library and Archives Canada, photo by William Rider-Rider/Department of National Defence collection/PA 002162; Plate 5 from the Beaverbrook Collection of War Art, © Canadian War Museum (CWM); Document 19 courtesy of Michael E. Hanlon of the Great Wear Society.

In some instances we have been unable to trace the owners of copyright material, and would appreciate any information that would enable us to do so.

CHRONOLOGY

Unless indicated otherwise, a place-name signifies a battle

1914
29 July: Austrians bombard Belgrade
3 August: Germany declares war on France, invades Belgium
7 August: Russians invade East Prussia
12 August: Austrians invade Serbia
14–25 August: Battles of the Frontiers
16 August: Germans take Liège
18 August: Russians invade Galicia
23–24 August: Krasnik
23–24 August: Mons
26–27 August: Le Cateau
26–31 August: Tannenberg
5–10 September: the Marne
9–14 September: Masurian Lakes
14 September: Falkenhayn succeeds Moltke
15 September: the Aisne, first trenches appear
15–21 October: Warsaw
12 October–17 November: First Ypres
2 December: Austrians occupy Belgrade
1915
19 February: Allies bombard the Dardanelles
10–13 March: Neuve Chapelle
18 March: Allied naval attack in Dardanelles
22 April–25 May: Second Ypres
25 April: Allied landings at Helles and Anzac Cove
7 May: Germans sink *Lusitania*
16 May–30 June: Second Artois (or Vimy)
23 May: Italy declares war on Austria
23 June–7 July: First Isonzo
12–13 July: British attack at Helles
18 July–3 August: Second Isonzo
6 August: British landing at Suvla

6–9 August: Anzac attack at Lone Pine
19 August: Germans sink *Arabic*
18 October–4 November: Third Isonzo
25 September–6 October: Second Champagne
25 September–8 October: Loos
10 November–2 December: Fourth Isonzo
19–20 December: Allies evacuate Suvla and Anzac
1916
8–9 January: Allies evacuate Helles
21 February–18 December: Verdun, including
21 February: first German offensive
26 February: fall of Fort Douamont
6 March: second German offensive
9 April: third German offensive
7 June: fall of Fort Vaux
24 October: French retake Douamont
2 November: French retake Vaux
11–29 March: Fifth Isonzo
22 March: Russians take Przemyśl
24–29 April: Easter Rising in Dublin
25 April: Germans bombard Lowestoft and Great Yarmouth
2–4 May: Central Powers' Gorlice–Tarnow offensive
31 May–1 June: Jutland
3 June: Austrians retake Przemyśl
4 June–20 September: Brusilov Offensive
5 June: Lord Kitchener drowned in sinking of HMS *Hampshire*
6 June: Start of Arab Revolt in Hejaz
10 June: Arabs capture Mecca
22 June: Austrians take Lemberg
1 July–18 November: The Somme, including
1–13 July: Albert
23 July–3 September: Pozières
15–22 September: Flers-Courcelette
26–28 September: Thiepval
5 August: Germans enter Warsaw
6–17 August: Sixth Isonzo
25 August: Central Powers take Brest-Litovsk
14–26 September: Seventh Isonzo
10–12 October: Eighth Isonzo
1–14 November: Ninth Isonzo
7 November: British take Gaza
7 November: Woodrow Wilson re-elected President of United States of America
6 December: Central Powers capture Bucharest

7 December: Lloyd George replaces Asquith as Prime Minister
1917
31 January: Germans declare unrestricted submarine warfare
15 March: Tsar Nicholas II abdicates: Prince Lvov forms provisional government
6 April: USA declares war on Germany
9 April–15 May: Arras
9–14 April: Vimy
16–20 April: Nivelle Offensive
12 May–8 June: Tenth Isonzo
7–14 June: Messines
l July: Start of Russian offensive
31 July–10 November: Third Ypres, including
31 July–2 August: Pilckem
16–18 August: Langemarck
20–25 September: Menin Road
26 September–3 October: Polygon Wood
4 October: Broodseinde
9 October: Poelcapelle
12 October: First Passchendaele
26 October–10 November: Second Passchendaele
18 August–15 September: Eleventh Isonzo
3 September: Germans take Riga
24 October–12 November: Caporetto (Twelfth Isonzo)
7 November: Bolsheviks seize power
16 November: Clemenceau becomes Prime Minister of France
20 November–7 December: Cambrai
9 December: British take Jerusalem
1918
8 January: Wilson issues 14 Points, four more than Moses (Clemenceau's joke)
21 March–5 April: German 'Michael' Offensive, including
21–23 March: St. Quentin
24–25 March: First Bapaume
28 March: Second Arras
9–29 April: German 'Georgette' Offensive
27 May–17 June: German 'Blücher–Yorck' Offensive
9–13 June: German 'Gneisenau' Offensive
18 July–5 August: Allied Aisne–Marne Counter-Offensive
8–11 August: Amiens
12 August–12 October: Assault on Hindenburg Line, including
26–30 August: Scarpe
2–3 September: Drocourt–Quéant Switch

27 September–1 October: Canal du Nord
29 September–2 October: St. Quentin Canal
8–9 October: Second Cambrai
12–16 September: St. Mihiel
26 September–11 November: Franco-American Meuse–Argonne Offensive
30 September: Anglo-Arab occupation of Damascus
24 October–4 November: Vittorio Veneto
29 October: German sailors mutiny
11 November: Armistice signed, taking effect on 11th hour of 11th day of
11th month

To Mariel
for putting the pieces together

PART ONE BACKGROUND

CHAPTER ONE

WAR KNOWN AND WAR IMAGINED

THE CIVILIAN VIEW OF WAR

The First World War began on 3 August 1914 when Germany declared war on France and invaded Belgium. Germany and Austria–Hungary* (the Central Powers) fought against Russia, France and the British Empire (the Triple Entente*). After the Pact of London of September 1914 which bound the latter three not to make a separate peace, they became known as the Allies. They were joined by Italy in 1915 and then by America in 1917, as an associated but not allied power. The war grew out of the diplomatic crisis that began when Gavrilo Princips, a Bosnian Serb, assassinated Archduke Francis Ferdinand and his wife. The archduke was the heir to the throne of Austria–Hungary. Austria–Hungary sought to punish Serbia for sponsoring such terrorism. Russia defended Serbia, a fellow Slavic state. Germany insisted that the rest of Europe keep out of the business that her ally Austria–Hungary had with Serbia. France was bound by treaty to assist Russia. Britain did not have formal treaty commitments to France or Russia, but informal military and naval arrangements seemed to the government to amount to a moral commitment to help France. People in the towns and cities of the belligerent nations welcomed the outbreak of war almost universally and assumed the conflict would be over by Christmas. It did not end until 11 November 1918. Historians estimate that the war led to approximately 9.5 million military deaths.

After the First World War, survivors across all of Europe looked back to the world before 1914 with profound nostalgia. They contrasted the bleakness of the war and its aftermath to the radiant light of a golden age the war seemed to have destroyed, an age of peace, prosperity and tranquility [*Doc. 10*]. This homesickness for a time rather than a place showed up more in personal memoirs or fiction than in academic history, which was instead obsessed with finding the diplomatic causes of the war.

Of all the myths about the age before 1914, that of the Long Peace is the most enduring, echoed as it has been in both high and popular culture. It is also the least realistic. After all, British people in their sixties in 1914 would have lived through at least twenty-four wars. Myths, however, usually rest on facts and for that reason should not be taken lightly. What matters in history is not only what happens but also what people think happens – or has happened. People living in 1914 thought peace was normal because the wars since 1850 had been brief and peripheral to their lives. War for most people had become war imagined. At the same time, without reality as a check, war had become idealized as a test not just of state power but also of the moral strength of individuals and nations. Social changes encouraged this perception.

Modernization arrived in force after 1870, in an era that Norman Stone has called 'the great transformation' (Norman, 1983). People were on the move – literally, with 30 million Europeans migrating outside Europe and 60 million more moving into the cities of Europe. They were also trying to move socially, climbing the new ladder of urban society. Movement brought contact with strangers, which in turn raised new questions such as 'who am I?' and 'who are we?' – questions that had not seemed important in the isolated, unchanging life of rural society. Together with self-consciousness about one's identity came a yearning for certainty in a world in which, as Karl Marx observed, everything solid melts into air. Historians are now paying close attention to the changing experience of women in this era. But change had an impact on masculinity too. When the role of women was starting to change and activities that had traditionally defined masculinity were mutating, what did it mean to be a man? Kipling wrote a sentimental poem outlining a modern version of Aristotelian gentility that avoided extremes of behaviour, although its title, 'If', suggests the limits of a stiff upper lip as a code of conduct. Being a gentleman meant juggling a lot of 'thou shalls' and 'thou shall nots'. Yet the ideal of chivalry that he evoked had an important revival in the Victorian era. Middle-class men found emotional satisfaction in imagining themselves to be knights in shining armour. It was not just a matter of a taste for literature set in the Middle Ages but a way of expressing the ideal of the gentleman. A gentleman devoted his life to fair play and to helping others. In this deliberately old-fashioned view of life, war served as the ultimate test of character. The gentleman-warrior, schooled on the playing fields of the public schools, put his life on the line for the sake of honour. Cowards and bullies thought only of themselves and their narrow, selfish interests. They broke the rules, violated the spirit of the game and so of course they lost, whatever the final score. Yet it was not just against cads that the gentleman-knight defined himself. What he did could not be done by women. Men made war and war made men. It was the surest way to define masculinity and test character. The cult of the gentleman rationalized the violence and terror of war by treating death as the ultimate challenge. The gentleman should aspire to die a good death, facing it as Peter Pan did, as a 'great adventure'.

War was imagined to be a purgative as well as a test. It was assumed to be the opposite of peace and therefore free of the sins peace had acquired:

individualism, materialism, cynicism, uncertainty, aimlessness or boredom. Eric Leed argues that people welcomed the war as an escape from the dispiriting realities of the new industrial world (Leed, 1979). They did not realize that war itself would be industrialized. It would not provide an escape from mechanized routine but only an intensification of it.

THE PROFESSIONAL VIEW OF WAR

Were the professional soldiers wiser than civilians about what would be the realities of war? Yes and no. By 1914 many of them factored new technologies and social realities into their guesses about the next war. Civilians might imagine that war was a gallant and uplifting adventure, and soldiers often shared the assumption that character mattered most in life, but soldiers also knew that the staggering increase in firepower brought about by a century of industrialization ensured a corresponding rise in violence and casualties. They expected the next war to be terrible. Like the public, however, they thought that it would be brief and mobile. In particular, they assumed that improvements in manpower, firepower and command would strengthen the attack. They did not realize that in the first instance the defence would benefit more, simply because it could be dug in while the attack had to move above ground [*Doc. 8*].

The experts and the public were in various stages of denial about the nature of warfare because the profound changes that had occurred over the previous century were not so much hidden from sight as they were unpalatable to those who believed that war ought to embody a purpose other than brute killing. Both the natural and the customary limits to violence had weakened. Total, unlimited warfare had at least become possible. The French Revolution led to the 'nation in arms', with an economy devoted solely to the demands of war production supporting the armed forces. The Industrial Revolution increased firepower exponentially, above all with artillery. Formerly cast in bronze or iron and loaded from the muzzle,* the new guns were bored out of high quality steel and loaded from the breech.* Mechanisms to absorb the recoil meant that guns stayed in place and retained their aim after they were fired. The simple division between light field artillery* and heavier garrison or siege artillery became more elaborate as specialized guns and projectiles appeared: howitzers with a plunging or steep arc of fire; quick-firing field guns using shrapnel against human targets; immense long-range guns on fixed mountings or railway carriages to destroy heavy defensive positions; early versions of trench mortars that gave the infantry portable artillery of their own; heavy machine guns that filled a niche between small arms and artillery.

Armies in the past had been limited in size by the inherent difficulties of co-ordinating a large group, by problems of supply and by the shortage of men willing to become trained, reliable soldiers. Hierarchic organization and training overcame the problem of control, although linking the sharp end of combat with the centres of command remained a problem throughout the First World War. Problems of supply and logistics* were less severe. The ancient custom of overestimating one's needs and producing more than enough to win was finally practical when mass production arrived. Getting the mountain of stuff to where it was needed was also easier because of the modern railway system and the existence of all-weather paved roads in Western Europe.

As for the traditional limitation on the size of armies, all the major powers except Britain and her Dominions solved the problem by adopting conscription, thereby making all men of military age liable, at least in theory, to serve. In Germany men were liable to serve at age 20 for two years in the infantry and three in the cavalry or field artillery. After that they might serve in the reserve for four to five years, which meant a fortnight of training each year. There could also be terms in the *Landsturm*, an emergency national guard, between age 17 and 20, and the *Landwehr* or militia for 11 years after that, taking a man to age 45. The *Landsturm* and *Landwehr*, however, were only mobilized in wartime emergencies.

With the Germans providing the model, the other continental powers followed with varying degrees of thoroughness. By 1914 the major powers had million-man armies made up of young first-line soldiers and huge reserves of older trained men.

Why was the impact of this seismic change not understood more clearly, especially by military professionals? The answer, perhaps, is that if war had indeed tilted to the defensive side, it had lost much of its apparent purpose. To be sure, states could be more confident about defending themselves against attack, even surprise attack, which is how most wars had started. But that seemed to point to mass armies digging in and going nowhere. What, then, was the point? Good question, and rather than answering it in a clear-headed way, people built optimistic assumptions into their plans and projections.

WAR PLANS

What did the military leaders plan to do when war came? Only the leaders of Germany planned to initiate a general European war, and then it would seem that they did so because they were convinced war was coming, probably by 1916, whether or not they wanted one. Better that it come when they could still expect to win or even survive against the perceived 'encirclement' posed by France and Russia. The great general Helmuth von Moltke, Bismarck's military partner in creating the German Empire between 1864 and 1871, had planned for a limited war that involved defending in the west against France and seeking limited gains in the east. His eventual successor, Count Alfred von Schlieffen (Chief of the Great General Staff 1891–1906), took a strong and united Germany for granted. He saw no reason to play it safe the way Moltke had; the safety that such caution would provide seemed temporary, given the danger Germany would still face on two fronts. If a two-front war were coming, he looked for a way to win it decisively. Whether or not he came up with a formal plan (the Schlieffen Plan*) is now a matter of historical debate, but it seems safe to say that he devised a formula or set of working assumptions which committed most of the German army to a sweep through the Lowlands into Northern France, then hooking south to the west of Paris. Assuming that the French advanced east into Alsace and Lorraine, the provinces they had lost to Germany in 1871, the Germans could hook around them going the other way. Germany would beat France within six weeks and then use her railway system to shift east to defeat France's ally, Russia. Schlieffen's approach was a bold gamble which had the considerable virtue of addressing the gravest problem the German leaders thought they faced: what to do in the event of a two-front war. By doing so, however, Schlieffen reduced the incentive to ask just how likely such a war was. Was there any evidence available to the Germans that the French and Russians were indeed going to attack? Were there no non-violent ways, such as negotiation, to deal with the neighbours? Was Germany in fact subconsciously inventing reasons to precipitate a war? Schlieffen might not have bequeathed his state with a plan but, after he left office, his state acted as if he had and, moreover, as if it were the only plan they could now follow. Every international situation Germany faced after 1906 increasingly led back to the assumed solution, the magic bullet, war against France – even if France were only marginally involved. When all you have is a hammer, everything looks like a nail.

Moltke's nephew, also named Helmuth von Moltke, succeeded Schlieffen in 1906. When Russia not only rebuilt much of her military power after her defeat by the Japanese in 1905 but also started to build railways in what had been the underdeveloped glacis of Russian Poland, Moltke began to worry about the prospects of attacking in the west and defending in the east. Russia might show up on Germany's eastern frontier in strength before France was defeated. What then? Increasing the size of the army* seemed one logical step to take. The problem here was that the German Navy was also eating up the scarce tax resources available to the central government (the Reich), and money bills to pay for arms increases had to obtain the approval of the *Reichstag*, the national parliament. Moreover, conservative elements in the Prussian Ministry of War were reluctant to dilute the traditional composition of the army, which constituted an aristocratic officer corps and a peasant rank and file. Expansion of the army would mean drawing upon the middle and working classes of the cities. In the end, the stark necessities of security overrode conservatism and political complications, and the *Reichstag* passed army bills in 1912 and 1913 that increased the size of the army by around 20 per cent.

Moltke was closer to having the manpower that would be required for his ambitious plans, but he was no closer to solving the problems of moving and supplying such a human mass and dealing with its exhaustion in combat than Schlieffen had been. Having willed the conclusion – that a pre-emptive attack in the west would save Germany from defeat in a two-front war – the leaders of Germany now willed the premise, the two-front war. The attack would work because it would have to work. When there are nails everywhere, what you are carrying had better be a hammer.

What of the military plans of the other powers? By 1914, most Austrian leaders of Germany's ally Austria–Hungary also wanted a war, but it was to be a limited war against Serbia, intended to curb Balkan nationalism. A wider war against Russia frightened them. The landed elite ruling Hungary, the Magyars, could not see how a war against either Serbia or Russia would serve their interests and resisted it until the last minute.

Following defeat in 1871, the French put their faith in fixed fortifications along the common border with Germany, hoping to guard against another invasion. Schlieffen was impressed enough by these defences to avoid them and so his plan called for an advance to the north. The fixed defences were meant to serve as a shock absorber that would buy the French enough time to determine where the main weight of the German attack was falling. Plan XV, adopted in 1905, assumed that the Germans would be attacking out of Alsace and Lorraine. When evidence from German railway construction and hints about Schlieffen's thinking pointed to an attack coming through Belgium, the French military at first thought they were being deceived. Such an attack would require a heavy commitment of reserves in the first line, and that seemed unlikely. By 1909, however, the omens had grown too persuasive to dismiss, and the new Plan XVI assumed that the Germans would come through Belgium and then turn south towards Verdun. The French response would be to keep their main force concentrated on their eastern frontier and then meet the Germans at Verdun (Strachan, 2001).

A change in organization in 1911 that brought operational and strategic planning under one roof in the General Staff also brought a new Chief of Staff, Joseph Joffre. His background was in military engineering, and in railways in particular. Historians have tended to cite his lack of interest in strategic thinking and innovation as evidence of his intellectual mediocrity, but more recent writers have been kinder, pointing to a practicality and imperturbability that served France well. He focused on the tasks at hand. The main challenge he faced by 1912 was the expansion of the German Army. In response, in 1913 he secured the increase in the term of service in the French Army from two to three years, improved training and by 1914 provided an overall increase in the regular forces of 200,000 men. Strachan (2001) argues that, despite the qualms Joffre and others had about relying too heavily on the reserves, of the 3.6 million men France mobilized in 1914, 2.9 million were reservists or territorials.

Joffre's pragmatism showed up in his new plan, Plan XVII.* Instead of waiting to see where the Germans attacked and letting them come, Joffre wanted to counter-attack as soon as possible, preferably in Belgium where the ground was most suitable. When concern for Belgian neutrality ruled that out, Joffre's alternative was to plan for early counter-attacks either in Lorraine or in the Ardennes along the eastern frontier. These attacks, however, were not planned in detail, so that Plan XVII was, in Strachan's judgement, a plan more of mobilization than of attack comparable to the German plan. It specified where the army would gather, not how it would then proceed. This in fact was one of the strengths of France in 1914. Joffre's experience with railways paid off in improvements for the system of quick mobilization, so that the German advantage was gone and Joffre had reason to believe that his army would begin a war in the right place, able to react to whatever the enemy did. What neither he nor his intelligence staff fully understood was the size of the move the Germans would be making. By 1914, they conceded that Germany would be using reserves in the first wave, but they also believed that up to 22 German divisions would be sent to the eastern front to hold off the Russians. The sheer length of the German front and its immense weight on the right wing did not seem possible given the numbers the French were crunching. When your hammer is not as large as you would like, you assume fewer nails.

The Russian armed forces had staged a remarkable recovery from the shambles of 1905, helped in part by Russia's spectacular economic growth and heavy investment from abroad, especially France. What had yet to be added to the military mix was an officers' corps competent at field command or staff work. So a Russian plan to strike first was ruled out by the inability to plan anything. As with Austria–Hungary, Russia was not contemplating taking part in, let alone starting, a general European war. Her interests were confined to the Balkans.

The British defied the trend to taking thought for the morrow by having no strategic plans of their own. Instead they intended to attach the small British Expeditionary Force (BEF)* to the left wing of the French army and conform to the French plan. Britain was not carrying out a formal treaty obligation to France when she declared war on Germany. The treaty obligation at work was the Treaty of London of 1839, guaranteeing Belgian neutrality. What shaped the British response was the moral obligation they felt to support France once the goal of the German thrust through the heart of Belgium became clear. In acting, the British were not just defending Belgium. Above all they were defending the target of the German invasion of Belgium, France.

THE NAVAL RACE

Britain had long depended more on the Royal Navy than on its small army of long-serving professionals to defend her vital interests. Once the challenge posed by the new Imperial German High Seas Fleet became clear after 1900, Britain committed her resources to staying ahead at sea, especially in numbers of up-to-date capital ships. The moving force other than the Kaiser behind the German programme of naval build-up, Admiral Alfred von Tirpitz, wanted a world-class battle fleet to rally the middle classes to the monarchy and intimidate Britain into making geopolitical concessions. However, once the First Sea Lord, Admiral John 'Jackie' Fisher, reorganized the Royal Navy to concentrate it in home waters, reformed the training of officers and manning of ships and launched a programme of super-battleships with HMS *Dreadnought* in 1906, the British were satisfied just to stay ahead. This they did, with 24 Dreadnought-class* battleships by 1914, compared with 13 for Germany, plus 13 under construction against 10 for Germany.

CHAPTER TWO

1914: OOPS! THE PLANS FAIL

We still tend to think that the war was all of one piece and that those who experienced it had a single, common experience. The war, however, developed what the historian Trevor Wilson, quoting the novelist Frederick Manning, calls its 'myriad faces' (Wilson, 1986). The soldier of 1914 encountered something different from the soldier of 1917; the French soldier something different from the German; the front soldier something different from the people at home, who often seemed to the soldiers to share nothing with them any more [*Docs. 6, 12* and *16*]; the mother worrying at home something different from the nurse at a base hospital [*Doc. 17*]; the war profiteer something different from the conscientious objector in jail. As the fighting tended to subside over winter, giving those in charge a chance to reconsider their approach, the war also changed over time. Each year it lasted formed a distinct period:

1. 1914. Manoeuvre on the battlefields, bogging down in the west into unexpected positional war while the war in the east remained more open and mobile; at home, 'business as usual'.
2. 1915. Improvised trench war and badly planned offensive disasters on the Western Front; German success against Russia; the state controlled war economy emerged at home.
3. 1916. The year of the most-remembered phase: well-planned disasters of attrition on land and sea; total war at home.
4. 1917. No end in sight in the field, until Russia collapsed; revolution, despair or grim determination at home.
5. 1918. Movement returned to the battlefield; the home fronts approached or moved past the tipping point. And then it was over.

THE BATTLES OF THE FRONTIERS

In compliance with the Schlieffen–Moltke plan, the Germans sent 1.5 million men across their western frontier in the first days of the war. First came cavalry patrols and an advance guard into Luxembourg on 3 August. Then the northern-most armies set off into Belgium on 4 August, the First Army under General Alexander von Kluck and the Second under General Karl von Bülow. With 320,000 men, Kluck's First Army was the largest of the seven German armies attacking in the west. With the advantage of surprise, the Germans were slowed only by problems with traffic and supply. The first real resistance the First Army met came at the fortress of Liège, the hub of the Belgian defensive system. When the Belgian defenders stopped the initial German attacks, the Germans brought up immense siege mortars. The main fortress at Liège fell quickly, and then the satellite fortresses. By 16 August, the Germans had opened the path through the central plain of Belgium towards France. Although Liège was still the only significant obstacle that the Germans had faced, the vanguard of their attack slowed down simply because men could not keep marching between 20 and 25 miles a day, especially in the unusually hot weather. Moreover, by blowing railway tunnels, the Belgians constricted the flow of supplies and reinforcements. When Belgian civilians resisted, the Germans treated them as *franc tireurs* or terrorists and killed them en masse to cow the rest into submission. In Dinant, 612 men, women and children were shot in the main square. Two days later, the great library at Louvain was set on fire when the occupying troops panicked for five days. The British later exaggerated the 'Belgian atrocities' of August and September 1914 for propaganda purposes, so that posterity came to think they were a hoax. They were not. They happened, and they set a terrible precedent for the century to follow.

Moltke thought briefly about shifting the main attack to Lorraine. He moved some reserve divisions there and gave the Sixth Army, under Crown Prince Rupprecht of Bavaria, orders to defend vigorously. Rupprecht was more than just a figurehead and had real abilities as a commander. He decided that the order to defend did not rule out attacking. By 20 August, his Bavarians had thrown the French out of Lorraine. So by accident, the bulk of the French army was retreating to positions between Paris and the greatest of the French frontier fortresses, Verdun.

By now Joffre knew that the Germans were advancing in strength in Belgium and that the centre of the German line was also surprisingly strong. Because of the prior underestimation of German strength, he naturally concluded that this strength in the north and middle meant that the Germans were weak somewhere else. At first, he thought this meant in Lorraine. When his attack into Lorraine failed, he decided that the centre of the German line must be weaker than it first seemed. That was where he sent the Third and Fourth Armies. With the French infantry resplendent in bright red trousers and blue jackets and the officers in full dress uniform, like targets on a shooting range, the result was a massacre. The French fell back to the river Meuse. Their initial attacks had failed badly at the cost of 300,000 casualties and had scarcely bothered the Germans. They were just beginning to roll.

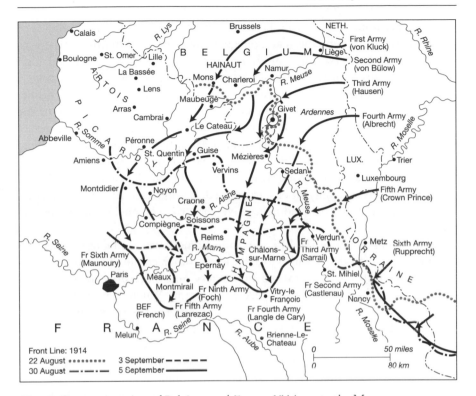

Map 1 German invasion of Belgium and France 1914: up to the Marne
Adapted from Richard Natkiel, *Atlas of Twentieth-Century Warfare*, Bison Books
(London, 1982, reprinted 1989), p. 30

THE BRITISH EXPEDITIONARY FORCE (BEF) UP TO MONS

On 5 August, three days after France began mobilization and a day after the
British Empire declared war on Germany, Prime Minister Asquith convened a
Council of War. The Council realized immediately that the BEF must go to
north-west Europe. As for what it would do when it arrived, the soldiers
admitted that the only plan they had was to stick to the left flank of the French
army. Britain thus backed into the Western Front as a very junior partner of
France, adding the four (later six) divisions of the BEF to the 70 of the French
army.

The BEF duly embarked, crossing the Channel and setting out for
Maubeuge without a hitch. By the time it approached Mons across the border
in Belgium on 21 August, the French were beginning to realize that they faced
disaster. Almost all of Joffre's armies had been decimated and thrown back.
Only the Fifth Army under General Charles Lanrezac, on the left of the French
line, remained intact, simply because the German First Army had yet to reach

it. Lanrezac, along with General Ferdinand Foch, had taught the supremacy of the offensive at the Supreme War College before the war. After the war, critics contended that the two men offered a one-sided gospel that stressed high morale and aggression and overlooked the basic realities of defensive firepower. A closer look at their arguments reveals a more reasonable concern for ensuring that attacks over open ground should succeed despite the power of the defence, primarily by employing what would now be called 'fire and movement' tactics by small groups of infantry. Certainly at this juncture Lanrezac was not about to leap into the attack. He was alarmed by reports that the German Army was strong not only in front of him but also on both his flanks. Rather than advance only to be surrounded, he preferred to wait. Nevertheless, his reports to Joffre used aggressive rhetoric, convincing Joffre that he was keen to attack.

The Commander of the BEF, Sir John French, was a cavalryman with a distinguished record. As with virtually every other commander of the early war, except Joffre, he was racked by anxiety and indecision, as if he knew he was out of his depth in an unexpected situation. When he visited Joffre on 16 August, Joffre spoke glowingly of Lanrezac's zeal to attack. Sir John discovered a different picture when he visited Lanrezac the next day. Belgian refugees were pouring through Lanrezac's sector to escape Kluck's steamroller and the next French army down the line was suspiciously quiet, leading Lanrezac to think it might be on the verge of pulling out.

Before the BEF could attack in support of the French, it collided with Kluck's First Army at Mons on 23 August; 200,000 Germans by now against 75,000 British. Mons was one of the first battles in history to take part in an industrial city, and the first in which aircraft* played a part, the Germans using them to range their guns. The professionals of the BEF quickly dug in among the slag heaps, while the Germans, impatient to brush aside this pesky obstacle to their advance, attacked frontally with little artillery support. The British riflemen, trained to fire an aimed shot every four seconds, held off the Germans for a full day. By the end of 23 August, Sir John learned that Lanrezac's Fifth Army not only had failed to join the attack but was even starting to retreat, without a word to the embattled British. They had no choice but to break off the battle and join the French in retreating to the south. They covered over two hundred miles in the next two weeks, the infantry marching in the late-summer heat for twenty out of every twenty-four hours.

THE END OF THE SCHLIEFFEN PLAN

On the other side of the hill, the German General Staff was moving step by step away from its original intentions, confirming the observation of Moltke's uncle that no battle plan survives intact after first contact with the enemy. Not only was Kluck peeling off large detachments to surround those pockets of the

Belgian army still intact, but Moltke was strengthening the left wing in Lorraine. On 25 August, he detached two corps from the right wing to relieve the crisis that seemed to be impending in the east. If he is to be faulted, it would be for taking these men from the all-important right wing, which had already started to bog down in Belgium. The fewer men the First and Second Armies had, the more they tended to pull apart as they fanned out when they moved into France. On 27 August, Moltke allowed Kluck to freewheel, moving independently of the Second Army next to him. Convinced that the British were retreating west to the Channel, Kluck wanted to sweep wide to the north to cut them off. The BEF, however, was retreating to the south, not west to the coast, and was closer to Kluck than he realized. The British 2nd Corps, under General Horace Smith-Dorrien, was too exhausted to march any further and dug in at Le Cateau. Once again, Kluck had the BEF in his sights, once again British rifle fire and artillery were deadly, and once again the Germans made the mistake of attacking frontally. The 2nd Corps stood its ground and finally retired in good order.

Thinking only of the hunt for the BEF, Kluck lost touch with Bülow's Second Army. The British marched into the gap between the two armies. They might have made something of their luck under a decent commander. By 29 August, however, Sir John French had lapsed into a total funk. His subordinate corps commanders, Generals Sir Douglas Haig and Sir Horace Smith-Dorrien, were still full of fight, but that only depressed Sir John the more and he actually issued orders to prepare the BEF to retire to England to refit. Sensing that Sir John was losing his grip, the British Cabinet sent the new Secretary of State for War, Field Marshal Lord Kitchener, over to instruct him to conform to the movements of the French army and not even to think of bugging out.

Joffre also hovered over Lanrezac's shoulder, and when Bülow's Second Army once again ran into the French Fifth Army, Lanrezac finally hit back. So came about the muddled battles of St. Quentin and Guise, the high point of which came when Lanrezac's 1st Corps, under General Franchet d'Esperey, threw the Germans back over the river Oise in the last old-style Napoleonic infantry charge in history. Kluck now had to double back to help Bülow, which meant turning south short of Paris instead of hooking around it to the west. Moltke eventually approved, because his hope now was to push the French to the south-east. To make sure the large garrison in Paris or the BEF did not attack Bülow's rear, Moltke ordered Kluck to stay between Bülow and Paris. Kluck thought this was too cautious, and on 2 September he ordered his First Army to cross the river Marne the following day.

THE MARNE

With Kluck only thirty miles from Paris, the French government prudently shifted to Bordeaux. On 3 September, the Military Governor of Paris, General

Joseph Galliéni, summoned from retirement to be Joffre's deputy, realized from air reconnaissance that the Germans were turning south short of Paris and heading for the Marne. He ordered the new Sixth Army under General Michel-Joseph Maunoury to prepare to attack the ripe German flank that had appeared when Kluck moved to the Marne. Joffre confirmed the attack the following day, and then went to work on Sir John French. After some spirited oratory from Joffre, Sir John promised that the BEF would do what it could.

On the German side, poor communications were wrecking the tidy world of peacetime plans, war games and staff rides. It was also messing up Moltke's willpower. Only a week before, the mood in his headquarters in Luxembourg had been euphoric, but by 5 September, victory was slipping away. The enemy was getting beaten like a drum, but it was still free to manoeuvre, a bad omen which Moltke deduced from the absence of captured men and guns. Worse still, Kluck's energetic tourism had exposed the entire German right wing to a Schlieffen plan in reverse. On 4 September, Moltke restrained the First and Second Armies and warned them to guard against a flank attack from Paris. By the time the order reached Kluck, he had already moved most of his army across the Marne.

On 4 September, Maunoury's Sixth Army ran into the reserve corps Kluck had left north of the Marne. Maunoury's sharp attack on the vulnerable German right flank had a ripple effect, leading to adjustments out of all proportion to the initial French blow. Moltke ordered Kluck to pull back. By 6 September, the entire French army and the BEF were attacking. Nowhere did they break the German line, and the net effect was little more than equal and opposite pressure. When Kluck pulled his two corps back across the Marne and sent them to counter-attack Maunoury, this opened another gap of almost twenty miles between the two German armies. By now, the rule was that when there was a gap, the BEF would pop up in the middle of it. The rest of the rule was that the British were unable to exploit their good fortune. Aside from the gap between their leading armies, the Germans were doing well. They repulsed the French Fifth Army, now under Franchet d'Esperey instead of Lanrezac. They drove back the French Ninth Army under General Ferdinand Foch, of whom more will be heard later.

In spite of the German steadiness in the field, they blinked first. On 9 September, Bülow ordered his army to pull back. Kluck had no choice but to conform and ordered a retreat in the direction of Soissons to the north-east. By 11 September, all the German armies were heading north, either under local orders or on direct orders from Moltke. The only reason the German retreat did not turn into a rout was that the French and British were too exhausted to pursue.

Thus dwindled out the Battle of the Marne, the 'miracle' as the French immediately called it. It did not mark the collapse of the Schlieffen–Moltke plan, because Moltke's indecision and Kluck's improvising had already forfeited a quick German victory before Maunoury jarred the German right flank. It was not a showcase for clever generalship. Joffre's main virtue was his equanimity, a quality not to be dismissed lightly in a supreme commander. What the British would call 'twitch' in the Second World War can spread like an airborne disease, especially from high office. Joffre's supporters tried to credit him with the attack on the German flank, but the initiative for that came from Galliéni. As it happens, the Germans stopped it cold, despite the presence of 3,000 soldiers rushed into the French line by 600 taxi cabs. What was significant during the battle was not what happened but what the Germans, and above all Moltke, thought might happen. Nor were their fears groundless, because if the BEF had been able to exploit the gap between the two main German armies, if Joffre had ordered a massive attack by his left wing in the east instead of a general attack along the line, the German army might indeed have been broken and a long way from home.

FIRST YPRES

Although the Battle of the Marne was a draw, it was also a strategic victory for the Allies. The German expectation of a short war was finished. As both sides regrouped and recovered, the leaders looked ahead to the next round. They realized that frontal attacks were best avoided. Outflanking the enemy to the north would be wiser. In pulling back to the Aisne, where the German First Army dug the first trenches of the war and held off a French attack, Kluck began what was to be called 'The Race to the Sea'. The description is misleading, because each side was trying to turn the other's flank before reaching the sea.

After the Marne, Joffre bowed to Sir John French's plea that the BEF be allowed to fight nearer to its Channel base. It was extracted from the Aisne and sent up to Flanders. By early October, the Germans had finally taken Antwerp. With this threat in the rear removed, they decided to use five of the reserve corps that had besieged and taken Antwerp to break around the north of the enemy line at Ypres. By then, the chief of staff and head of the OHL* (High Command) was no longer Moltke, who had suffered one nervous collapse too many, but Erich von Falkenhayn, the Minister of War. Falkenhayn seemed more politician than soldier to some of his fellow generals, and to posterity his short-cropped hair, silver moustache and cold-blooded command decisions made him seem like an earlier version of Darth Vader. Looking past appearances and the jealousy of rivals, Falkenhayn analyzed situations with a clear intelligence [Doc. 2]. To help the flanking attack he used replacement divisions made up of untrained student volunteers. By the end of the battle, between a third and a half of them, around 40,000, were killed or wounded. Among the minority to emerge unscathed was an older member of the 16th Bavarian Reserve Regiment, Adolf Hitler. The BEF by then included units of the Indian army. By the end of the battle, a third of the original BEF was dead.

Both the Germans and the British actually broke through, but in each case the defending side brought up reserves to seal the breach quicker than the attacking side exploited its gains. The climax of the battle, actually witnessed by the Kaiser, came when the Germans broke through at Gheluvelt, and the British, led by a few hundred survivors of the 2nd Worcestershires who formed the only reserve left, counter-attacked and threw the Germans back. After a final attack by the elite Prussian Guards failed, the battle petered out. By holding Ypres itself but giving ground slightly to the north, the British gained a bulge or salient in the Front, which now ran from the Channel to the Alps. They lost 50,000 dead and wounded at Ypres, the Germans around 100,000.

EASTERN FRONT: TANNENBERG TO LEMBERG

On the Eastern Front, plans and expectations also fell by the wayside. The Russians had not obliged the Germans by waiting six weeks to attack. Instead, they threw two huge armies into East Prussia as soon as the war started in August. The First Army, led by General Pavel Rennenkampf, advanced from the east towards Königsberg. General Alexander Samsonov's Second Army came up from the south. These armies were little better than feudal levies, badly equipped and worse led, but they rolled over the German screen by sheer weight of numbers. When the German commander in the east, General Max von Prittwitz, appealed for reinforcements, Moltke, as mentioned, detached two corps from the west and sent them to hold back the Russians. By the time they arrived, the new commanders in the east, Paul von Hindenburg and Erich Ludendorff, had turned the tide with the forces on hand, following a plan that Col. Max Hoffmann, operations officer with the German Eighth Army, had prepared earlier.

Hoffmann realized that Samsonov's Second Army, moving slowly towards the town of Tannenberg, was out of touch with Rennenkampf's First Army. Legend has it that the two Russian generals hated each other, but their failure to co-operate was common enough among Russian officers. Even worse than any personal feuding, the Russians did not encode their radio communications, which allowed the Germans full access to their plans. Hindenburg had been plucked from retirement to steady the new command team. Ludendorff provided the brains. As a talented staff officer of bourgeois origins, he had worked tirelessly before the war on the expansion of the German Army. Despite his high rank as Quarter-Master General of the Second Army, he personally led the capture of Liège, and then moved to the east. He was known to be erratic and tempestuous, which is why he was paired with Hindenburg. They became a remarkable team.

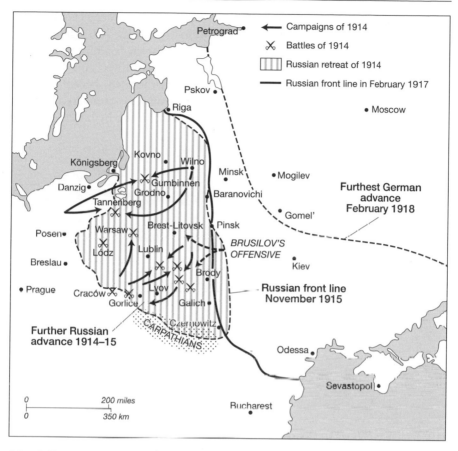

Map 2 Eastern Front
Adapted from Orlando Figes, *A People's Tragedy*, Viking (New York), p. xviii

On 26 August, the outnumbered Germans attacked Samsonov's Second Army near Tannenberg. Three days later the Second Army had ceased to exist, with 120,000 Russians taken prisoner and most of the rest of the original 200,000 dead. Samsonov shot himself. Ludendorff quickly moved the Eighth Army to face Rennenkampf's First Army in the wastelands formed by the Masurian Lakes. The Germans mounted a holding attack,* pinning the Russians while a flanking force worked north through a gap in the Russian lines. By 11 September, the First Army had lost 125,000 men; Rennenkampf abandoned the field and headed back to Russia.

On the same day, 11 September, the Austro–Hungarian offensive in Galicia, which had begun successfully in August with the capture of Krasnik and Komarow in Russian Poland, fell apart when the Russian Eighth Army, led by the ablest Russian commander in the war, General Aleksei Brusilov, smashed into the right flank of the Austro–Hungarian advance. The Austrian Chief of Staff, Conrad von Hötzendorf, originally intended to operate only against Serbia. When Moltke virtually ordered him at the last minute to move against Russia, he tried to mount two attacks in opposite directions. When the Russians took Lemberg, the Austro–Hungarian withdrawal became a rout. With 350,000 men lost, the Austro–Hungarian Army never recovered from its opening fiasco. The Serbs then completed Conrad's misery by holding off his invasion of Serbia in September.

CHAPTER THREE

TAKING STOCK

THE SOLDIERS

The military leaders might not have expected the defensive stalemate that emerged, but when it did, they, or more often the new men who replaced them, analyzed the unexpected dilemma with a good deal more acuity than the post-war legend about bone-headed generals would suggest. As Trevor Wilson points out (Wilson, 1986), they realized that there were essentially only two ways to bring back open and mobile warfare. One was to attack faster than the defence could entrench itself. Speed to achieve this came through the railway systems. For example, in the race to the sea in 1914, the battles between the Marne and Ypres took place where east–west spur lines delivered men who had been moved north on the main lines. Speed was constant for both sides because both were using the same railway network. Space was the other variable. The 475 miles of front might seem to present opportunities for open attack somewhere, but much of the territory was unsuitable for attacking, especially between Verdun and the Swiss frontier. In the flatter areas where manoeuvre was possible, the increase in firepower and manpower of the previous half-century ensured that both sides could pack in more than enough to stand their ground. Even before 1914, modern trenches had evolved far beyond being holes in the ground. Reinforced with barbed wire (one of the underrated basics of trench war), sandbags, deep dugouts, modern rifles, quick-firing field artillery and machine guns (one of the overrated basics of trench war), entrenched defences would yield only to infantry well supported by artillery. So artful manoeuvre and power drives were both impractical, at least for the moment. Moreover, by the end of 1914, everyone had run out of shells. Starting virtually from scratch, both sides converted to war economies to feed the guns. Yet the same artillery backstopped the defences. The more things changed, the more they were likely to stay the same, if only because the two sides had the same technological capacities, and whatever device one side lacked, it soon was able to copy.

THE POLITICIANS

The warring powers objectively still had a range of choices; all chose at this early point to limit the war. The shortage of shells gave them no other choice. Subjectively, however, each power faced a different situation. The French had the least freedom of choice. As Foch is alleged to have said after the war, 'when I last looked, France had not invaded Germany'. Other than surrender, the only option open to the French was to expel the invader. The Germans had a choice of fronts and therefore some strategic leeway. Looking ahead to the coming campaign season, they chose to defend in the west and attack Russia in the east. Hindenburg and Ludendorff wanted to commit everything to an eastern victory, but Falkenhayn doubted that he had the resources to force a Russian capitulation. Russia could always trade space for time, withdrawing into her vast interior to fight another day, the way she had when faced with Napoleon. Falkenhayn preferred to combine military pressure with diplomatic moves to detach Russia from her Western allies. As it happened, the German victories in the east in 1915 were too humiliating in their scope and their diplomatic concessions too minor to alter the will of the Tsar to fight on. Austria–Hungary still faced the threat the South Slavs seemed to pose to the survival of the multinational Empire, but it was now magnified by the struggle against the Slavs of Russia and the fissures that war brought. That the Habsburg Empire fought on despite its sorry start in 1914 is still hard to understand. Patriotism of the sort that France or Germany could muster was insignificant in a state whose ruler at most wanted, in his words, 'a patriot for me'. Yet there was perhaps an underlying affection for Franz Josef, who had been on the throne since 1848. Even for disgruntled nationalists he had become rather like unsightly wallpaper that is too familiar and inconvenient to replace. The Dual Monarchy kept going by sheer inertia.

Britain seemed to have the most freedom of choice by the end of 1914. Her new army was still embryonic, so that the Royal Navy remained her main strength. As early as the winter of 1914–15, members of the War Cabinet understood that the impasse on the Western Front might not be temporary. Winston Churchill wrote to Prime Minister Asquith to insist that the new army not be forced to 'chew barbed wire in France' (Wilson, 1986: 104). David Lloyd George, the Chancellor of the Exchequer, had gone from being a critic of militarism to a staunch believer in the war. Not, however, any kind of war nor war at any price. He too did not want the main British effort on land to be on the Western Front. There Britain would always be a junior partner to France and might well be drawn into the French manner of war which seemed to him to involve enormous and wasteful attacks to wear down the Germans. Lloyd George looked instead to the Balkans. The growing conviction of the politicians that Britain should fight anywhere but the Western Front testifies to their compassion, but also to their evasion of the central reality Britain faced in the war. Between 1914 and 1918, most of the German army was on the Western Front, making it the main front. To fight elsewhere ignored the reason Britain was at war in the first place, the need to defeat Germany. Whatever freedom of choice Britain had in theory, or in the imaginations of Churchill and Lloyd George, in fact she had as little as the others. She could see it through on the Western Front, tiptoe off to an unimportant sideshow, or drop out altogether. The generals accepted this point and its implications. The politicians had to deal with the political and social implications and under-standably turned waffling into high policy.

CIVILIANS AND THE SUSPENSION OF PARTISAN POLITICS

Side-stepping the point was not an art form exclusive to the British. Politicians in all the warring countries had to tread carefully. As war approached, civilian leaders worried that an outraged public would regard war as a calamity and hold them responsible. When instead crowds everywhere welcomed the war rapturously, and even militant socialists supported the war on behalf of the working classes, the leaders issued a collective sigh of relief. Had the war not been so popular, at least in the larger cities, it might indeed have been over by Christmas. What turned another war into the Great War was its extraordinary popularity [*Doc. 10*].

In Germany, Theobald von Bethmann Hollweg had been Chancellor (head of the central government) since 1909. A civil servant by training who in office was responsible only to the Kaiser and not to the elected parliament of the Empire, the *Reichstag*, Bethmann had hoped to concentrate on domestic matters. Foreign policy, in which he was relatively untrained, came instead to dominate his attention. After his wife died in 1912 he seems to have become fatalistic, and by 1914 to have convinced himself that war was inevitable. All he could do was ensure that Germany was prepared for it when it came. That meant hoping for British neutrality and keeping a watchful eye on the Social Democratic Party (SPD), which in 1912 had won a third of the seats in the *Reichstag*. In its official programme, the SPD was committed to oppose any war the capitalist classes foisted on the workers. In practice, the SPD gradually became less radical and more patriotic. Bread and butter issues and parliamentary politics displaced revolutionary ideology. When Bethmann delayed acting until Russia mobilized first, the SPD joined the rest of the nation in believing that Germany was the victim of Tsarist aggression. It was thus not just war with all its romantic associations that Germans embraced in August. They were also celebrating their new-found unity. When the Kaiser declared on 4 August that he no longer recognized parties but only Germans, he gave voice to a deeply felt yearning and for once spoke to and for his people. The government declared a *Burgfrieden** or 'truce of the castle', to signal the suspension of normal partisan politics.

Plate 1 Postcard. Inscription on the back reads: 'Born to Command. With the shortage of qualified officers during the war, Emma's natural leadership abilities were finally recognised' (© Wildwood Design Group 1987 All Rights Reserved Box 3140 McLean VA 22103).

Like the influenza pandemic that struck the world at the end of the war, the 'spirit of August' was not confined to one country or class, although contrary to legend it did not carry away everyone. People less engaged in the modern world were less susceptible, so that the 'spirit' was less evident in the countryside in Europe or in the longer-settled areas of the Imperial Dominions such as Nova Scotia or Quebec in Canada. France matched the German *Burgfrieden* with a *Union sacrée*. The Austro–Hungarian Empire was too fractious even to pretend to be united. Russia had little in the way of civic politics to suspend, but she too had a sudden abundance of patriotism. The Liberal government in Britain did not bother to proclaim a truce, yet the end result was much the same. The women suffragettes, Irish nationalists and trade unionists who had been so militant in the years before 1914 either suspended their agitation or backed the government enthusiastically. The legal side of consensus was secured by the Defence Of the Realm Act [*Doc*. 9]. Under Andrew Bonar Law, the Unionists (Conservatives) moderated their bad temper and kept a close watch over the Liberals.

Although an interest in war had been growing before 1914, so had pacifism. Its most popular expression was *The Great Illusion* by Norman Angell. He argued that modern states were too integrated economically to make war a rational option. Following this vintage liberal argument, businessmen assured themselves that a long war was out of the question because it would ruin trade. When war came, the main economic worries concerned trade and finance. Only when the war did not end after a few months did government and business think about problems that would occur in the longer run: shortages of raw materials, the disruption of the workforce with so many men in uniform, and paying for the war, which was proving to be expensive beyond all expectations. When Winston Churchill used the phrase 'business as usual', he hoped to dispel the fear that the situation was heading into unknown dangers. The trouble with this breezy complacency was that the need for victory was making old ways of managing obsolete. War tests everything. Whatever obstructs victory is dumped overboard; whatever works passes the test; and measures, manners or mores that once were unthinkable are adopted 'for the duration' if they bear the promise of victory.

WAR AIMS

Victory was pretty much the only war aim the powers formally declared. Of course they also tried to explain why they were fighting. Germany was fighting to avoid encirclement and to secure a free hand to grow to be a world power. France was fighting to expel the invader. Britain was fighting to rid the world of bullies, or at least bullies who wore pointed helmets. Canada, Australia, South Africa and India were fighting because the Empire (read Britain) was fighting. Austria–Hungary was fighting against the threat of disintegration.

Russia was fighting for the rights of the Slavic peoples. All the states claimed to be defending themselves against the aggression of others. All left the public expression of what they were fighting for, of the details of war aims and peace settlements until the fortunes of war decided the outcome.

This omission of clear and explicit war aims was more than an oversight. What a state wants to achieve through war affects the sort of war it gets. When the aims are unlimited, the war tends to be as well, as with the Second World War. The curious thing about the First World War is that, even though the avowed aims of all of the powers were either unexpressed or, when finally articulated, limited and defensive, the means by which the war was fought became increasingly open-ended and unlimited. The belligerents defined victory simply as the collapse of the enemy and dedicated all their resources to that end. So it was that after the first deaths, war was the cause of more war and seemed to take on a life of its own. In effect, the civilian leaders asked the soldiers to fight until the other side gave up. The civilians would then revise the maps and sort out the details. The soldiers in turn asked the civilians not to be back-seat drivers and to keep quiet until victory came.

In private, people high and low had war aims that were anything but defensive and limited. The best example of such a private agenda is the September Memorandum of Bethmann [*Doc. 1*]. When Professor Fritz Fischer discovered the document in the archives, he thought it proved that the government of Germany, and not just Pan German* extremists, was committed to annexations and European supremacy (Fischer, 1967). Bethmann's private aims were indeed indistinguishable from Pan German aims. They were, however, private. He drafted the memorandum before the Battle of the Marne negated the hope of a quick victory. When the god of battle left the enemy able to fight on, Bethmann refused to endorse or deny annexations. Not only would any declaration of aims play into the hands of the enemy, but it would offend either the Social Democrats, who wanted the peace to reflect the situation before the war, or the growing movement for annexations. To uphold the *Burgfrieden*, he asked the parties and interest groups to say nothing about war aims. They would trust him, he would trust the army, and the result of this stoic solidarity would be a peace that would reward Germans for their sacrifices. The British were similarly vague about their avowed aims, but they had the advantage of publicists like H.G. Wells, who provided phrases that were a substitute for policy. 'War to end war' and 'war to make the world safe for democracy' went over well at home and in America.

CHAPTER FOUR

THE WAR IN 1915: BADLY PLANNED DISASTERS

RUSSIAN POLAND, SECOND YPRES

The muddled state of war aims in 1915 corresponded to the muddled state of the war itself. Germany had failed to carry its plan to the intended conclusion but still held the strategic initiative in the east and west. In particular, Falkenhayn had the advantage of a reserve of manpower which, thanks to the central position of Germany and to the railway system, he could deploy where he wanted. Brusilov's success in September led Falkenhayn to fear that Austria–Hungary was too weak to resist Russia by herself. So he moved his reserve from west to east, using a chlorine gas attack at Ypres on 22 April to cover the withdrawal of eleven divisions and to test the effectiveness of poison gas as a weapon. Gas had not been used on the Western Front before, and the Algerians and French reservists who were its first victims broke and ran. The BEF, including the 1st Canadian Division, stood its ground on the second day and, at the cost of 2,000 lives, plugged the gap [*Doc. 7*]. Because the gas attack was experimental and the Germans intended to stay on the defensive in the west, they were not ready to exploit their initial success. The Allies quickly improvised gas masks, and poison gas became a feature of the new warfare, limited because of its dependence on the wind and terrain but increasingly part of the dehumanized environment of the Front and always deadly to the unwary [*Docs. 13* and *17*].

To attack in the east, Falkenhayn set up a two-pronged offensive in Russian Poland, with General August von Mackensen commanding the Austro-German thrust north-east in Galicia and Hindenburg attacking in the north towards Kovno [Map 2]. Hans von Seeckt was Mackensen's chief of staff; Ludendorff continued to serve with Hindenburg. Both Seeckt and Ludendorff were innovative. Seeckt put his assault divisions in the line without tipping off the Russians to the impending attack; the brief but intense preliminary bombardment also confused them, and when the German first wave attacked on 2 May, it was ordered to flow around resistance, leaving these positions to be taken by later waves. The attack went as planned and the Russians collapsed. The Austrians regained their fortress city of Przemyśl on 3 June and Lemberg on 22 June. Falkenhayn then directed Mackensen to move north. Warsaw fell on 4 August, and then the fortress city of Brest-Litovsk. To the north, Hindenburg took Kovno. By the time Falkenhayn closed down the eastern campaign, his forces had advanced 300 miles, occupied most of Russian Poland, taken a million Russian prisoners and inflicted a further million casualties. It was the most successful German campaign in the war. The loss of prestige was devastating for the Tsar, especially after he sacked the Grand Duke Nicholas as commander in chief and took his place. Tsar Nicholas could not have organized a rummage sale let alone an army. From now on, defeat would be a personal matter, bringing the very survival of the autocracy into question.

Falkenhayn was not thinking of driving into Russia proper but rather of inflicting such a defeat that the Tsar would abandon France and ask for a separate peace. Humiliation, however, made the Tsar stubborn. Nor was he alone. The loss of Russian Poland finally gave the patriotic classes of Russia something tangible for which they could fight. Seeing the helplessness of the autocracy, the middle classes started to take over the organization of the war economy. As production rose, so did inflation, making the cause of 'bread', or affordable food, into a revolutionary issue.

THE TRENCH SYSTEM AND THE CODE OF THE FRONT

Fewer men spread over greater distances kept the war in the east mobile. The war in the west was different. To understand why trench warfare prevailed there, one must first realize that it was nothing new. Since the first appearance of rifled arms with a greater zone of accurate fire, infantry had dug in for protection. In the First World War, trenches* appeared as early as the Battle of the Aisne. When the opposing armies connected the strongest defensive positions they held with trenches and barbed wire over the winter of 1914–15, the trench system emerged as a temporary improvisation. The trenches in turn were reinforced, in the German and British positions with sandbags piled to form parapets in front and paradoses to the rear (both terms derived from medieval siege warfare), in the French lines with bunches of branches to 'revet' or strengthen the constantly collapsing walls. In front of the trenches, in No Man's Land, each side staked rolls of heavy barbed wire. The teeth were razor-sharp; men could tear themselves to pieces if they were caught [*Doc. 5*]. Wiring parties worked through the nights while raiders tried to cut gaps. These gaps then showed the enemy where an attack would likely come.

Trench systems evolved gradually. They were different for each army. The British had to build on the ground in Flanders rather than dig in because of the high water table. In theory their system used three lines. The front line contained the fire and command trenches. The fire trench was zig-zagged with traverses,* with thick buttresses blocking off each section, and an infantry section of 14 men in each separate bay. The command trench, about twenty yards back, contained the dug-outs and, where possible, the latrines. The second line was the support trench, from seventy to a hundred yards behind the front line. The third line was the reserve trench, four to six hundred yards behind the support line. The French, who were still committed to attacking, used only front and support trenches and, like the British, manned the front line heavily. The Germans, who had shrewdly taken the high ground when the front stabilized, built a trench system up to 5,000 yards deep, with the forward lines lightly held and the reserves safe in massive bunkers, some dug up to a hundred feet underground.

By and large, the Germans learned about trench warfare faster than the Allies not because they had expected it, which they had not, or because they were wiser in the arts of war, which they were, but because they had an incentive to learn. They chose to stand on the defensive on the Western Front, which concentrated their mind on using their firepower and higher ground to maximum advantage. In this learning period, the Allied commanders were still thinking of attacking, leaving the unexciting details of figuring out appropriate tactics to field officers, who improvised stop-gap solutions. Few realized that in war, and perhaps in modern life, nothing is as permanent as the temporary (Daylight Savings Time, income tax, trenches). Then again, nothing is as temporary as the permanent, for the layout of the trench system was constantly modified by bombing, the weather and reconstruction. In effect, the infantry rebuilt the trenches each night. Because the trenches were always changing and the men in them usually on the move, unless they were in a front-line trench in daylight, it was almost impossible for soldiers to comprehend the labyrinth they were inside.

As trench fighting developed, a myth about the war took hold, especially among British junior officers. Myth in this case does not mean a falsification of the war experience but rather a heightened explanation of it that confirmed certain beliefs and made sense of the situation. According to the myth, young men went to war full of innocence and idealism, hoping to make the world a better place and to purge themselves of such peacetime vices as selfishness and materialism. They were murdered *en masse* by the old men, the generals, politicians, and profiteers, the noncombatants. This bitter disenchantment was muted at first, appearing occasionally in outbursts such as the declaration of the poet Siegfried Sassoon in 1916 [*Doc. 12*]. But eventually it became the dominant way of imagining and understanding the war. This myth of the Massacre of the Innocents made sense of the disjointed experience by refusing to look for any overall meaning, or indeed denying the possibility of such meaning in the world the war created. Paul Fussell (1975) has argued that instead of offering a meaningful narrative, the myth of the war imposed a binary structure:

then (naïve and innocent) and now (grizzled and world-weary), here (the trenches) and there (home), them (the noncombatants) and us, before and after [*Doc. 16*]. After the war, this myth became virtually the only way of remembering the war especially in Britain and France, expressing as it did a disillusionment not just with the war but with the peace that followed it [*Doc. 18*].

What should be noted is that the dominant myth of the war grew out of the experience of a small minority of the front soldiers, junior officers from relatively privileged backgrounds. Indeed, it could be argued that these young men were not actually front soldiers in the strict sense, because as officers, even junior officers, they visited the front lines and led raids and attacks but did not live continuously in the front-line trenches. That honour was reserved for the other ranks. For the educated officers, it was a 'literary war', to quote Paul Fussell. The overwhelming majority of front soldiers, however, came from the urban and rural working and lower-middle classes. These less educated and literate men did not preserve their experience in letters or works of the imagination, although many of the survivors later provided invaluable interviews and memoirs. Their attitude to the war can be gauged from the language they used [*Doc. 15*], the songs they sang [*Docs. 4 and 5*], the trench newspapers they wrote and read and the way they behaved. On the whole, whereas the officers saw the war through the prism of duty and service, the other ranks saw the war as unavoidable work to be carried out as part of a team, and treated it much as they had treated their civilian work.

According to the myth that arose after the war and coloured the way the war was remembered, the ordinary soldiers were doomed to their fate, which they had to endure passively. In fact, the soldiers had choices – not many to be sure, but enough to affect the conduct of the war. Seeking to show 'not . . . how the decisions of a few generals affected thousands of soldiers, but, rather how the decisions of thousands of soldiers affected a few generals', Tony Ashworth shows that front soldiers on both sides worked out a system of 'live and let live'* that prevailed in about one-third of the trench tours made by all the divisions of the BEF [7: *Chapter 7*]. Both the astronomical casualty rates for certain days and the attitude of utter disenchantment were exceptional rather than typical [*Doc. 16*].

According to Ashworth, as the trench system emerged, the front soldiers exercised the first of four choices open to them. They exchanged peace openly, with the most famous but by no means the first or last truce coming on Christmas Day 1914 on the British front. High Command was not amused and, as its grip over the war tightened, it forced the front soldiers to try a second option, inertia. They refused to take aggressive action because it made no sense against someone who could hit back. Equal vulnerability and a latent sense of fair play thus reduced the violence. Once again, High Command imposed rules to ensure that the men had the proper 'offensive spirit' [*Doc. 15, Offensive*]. Specialist units, recruited from men who wanted to be aggressive,

Plate 2 The most famous of the cartoons by Bruce Bairnsfather. The caption became a watchword for the British soldiers: 'Well, if you knows of a better 'ole, go to it' (originally printed in *The Bystander*, 1918, then *Fragments From France*, Part Five).

were sent to the Front to use mortars, grenades, sniping rifles and gas to irritate the enemy. Once again, the men refused to submit passively. They worked out a third response, ritualization. Because they were under orders, they could not openly engage in truces or refuse to be aggressive. They had to act, but they could try to ensure that what they did was not lethal, hoping that the other side would return the favour. Patrols avoided each other, gunners fired predictably at the same time and place, and each side was careful not to harass the other's ration parties. As the violence became ritualized, 'the other side' came to refer more to the other team, as in a sport, than to the enemy. The real enemy were all those outside the Front, the staff officers and civilians who were keeping the war going while imagining it to be different than it was [*Docs. 4* and *16*].

According to Ashworth, truces, inertia and ritualization made up the live and let live system, a way of improving the chances of survival that was carefully handed on to the new units that came into and took over the line. Soldiers were really civilians in uniform, and usually could not and would not abandon their civilian view of life, including the commandment of the Gospel not to kill. They fought not for King, Emperor or Country but for each other. When and if they abandoned live and let live, it was often to avenge the loss of comrades. They soon became disenchanted with the home front and its perception of the war as glorious. This created a rift between combatants and noncombatants [*Doc. 16*]. How then did nine and a half million men die if hatred was either episodic or absent at the front? By and large it happened because most of the killing was distant, mechanized and impersonal rather than face to face. Front soldiers were no killers. They were the killed.

NEUVE CHAPELLE, CHAMPAGNE, ARTOIS AND LOOS

The British discovered the strength of the German defences when they attacked at Neuve Chapelle on 10 March. The staff planners tried to approach the problem of attacking with fresh ideas. They saw that it was a gunner's war, and brought in 340 guns to fire off more rounds than in the entire Boer War. The artillery was asked to co-ordinate a fire plan instead of freelancing at targets of opportunity. The Royal Flying Corps (RFC) provided aerial reconnaissance and photography. Finally, the infantry was made familiar with the ground over which it was to attack. Haig insisted on the need for surprise and the British concealed their intentions completely.

If wise precautions and thorough preparation were enough, Neuve Chapelle would have been a success. Indeed, the first British rush advanced 1,200 yards and took the village of Neuve Chapelle. Haig got ready to pass the entire First Army through the village, including the cavalry, but nothing came of it. The second wave of infantry got entangled with the first, and then General Henry Rawlinson, commanding 4th Corps, was slow bringing up the reserves. The

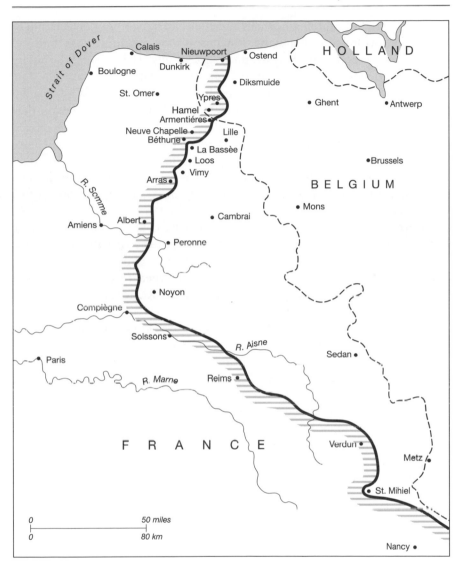

Map 3 Western Front, 1915
Adapted from Lyn Macdonald, 1915, *The Death of Innocence*, Henry Holt (New York, 1993), p. 343

German defences stiffened as the British lost their initial advantage. The whole point of a competently set defence is that it does stiffen. It lets the defenders ride out the disadvantage of being surprised or outnumbered. As long as they can hold their ground, time will be on their side, because their reinforcements will be able to arrive quicker than those for the attacking side. Moreover, the firepower of the gunners was not a magic wand. The fire had to be observed to be accurate; the shells and guns had to be free of defects and of the proper sort for the job at hand. Rawlinson soon concluded that 'bite and hold' attacks were the only way to attack successfully. The guns did the biting; their range dictated what the infantry could take and hold. He was right. Bite and hold was one of the secrets to success hidden in plain sight. Why then did he and the other responsible commanders forget or ignore the lesson they learned so early? The answer seems to be that their initial successes encouraged them to go too far, to bite off more than they could hold. In the case of Neuve Chapelle this very human flaw showed up in the hope that a whole army could funnel through the village and break out. It was not stupidity that bedevilled high command but impatience, not too little imagination, as critics often complained after the war, but too much.

Joffre remained supremely confident that he could pinch off the huge German salient formed where the front turned to the south-east. The two avenues of ground suitable for attack were at Arras and in the Champagne district. The first French offensive came in May, when 18 divisions attacked near Arras, aiming to take the high ground of Vimy Ridge that dominated the Douai plain. The main attack foundered on the elaborate German trench system, as did the British attack on Aubers Ridge. Nothing daunted, Joffre claimed that his real objective was to wear down the Germans, not to break through their lines. Wearing down, *usure* in French, was then elevated into higher diction as 'attrition'.* For the set piece in the autumn, he devised the greatest offensive of the war to date, the main blow coming in the Champagne region where the front turned and ran due east, with a supporting attack in the Artois again, including Vimy Ridge.

The French three-day bombardment in the Champagne offensive, heavy though it was, failed to breach the defences or cut the wire. The French repeated the pattern they and the British had set at Neuve Chapelle and Arras: success on the first day (25 September), soon giving way to uncoordinated local actions, and finally, after ten days of thrashing around, a futile attack against the German second lines. For a two-mile dent in the German lines, the French lost 145,000 men. To the north in Artois, the Allies fared even worse. Joffre had pressured Sir John French to attack the industrial sector north of Lens. Haig, who was to command the attack, argued that the target area was heavily fortified and of little military value. After a bombardment that was light because of the shortage of shells and thus brief enough to surprise the Germans, the British took the village of Loos and pushed on to break through the second German line near the suburbs of Lens. They released 150 tons of chlorine gas, killing 600 Germans but also, when it blew back, killing or disabling many of their own men. Sir John French unwisely kept his main reserves 16 miles to the rear, and by the time they reached the battle, the Germans had sealed the breach. With confusion reigning, the British second wave advanced in column into German machine-gun fire. When Sir John finally shut down the attack, the British had lost around 8,000 officers and men, killed and wounded. All they gained was another useless salient. It was at Loos that medical officers first observed 'hysterical manifestations' in some of the younger soldiers, the first trickle of what was to be called 'shell shock'. In an official dispatch, Sir John tried to blame Haig for the delay with the reserves. Haig, however, was better connected than Sir John and, on 17 December, became Commander-in-Chief of the BEF. From the Scottish family that produced the famous whisky, Haig started his career in the cavalry and rose quickly, helped by his wife's friendships with the Court and his own real abilities as a staff officer. Taciturn of speech, he was a clear-headed writer, in some ways like a top commander in the next war, Dwight D. Eisenhower. Haig was much better than the pig-headed Presbyterian of later legend. He had long been convinced that modern wars would be protracted, with the decisive battle coming only after a long wearing-down struggle.

GALLIPOLI

Lord Kitchener complained that what was going on was not war and he did not know what to do. In fairness to him, this should be coupled with his hunch at the start of the war that it would be long, and his certainty at the start of 1915 that the German lines in France could not be carried by assault. By that time the War Council agreed with his view, but it could not offer an alternative to the Western Front. It could not because there was no alternative except a negotiated peace, and with Kitchener's New Army* still training and the prospects of the Allies likely to improve in the long run, the War Council saw no reason to quit. However, responding to a request from the War Council for options, the Admiralty in early 1915 proposed 'a naval expedition in February to bombard and take the Gallipoli peninsula, with Constantinople as its objective' (Wilson, 1986: 107).

At the eastern end of the Mediterranean, the Dardanelles Straits ran into the Sea of Marmora, on the coast of which lay the capital city of the Ottoman Empire, Constantinople. The Straits were 41 miles long, four miles wide at most and as narrow as three-quarters of a mile. The Gallipoli peninsula formed the north coast of the Straits, Asiatic Turkey the south coast. To pass through the Straits, the Royal Navy would have to destroy the forts along the shore and neutralize the minefields, which meant destroying the shore batteries protecting them.

The Royal Navy began to bombard Gallipoli on 19 February. The fortresses were scarcely touched, but the assault committed Britain to carry on. So Kitchener quickly authorized the dispatch of a regular division, the 29th, to Gallipoli. Even with the Australians and New Zealanders (the Anzacs) and some French added to the 29th, the military force would amount to only 75,000 men, half the total he had earlier promised.

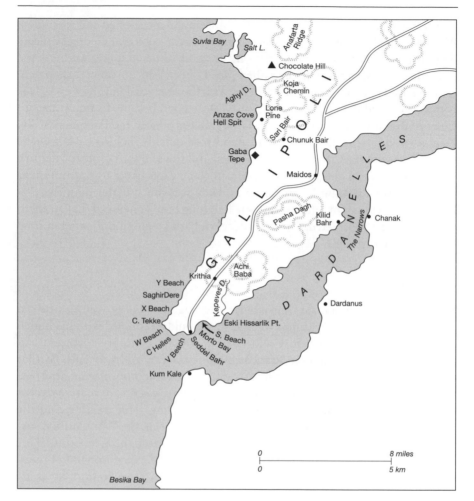

Map 4 Gallipoli
Adapted from Lyn Macdonald, 1915, *The Death of Innocence*, Henry Holt (New York, 1993), p. 343

Meanwhile, the naval attack had bogged down. The navy could not suppress Turkish fire from the land and so could not sweep the minefields. When the naval commander fell ill, Admiral de Robeck took over command and carried out the original plan, a daylight attack on 18 March using 16 obsolete battleships to hit the forts. Unexpected mines sunk three of the battleships, although in shallow water, and put three more out of action, and the mine-sweepers never reached the minefields. De Robeck withdrew, promising to return to support an amphibious landing.

General Sir Ian Hamilton, in command of the landings, was given no staff for planning and logistics and had only six weeks to figure out where and how to land his men. He chose Cape Helles at the tip and Suvla Bay and Gaba Tepe halfway down the north coast. The invasion kicked off on 25 April, which later became Anzac Day, commemorating the coming of age of the Dominions of Australia and New Zealand. The Anzacs missed Gaba Tepe and landed on a smaller beach, but they managed to advance inland despite the rough ground and fierce resistance from the Turks. The main force of the Anzacs landed at Anzac Cove and dug in. The landing at Cape Helles had a mixed result. The British and Anzacs scratched out perimeter defences on the beaches and hung on.

By now, the navy had stopped promising any result even if it did force the Straits, while Kitchener had decided not to divert any more men from the Western Front. By July, several attacks from the Cape Helles beach heads had failed dismally, and the only point from which an attack seemed promising was Anzac Cove, originally a secondary position. To achieve surprise, Hamilton tried night attacks. Once again, despite the courage of the Anzacs, the inherent difficulties of the situation prevailed and the attack stalled. On 6 August, Hamilton landed his New Army divisions at Suvla Bay, north of Anzac Cove and behind the Turkish front. The Turks were surprised and by the end of the first day, the British were close to a victory. But the local commander, Sir Frederick Stopford, dithered and let the beach head degenerate into a shambles, giving the Turks time to organize their defences.

By September, the summer heat, the flies, dysentery and disappointment had worn out everyone on the British side. Hamilton was sacked in October. To cover up the fiasco as much as investigate it, a Dardanelles Committee of Inquiry was set up in London, and then promptly changed to a smaller War Committee from which advocates of Gallipoli were excluded. That meant Churchill, who had earlier been demoted to a junior Cabinet portfolio. When Kitchener went to Gallipoli, he agreed to evacuate. The Cabinet fell in line on 7 December. Because the Turks were glad to see the British leave, the evacuation was the one aspect of this badly planned disaster that went right. From its muddled origins through its tragic course to its pointless end, Gallipoli was a textbook example of the dangers of making things up as one went along. 'Plan' might seem like a four-letter word when its military results are contemplated, but Gallipoli serves as a reminder of the grimmer fate in store for those who proceed without planning. Of the 410,000 British and Commonwealth and 79,000 French soldiers who served at Gallipoli, 205,000 of the former and 47,000 of the latter were killed, wounded, sick or missing.

CHAPTER FIVE

THE HOME FRONTS

On the home fronts, 'business as usual' was a hollow pretence by 1915. In Britain, the grim reality of war arrived with the shell crisis and the lists of dead. In Germany, it took the form of an increasingly bitter debate over war aims and submarine warfare. The occupation of a tenth of France concentrated the mind of the French wonderfully and ruled out any fond hopes of an easy war. Severe inflation saw to it that staying alive preoccupied the people of Russia. Ethnic nationalism had divided the subjects of the Habsburg Empire long before the war and now intensified, with the added complication that Slavs in the Empire were pitted against fellow Slavs in Russia. When Britain and France bribed Italy to enter the war in May 1915, the peoples of the Habsburg Empire finally had an enemy they could all dislike. Unfortunately for both them and the Italians, the only place they could meet to fight was in the valley of the Isonzo river and in the Dolomite Alps north and east of Venice. Between June 1915 and June 1917, there were ten distinct 'battles of the Isonzo', none conferring an advantage to either side for long and all adding up to abject misery comparable to the suffering the Germans and British endured in the flood plains of Flanders. German help gave the Austro–Hungarians a thin edge, culminating in the rout of the Italians at Caporetto in October 1917, sometimes called the Twelfth Battle of the Isonzo. A year later, the Italians with British help broke through to Austro–Hungarian headquarters at Vittorio Veneto, in effect applying a finishing blow to the ancient Habsburg Empire.

BRITAIN: DORA AND CONSCRIPTION

The British saw no option but to use illiberal means to defend their liberal way of life. At the outset of war, in response to the public frenzy about the danger posed by German spies, the Asquith government passed the Defence of the Realm Act (DORA) which in a few sentences conferred sweeping powers on the Cabinet to maintain order and security [Doc. 9]. The spy craze soon abated, in part because there were so few German agents in Britain, and public support for the war remained solid, if not at the near-hysterical intensity of 1914, but the restrictions on civil liberties increased. The Irish Nationalists under John Redmond, disappointed when Home Rule for Ireland was postponed for the duration, nevertheless supported the war. Strikes suddenly gave way to labour peace, and the unionized working class proved just as willing to volunteer for service as the rest of the nation. The suffragettes in the Women's Social and Political Union (WSPU) abruptly broke off their militant campaign to get the vote for women and supported the war. The united front of the British people ran deep.

The flood of volunteers shows the unity. Over a million men enlisted by the end of 1914, and 2.2 million by September 1915. They swamped the makeshift organization Kitchener and the War Office set up for the New Army that was to replace the Regular Army that was being decimated in France. Thousands of the volunteers went not into the New Army, however, but into existing Territorial divisions. These were units of part-time reservists formed as part of the reforms of the British Army that the Minister of War, Lord Haldane, introduced after the Boer War. Professional soldiers like Kitchener doubted the effectiveness and reliability of the Territorials, but necessity overrode such prejudices and in the end the Territorials proved to be a vital part of the British military effort. On the other hand, the ramshackle arrangements for the New Army resulted in such tragedies as the Pals battalions,* by which men joined up with their mates on the promise that they would serve together. The social catastrophe this unleashed when men from a city, town or common workplace all too often died together is still difficult to measure or grasp. Yet the example of the Pals (or 'Chums') points to the innocence of these early days, in which men joined because their family expected it, because the idea of a brief holiday with pay was attractive, because, as the song said, 'every girl loves a soldier', or because the men believed in the nation's cause.

The flood of volunteers left the authorities with two messy problems: how to train them and how to replace them in the workforce. Training remained haphazard. Retired officers and non-commissioned officers (NCOs) were 'dug out' to provide experienced leadership, which all too often was experienced to the point of being antique. In the end, the New Army used its time in camp to become physically fit and to learn the rudiments of drill. Given the novelty of the trench experience lying in wait, its real training would have to come on the job when it reached the trenches. As for replacing the volunteers, the obvious solution was to use women but this required delicate negotiations with the trade unions, who feared that their hard-won rights and privileges would be diluted. Men who left their jobs to fight were guaranteed their positions when they returned. Because of the importance of industrial workers to the war economy, especially in metal-working and mining, they tended to be retained in their pre-war jobs more than white-collar workers were in theirs. J.M. Winter has estimated that if the same proportion of blue-collar workers had served as did white-collar, an additional 600,000 men would have been freed up to serve over the duration of the war (Winter, 1986). Although the appearance of women in industrial jobs was much publicized, especially in munitions, most of the substitution for men took place in the commercial and non-industrial sectors. Replacement labour also came from the servant class and from the underclass that had been almost permanently unemployed before the war. Because families at the bottom of the social order received a steady income for the first time, the war improved their situation dramatically. This showed in the sudden decrease in infant mortality despite the absence of half the doctors, who were serving in the army. Mothers were able to feed their children and themselves properly.

As the rush to volunteer abated, the government had to reconsider its antipathy to conscription, which meant rethinking a basic tenet of liberalism, the aversion to state coercion. Asquith was not one to hurry a decision and handled the issue in stages. First came Lord Derby's scheme by which the eligible male population was divided into annual classes. Only single men would join up when they came of age, and instead of conscription, which smacked of Prussian militarism, they would be persuaded to 'attest' or promise to serve. Tribunals were set up to consider exemptions. Canada and Australia tried similar compromises, but the casualty rate for the infantry rendered them futile. In January 1916, the Military Service Act conscripted all single men between 18 and 41. After a muddled effort to honour Liberal principles, the government introduced universal conscription in May 1916. Even though voluntarism increased the army by 2 million men, despite 400,000 casualties, it seemed by the spring of 1916 to be another part of the old world that was vanishing. Canada followed the British example in 1917, but Australians twice rejected conscription in plebiscites. In August 1917, then Prime Minister Lloyd George put Sir Auckland Geddes in charge of the Ministry of National Service and empowered him to allocate manpower between the army and industry. In setting his criteria, he retained the existing policy that protected manual over white-collar workers.

PROPAGANDA AND CENSORSHIP

It is tempting but misleading to attribute the unity of the nations at war to propaganda. The British in particular seemed to have mastered the dark arts of persuasion. In fact, German behaviour, as with the execution of British nurse Edith Cavell and the sinking of the passenger liner *Lusitania*, both in the spring of 1915, sold the war to the British public. The government did not see the need for an official propaganda organization aimed at the home front until 1918. Up until that time the main concern of the government was neutral opinion. In 1914, C.F.G. Masterman, head of the National Insurance

Plate 3 Women of the Land Army in Britain (Imperial War Museum Q30679).

Commission, was asked to recruit well-known writers to influence foreign opinion. Masterman's group took the name of the building in which he worked, Wellington House. It was a secret organization set up with separate bureaus to handle target countries, America being the most important. The propagandists studied the local media in their assigned countries and published pamphlets and books geared to local opinion. Even today, most of these publications appear to be impartial rather than hate-the-Hun ranting, and of course they bear no indication of their connection to the British government. For America, the Canadian-born novelist Sir Gilbert Parker analyzed press opinion and set up a mailing list of 33,000 prominent Americans. He gave American publishers commissions to publish books that Wellington House approved, which were then sent to those on the mailing list. He also organized film and lecture tours. The rule of thumb at Wellington House was to keep the message balanced and seemingly academic. The lack of any obvious connection between the British government and the propaganda helped to maintain the impression of objective honesty. The Germans also concentrated on American opinion, but their efforts were more obvious and heavy-handed and were no match for the more adroit British.

In all the countries, those on top kept popular feelings on a short leash by censoring the news. The military clamped down immediately in Germany, but neutral press reports available through Holland and Switzerland helped to offset the official version of the war. Lord Kitchener allowed a journalist to be assigned to the staff of the Commander in Chief. After Kitchener approved the reports, they were published under the byline 'Eyewitness'. Then in May 1915, the press managed to have permanent correspondents assigned to the BEF to supply more useful news. If the war correspondents failed to report the truth about the war, this was in part because, even if they were experienced and honest, grasping what exactly was happening and then expressing it clearly were almost impossible tasks. After all, not many front soldiers found the truth about the war easy to comprehend or express. Why should it have been easier for outsiders? Truth was not the first casualty of war. Truth lived, but it lived in isolation, unknowable and silent.

WAR ECONOMIES

The sword was, for the moment, as powerless as the pen. To explain the failures at Loos and Neuve Chapelle, Sir John French claimed there was a shortage of shells. The press took up his complaint. The government in turn blamed the munitions workers, and to ensure that they concentrated on their work, pubs were closed from mid-afternoon until evening. This did little to increase productivity but did play a role in improving the health of the lower classes. The BEF did indeed face a shell crisis. It lacked enough of them and those it had were often faulty and of the wrong type. Yet the same was true of every army in 1915. No one had fully anticipated how important heavy artillery would be. Because the habit of planning and government intervention were far more prevalent in France and Germany than in Britain, these states moved quickly to set up command economies for war production. Despite the British faith in *laissez-faire* principles, part of the liberal civilization for which they believed they were fighting, they moved over to what was becoming known as 'war socialism' almost as quickly as the others. This became clear when the muddle surrounding the War Office forced the government to create the new Ministry of Munitions, under the dynamic leadership of the Chancellor of the Exchequer, David Lloyd George.

GERMANY, WAR AIMS AND WAR MEANS: SUBMARINES

In Germany, meanwhile, the euphoria of August evaporated after the dead-lock on the Marne but the *Burgfrieden* persisted. Although the left wing of the Social Democrats became increasingly sceptical about the justice of the German cause, and in particular the claim to be acting only in self-defence, the party remained loyal to Bethmann. So did the left-learning liberals, the Progressives. The more right-wing National Liberals had been deeply divided before the war between those dedicated to serving the interests of heavy industry and the status quo and those tied to commerce and light industry and interested in a modicum of political reform. Now war aims provided the line of fracture, with a majority of National Liberals favouring annexations in the east and west. The Conservatives, representing the interests of land-owners and old Prussia, and the Free Conservatives, who were close to heavy industry, were the most committed to a so-called 'peace of victory', and were angry at the refusal of Bethmann Hollweg to commit himself to such a peace openly. By the spring of 1915, the right-wing parties had formed a war aims majority in the *Reichstag*. It worked with a war aims movement outside the *Reichstag*, made up of pressure groups representing heavy industry, large agriculture and the free professions, especially academics.

The means of waging war rather than the ends for which it was waged came to threaten Bethmann's delicate balancing act and the *Burgfrieden*. In 1914–15, submarines were too new a weapon to be fully covered by interna-tional conventions and rules governing blockading at sea. With Britain's huge surface fleet and her great advantage in merchant shipping, she had only a secondary interest in an undersea weapon of stealth. By the logic of Germany's continental position and restricted access to the open sea, she should have concentrated on submarines, but Tirpitz's obsession with matching the Royal Navy in the North Sea and his exploitation of the prestige which only battle-ships offered led him to give the submarine a low priority.

Right from the start of the war the British turned the entire North Sea into a war zone in which they prescribed safe routes for neutral shipping, which had to travel under British escort. They further declared that all goods heading for Germany, including food and raw materials, were contraband liable to seizure. This was economic war with a vengeance, and it could be argued that the British blockade* and not the German use of Zeppelins to bomb East Anglia in April 1915 or the sinking of the passenger liner *Lusitania* was the first instance of intentionally total war, making no distinction between soldiers and civilians.

Diplomatically, the Germans had no effective answer. They already guessed that the submarine would be the only way to counter-blockade and were reluctant to denounce ruthless methods they might have to use themselves. Yet they were cornered strategically as well, because the only way that they could gain the advantage at sea would be if the Royal Navy was inept enough to be lured into a pitched battle on German terms. The Royal Navy, however, had seized the initiative at the start, much like the Germans did on land, and was determined not to lose it through careless adventures. Late in 1914, the German admirals threatened to use submarines to blockade the British coast, but the threats were hollow, if only because the Kaiser flatly opposed all-out submarine warfare and Germany had only a handful of submarines available.

The Kaiser's scruples get to the heart of the German dilemma. He thought that drowning innocent civilians was frightful. Yet why should the German counter-blockade with submarines be more frightful than the British blockade with surface ships? It was because of the nature of the particular weapon. Using surface ships, the British could board a neutral ship, inspect the cargo and confiscate any war goods, with a promise to compensate shippers after the war. The intercepted ship and crew could either be sent on their way or escorted to a British port. Submariners worked differently. They preferred to attack on the surface, using torpedoes and deck guns to sink ships. Travelling submerged was reserved for running to and from station by stealth. Such attacks meant destroying the cargo and drowning the crews because the small size of the submarines prevented them from picking up survivors.

The Germans wrestled with the problem of what to do for six months. Neutral nations, led by America, were unwilling to pay Germany the respect they showed Britain for the simple reason that Germany had only 22 submarines, of which only a third could be patrolling on station in the war zone at any given time. In February 1915, the Germans formally initiated submarine warfare. They declared that German submarines would sink every enemy vessel encountered in the waters around the British Isles. They would spare neutral ships, but given the British habit of sailing under neutral flags and given too the accidents normal to war, neutrals would be well-advised to stay away. The Chief of the Naval Staff, Admiral von Pohl, actually wanted to sink neutral ships on sight, thus launching unrestricted submarine warfare right away, but Bethmann and the Kaiser, already nervous about the American reaction, overruled him.

The February declaration gave Britain the excuse to make her blockade of Germany total, so that all trade with Germany, even through neutral ports, would henceforth be stopped. The German decision brought an angry protest from President Wilson, who informed Germany that America would hold her fully accountable for any indiscriminate attack on American ships and would even go to war to defend the freedom of the seas. The worst thing about the German bluff was that it was quickly seen to be hollow, so that the neutrals kept on trading with Britain.

On 7 May 1915, a German submarine sank the British Cunard liner *Lusitania* off the Irish coast. The attack conformed to the policy that Germany had announced in February, and technically the liner could be classed as an auxiliary cruiser and thus a legitimate target. Although only 128 of the 1,200 victims were American, the earlier German attempt to frighten neutrals now came back to haunt them, and in America, one would have thought the *Mayflower* had been sunk. In a series of notes, Wilson first insisted that all forms of submarine warfare were illegal, because even if a submarine attacked on the surface like a cruiser, it could not take care of survivors. His third note, in July, admitted the novelty of the submarine and thus the irrelevance of any appeal to traditional restraints. It went on to point out that, since the sinking of the *Lusitania*, the Germans had indeed found it possible to limit the use of submarines to surface interception and thus to abide by 'cruiser rules'.* So the war at sea could be limited, and if the Germans nevertheless reverted to terrorism, America would be forced to consider war. Germany quietly backed down. The German navy fitted the submarines with deck guns, which allowed them to surface, inspect neutral ships to ensure they were not carrying contraband and, if they were, to evacuate the ships before sinking them. In the period between May and July 1915, submarines were able to deal with 86 per cent of the merchant ships they sank in this limited or cruiser method.

In August, a U-boat sank another British liner, the *Arabic*, despite explicit orders from the Kaiser that all large passenger liners were to be spared. Again, President Wilson protested angrily, and this time, thanks to the support of the Kaiser, the civilian leaders of Germany prevailed over the admirals. The U-boats were ordered not to sink enemy passenger liners without warning. When Tirpitz denounced such a weak response to American threats, his loyal supporter, the chief of naval staff, was replaced with one more in tune with the chancellor. By late 1915, nine months of crisis over the submarine had settled down into a German-American detente.* The Germans had forced the world to concede that the submarine, when used like a surface cruiser, was a legitimate means of war, while the Americans had forced the Germans to forego the most ruthless and effective use of the weapon. For Americans, there was still the parallel outrage of the British blockade, but by helping to support the price of cotton, hard-hit by the loss of German markets, the British appeased American opinion more effectively than the Germans could or would.

Bethmann had dodged a political crisis and preserved the shell of the *Burg-frieden*, but at a heavy cost. If and when the German admirals built a fleet of U-boats sufficient to counter-blockade effectively, his concern about the American reaction would pale beside the imperative of using a war-winning weapon [*Doc. 2*].

CHAPTER SIX

1916: ATTRITION AND
THE WELL-PLANNED DISASTERS

The third year of the war featured human misery of a type and scale that defied understanding or conventional description, a sense among some of the front soldiers that they had been betrayed and abandoned, and at home a growing weariness with the war, which translated either into defeatism or a grim determination to stay the course. In other words, the war we now remember finally arrived. One might think that the alternative to badly planned disasters would be well-planned triumphs. Instead, the world got well-planned disasters that took on a horrific scale because of the thoroughness and ingenuity of the planning. They were disasters not because of incompetence, cold-bloodedness or bad luck but because of their context. They took place in a titanic struggle in which the two sides were more or less equal, especially in their capacity to mess up the hopes and plans of the other side. What the Prussian writer Clausewitz called the 'friction' of war, the inability of those in command to impose their will effectively, dominated the course of events. Accounts of the war that stress how badly it was managed usually imply that it could have been much tidier or better run. Such critiques are like moving flags around a map of a battlefield well after the battle. They use hindsight to predict the past and to say, in effect, that things would have gone much better if Napoleon, Caesar or maybe even if the author had been in charge. The starting point to understanding the war in its maturity, however, is to accept that its horrors and its waywardness were built-in. Of course the fighting could have been better managed. There is room for criticism or for speculation along the lines of 'if only this or that had been done'. But not much. What happens at the sharp end of modern wars is remarkably resistant to close control from above. Just look at today's headlines – whatever day it is.

JUTLAND

The first battle to typify the stalemate took place at sea. On 31 May 1916, the German High Seas fleet under Vice-Admiral Reinhard Scheer set out from Wilhelmshaven to lure the British Grand fleet to its destruction. Still facing a disparity in ship totals, Scheer intended to use his battle cruisers, under the command of Vice-Admiral Franz von Hipper, as bait to lure the British battle cruisers under Sir David Beatty within range of the main High Seas fleet. The British sailed, hoping that Beatty's ships would lure Hipper's. The six-hour battle conformed more to British than to German expectations, so that twice the Grand fleet crossed the German 'T' – that is, formed the top of a T so that every one of its guns could bear on the enemy while only the forward German guns could fire back. Yet the Germans sank 111,980 tons of British warships and killed 6,945 sailors; the British sank half the tonnage, 62,233 tons, and killed 2,921 German sailors. The discrepancy was due in part to British complacency; the Admiralty had known for over a year about the problem of flash control in its battle cruisers, whereby flames from exploding shells could penetrate to the main ammunition magazines* because safety systems were disconnected to speed the transfer of shells to the guns. This uncorrected problem led directly to the explosion of three battle cruisers at Jutland with the loss of virtually all hands. In addition, British signalling was deficient, British ammunition was inferior to the German, and the British commanders' overall handling of the Grand fleet was cautious to the point of paralysis. Yet Churchill was right to comment later that Admiral Sir John Jellicoe, the Commander of the Grand fleet, was the only man who could lose the war in an afternoon. By not losing at Jutland, Jellicoe won. Although the Germans won a rare propaganda victory when their dispatch came out before Jellicoe had returned to Scapa Flow and the British public believed the German version, the Kaiser and the German admirals did not. They knew the British remained in control of the seas. The German fleet returned to its harbour at 4.30 a.m. on 1 June and in effect stayed put thereafter.

VERDUN

By the end of 1915, France had lost half her regular officers and as many men as Britain was to lose in the entire war. Joffre was undisturbed. The only original commander left, he was in effect the Generalissimo of the Entente. On 6 December, the Allied commanders met at his sumptuous headquarters in Chantilly. He proclaimed that the Artois and Champagne offensives had brought 'brilliant tactical results'. Only bad weather and a shortage of munitions, he claimed, had prevented them from ending the war. Because war production was improving and the British New Army would soon take the field, Joffre intended to repeat these frontal attacks on a grander scale in the coming years. For the location of the final battle, Joffre chose the valley of the Somme river, hitherto a quiet sector. To support this offensive in the west, the Russians would hit the Austro–Hungarians in the east and the Italians would attack in the south.

Falkenhayn was making his own plans for 1916. His cool overview of Germany's situation was clear in the analysis of the war he prepared for the Kaiser in December 1915 [*Doc. 2*]. With relentless logic, he argued that a limited attack on the hallowed fortress complex in and around Verdun would force the French to defend at all costs. This would lure the French within range of German guns, bleed France white and cost the real enemy, Britain, her main ally. On 20 December, the Kaiser approved Falkenhayn's proposal, and on Christmas Eve, planning began for Operation *Gericht*, Execution Place, a limited attack that turned into the longest continuous battle in history.

In theory, Falkenhayn had chosen the ground well. Verdun had been a fortified city since Roman times, and by 1914, succeeding generations of French military engineers had turned it into the most formidable defensive position in the world. When the Western Front took shape, it draped itself around Verdun, so that the fortress was at the tip of a huge salient. Successive rings of hills surrounded the city itself, which had been reduced from its peace-time population of 15,000 to around 3,000 garrison troops. On the ridge of each outlying hill there were fortresses; German maps showed no fewer than twenty major and forty intermediate satellite forts. The river Meuse ran through the town, cutting the whole sector into two parts, the Right Bank or eastern half and the Left Bank or western. There were two fortified lines on the Left Bank and three on the Right Bank, where Falkenhayn intended to attack, with the outer line anchored by the massive forts of Moulainville, Vaux and Douamont. The Germans did not know that the French General Staff had come to scorn fixed defences and fortifications, which they assumed from the experience of Liège in 1914 could not stand up to German heavy guns. So Verdun had been stripped of its guns and most of its garrison.

Some of the French soldiers on the spot began to suspect that an attack was coming, but Joffre and his staff treated their reports as alarmist and continued to weaken Verdun. The strict secrecy with which the Germans covered their massive preparations reinforced Joffre's habitual deaf ear for bad news. For the first time in the war, the Germans used aircraft to achieve protective air cover over an entire sector. The French were unaware of the miles of new railway lines laid down to bring in munitions and supplies for the 140,000 men of the Fifth Army due to attack. In all, the Germans deployed 850 guns, including 13 of the howitzers that had smashed Liège, two 15 inch naval guns for long-range work; 17 Austrian 305 mm mortars, 306 field guns; 152 mine-throwers; and several new additions to the horror, flame-throwers. All this firepower faced only 270 French guns. The 72 German battalions in the first wave would face only 34 French battalions.

The preliminary German attack began on 19 February. The bombardment stunned the French front soldiers with its intensity, but enough of them survived to break up the attack. The Fifth Army launched its main push on

21 February, quickly taking the village of Haumont, which opened up a ravine leading south to the next strong point and exposed the flank of the Bois de Caures, where Colonel Émile Driant was holding out valiantly. Driant was in his sixties. After a distinguished Army career, he had been elected to the National Assembly. Rejoining the Army when war broke out, he was assigned to the Verdun sector and soon predicted that Joffre's policy of weakening the defences there would lead to disaster. Knobelsdorf finally had to send three entire Army Corps and around 10,000 tons of shells against Driant. Down to eighty men, he stood in the open directing counter-fire until he was killed.

The weak second line on the Right Bank collapsed on 24 February, and when the third line broke, a path opened to Fort Douamont. By the end of the day, the entire Verdun position was tottering. With superior range and technique, German gunners had silenced their French counterparts. The French wounded were in danger of freezing to death. Verdun was wide open, but the Germans did not know it. They were trying to figure out what had happened at Fort Douamont.

Fort Douamont was situated at 2 o'clock if one thinks of Verdun as the centre of a clock. Taking it was an honour that the tough Prussians in the 24th Brandenburg Regiment coveted, and they were considerably miffed when their neighbouring regiment, the Westphalians from West Germany, drew the assignment. Among the Brandenburgers was Sergeant Kunze. All afternoon, Kunze and his unit of ten men pushed south until they stood before Fort Douamont. He had orders to remove any obstacle to the advance of the infantry, and he reckoned that Fort Douamont was definitely an obstacle. It did seem odd that the French guns were aimed far off and there were no garrison troops visible. He pushed on through a gap in the wire, across the moat, and by forming his men into a gymnastic pyramid, into the fort. Still no sign of the enemy. He went on alone. After one small group of French gunners escaped capture, he surprised a larger group and barricaded them in their room. By now, three other German units, also acting independently, had crept into Douamont. They joined Kunze around 4.30 p.m. They had captured Douamont in forty-five minutes without firing a shot. No wonder. Joffre had reduced the garrison to fifty-six elderly gunners, and when it had occurred to the French to reinforce the place, everyone thought someone else was doing it. To get Douamont back, the French lost 100,000 men.

While Germany rang its church bells and celebrated, Falkenhayn worried that Verdun itself might fall as easily as Douamont, undermining his whole scheme. French honour had not yet been engaged, mainly because the French army was issuing communiqués ranging from outright lying to solemn assurances that losing fortresses was a cunning way to win the war. When the commander of the 37th Division panicked and pulled back to the Meuse, the entire Right Bank seemed ready to fall, and no amount of spin control could cover the threat to the honour and security of France.

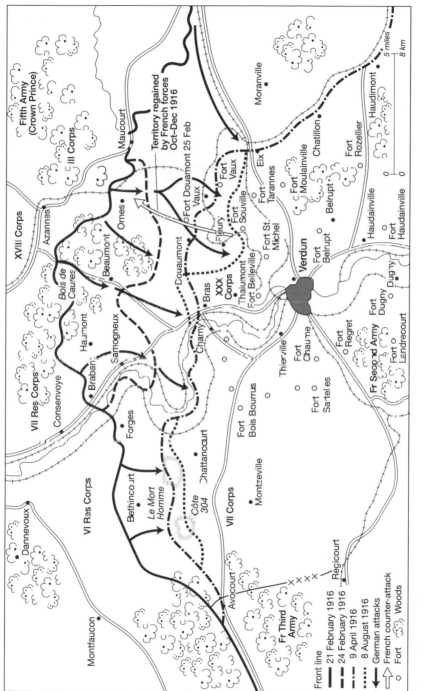

Map 5 Verdun, 1916
Adapted from Richard Natkiel, *Atlas of Twentieth-Century Warfare*, Bison Books (London, 1982, reprinted 1989), p. 45

The situation was saved by de Castelnau, Joffre's Chief of Staff. As a devout Catholic aristocrat, he was a misfit in the army. Making him stick out even more, he was able and intelligent. He had been promoted to Chief of Staff by another clever misfit, Galliéni, by now the Minister of War and Joffre's bitter rival. By the evening of 23 February, he had decided that the situation was grave enough to warrant waking Joffre after he had gone to bed. Joffre agreed with de Castelnau's offer to visit the battlefield and take stock. He also agreed that the Second Army, under General Philippe Pétain, be sent in to reinforce Verdun, with Pétain assuming command. Once at Verdun, de Castelnau decided that Pétain should be ordered to defend not just the Left Bank west of the Meuse but also what remained on the Right Bank, including Verdun itself. Critics have suggested that de Castelnau should have stuck to his first notion, giving up Verdun and holding a shortened salient on the Left Bank. But would the French troops hold on the Left Bank, or would they keep retreating? De Castelnau feared the latter. So he preferred to take a stand. He was doing precisely what Falkenhayn hoped.

Until 1914, Pétain's icy personality, peasant pessimism and unfashionable contempt for offensives had blighted his career. His passion for the defence rested on his sensible appreciation of the stopping power of rifles, machine guns and artillery, summed up in his remark that 'one does not fight with men against *materiel*'. In the first phase of trench war, he and the times finally coincided. As one general after another was dismissed, Pétain kept making sure that more Germans were hurt by his decisions than Frenchmen and his star kept rising.

Pausing at Headquarters to consult Joffre, Pétain sensed a hint of panic, and more than a hint at Verdun, which he reached late on 25 February. De Castelnau still remained calm, and together the two men agreed to hold on the Right Bank. Pétain's first move was to institute proper barrages from carefully selected positions. Then he made sure that men and supplies could reach Verdun, even though there was no railway and only a narrow fifty-mile road. He organized the maintenance of this road, the *Voie Sacrée* or Sacred Road, despite constant German fire and a thaw on 28 February that turned the road into a swamp. The lifeline held, and Verdun was able to get reinforcements and the 2,000 tons of supplies it needed each day. Finally, he ensured that the remaining strong-points on the Right Bank were properly defended. There would be no more cheap wins for the Germans, no more Douamonts.

The appointment of Pétain marked a turning-point, in part because it coincided with setbacks for the Germans. The same rains that turned the *Voie Sacrée* to mud made it almost impossible to bring up the heavy guns to support the infantry. As German guns became less effective, the French guns, reorganized by Pétain, became deadly, especially when they could fire across the Meuse into the exposed flanks of the German advance on the Right Bank. By the end of February, German losses had caught up to the French. Falkenhayn could have diverted reserves from Flanders and Picardy, but he still wanted to keep the battle limited.

Falkenhayn had nothing much to say when he conferred with the commanders of the Fifth Army at the end of the month. The Crown Prince and Knobelsdorf could only repeat their plea for more resources to allow them to spread the attack to the Left Bank and cut off the single road supplying Verdun. In the end, Falkenhayn agreed. In effect, once the German attack down the centre stalled, they decided to get it going again by attacking on both the wings, on the Left Bank and Fort Vaux. So much for the limited offensive Falkenhayn had planned. He had doubled both the frontage and manpower of the German commitment, and he no longer held the advantage of surprise. Pétain expected a heavy attack on the Left Bank, where the open and rolling ground was dominated by Mort Homme, a hill with a double summit. He positioned his guns to good effect and when the Germans attacked on 6 March, French artillery, together with infantry counter-attacks, stopped them short of Mort Homme. On the Right Bank, the attack on Fort Vaux stalled. The Fifth Army attacked Mort Homme again a week later. Once again, the first wave overran the French but was caught in the open by the French guns firing from the next hill to the south, the Bois Bourrus. When the Germans struggled closer to the Bois Bourrus, they were caught by guns firing from Côte 304 to the west of Mort Homme. They were now discovering the grim logic of attacking a continuous front. All the planners could do was to widen the attack, hoping to neutralize the guns at the shoulders and so free the push up the centre. To take Verdun, they had to take Mort Homme on the Left Bank; to take that, they had to take the Bois Bourrus; to take that, they had to take Côte 304; and to take that, they had to take Avocourt, at the western end of the Verdun sector. In fact, they did take Avocourt when a French division ran away, demoralized by too much Verdun. Once in Avocourt, French guns pinned the Germans down, and for the first time in the war, the OHL heard reports of poor morale, and even of units refusing to go over the top. In part, this was because of the policy of keeping divisions in the line for long periods instead of rotating them through reserve and rest, as Pétain was now doing and the British had done all along. Mainly, however, the Germans were reacting to the tenacious French defence. Both sides had too much Verdun.

By early April, the Germans decided to attack along the entire Verdun sector. The assault on Mort Homme reached the lower of the two summits, at which point the exhausted Germans looked up to see the French on the higher crest. A few days later, the French recaptured the lower summit. Early in May, with oppressive heat replacing the snow and rain of the earlier battle, the Germans took Côte 304 by blowing it up with the most concentrated shell fire of the war so far. With this, the line of defence that Pétain had established when he arrived suffered its first breach. The second came in May when Mort Homme fell. Nevertheless, in clearing the obstacles on the Left Bank and holding up their advance on the Right, the Germans had taken greater losses than the French, doubled the limited offensive Falkenhayn had intended, and joined the French as fellow victims on the Execution Ground.

At this point, the Germans should have been able to resume their original attack on the Right Bank. The weather was bad, however, and the commanders were once again at odds. Falkenhayn tried to return to his original idea of limiting the attack by constricting the flow of reserves. He worried that Haig might attack to relieve pressure on the French, and that the German losses were as heavy as the French. The Crown Prince could see the glorious triumph he had expected slipping away. He concluded that if Verdun could not be taken, it should not be attacked. However, Knobelsdorf, his Chief of Staff, wanted to mount an all-out attack on the Right Bank, and persuaded Falkenhayn to let the Fifth Army have one more go.

It is ironic that, as the Battle of Verdun reached its climax, Pétain shared the Crown Prince's doubts about the battle. Since arriving at Verdun, he had known that abandoning the Right Bank and Verdun to stand on the Left Bank would have been the most sensible course of action. But de Castelnau had decided otherwise, for reasons of morale which Pétain, as a realist, might not share but could not dismiss. At least he had been able to limit costly offensives and bring in a system of replacement which ensured that his infantry divisions stayed in the line for only a few days at a time. Although this meant that two-thirds of the entire French Army was cycled through the meat-grinder, it at least allowed the soldiers in the front lines to be as fresh as possible and prevented the destruction of entire divisions.

Joffre knew that while Pétain's star was rising, his own was falling as word spread about how unprepared Verdun had been. Joffre wanted action and yet would not allocate the men and guns Pétain demanded before he would agree to attack. So Joffre had Pétain promoted to command the whole central sector of which Verdun was a part, replacing him with Robert Nivelle.

On 1 June, the Germans launched the general offensive Knobelsdorf had been preparing for two months. The centre of the attack was the siege of Fort Vaux, to the south-east of Douamont. The fort itself was the smallest in the Verdun system, with only machine guns for its defence. But it did have Major Sylvain Raynal in command, a veteran who had worked hard to put the fort in order. He was unable to fix the water supply or send away the horde of wounded stragglers who had taken shelter. Thus, when the Germans surrounded the fort and seized the roof, Raynal was trapped with around 600 men, most of them unfit for fighting and desperate for water. For five days, the two sides fought in the tunnels under the fort. One man managed to lead some of the wounded out and even to return with news that Nivelle was sending relief. Raynal and his men had to watch the undermanned relief force get cut to pieces. The last link to the outside was a carrier pigeon, one of four Raynal had when the siege began. Although weak from gas and unsure of its direction in the moonscape of Verdun, the bird made it to French lines, delivered Raynal's message and fell dead. In the end, Raynal lost a hundred men defending Fort Vaux, but the Germans lost 2,600, and only the lack of water broke the French defence.

With Fort Vaux taken, the Germans had only to capture Fort Souville to reach Verdun itself. Knobelsdorf thought that victory was within his grasp. Pétain agreed. Even Nivelle began to consider evacuating the Right Bank. Everything hung on Fort Souville, the key to which was the crossroads at Thiaumont. For two weeks, the fighting centred there, with Thiaumont changing hands fourteen times. Nivelle foolishly ended Pétain's system of rotation. The divisions at Verdun were now condemned to stay, and by mid-June, morale was falling, if only because the divisions chained to Verdun were losing around 4,000 men each time they saw action and the men still alive were seeing action at Verdun for the second or third time. Pétain had allowed for the loss of one division every two days, but German pressure and Nivelle's costly policy of counter-attacking raised this to two divisions wasted every three days. The Germans almost had Verdun and the French desire to keep it was wavering. Around 12 June, Germany was within an inch of winning the war on the Western Front, which meant winning the war. Two days later, the chance had gone and the tide had turned. Nothing in particular changed at Verdun, but something had changed in the German High Command. The man who saved France was Erich von Falkenhayn, with assistance from the Russian Alexei Brusilov.

The cause of Falkenhayn's crucial decision in June was what had shaped German military policy in 1914, the way Germany had yoked herself to an ally she despised and ignored. When Conrad asked Falkenhayn for help against Italy, he was brushed aside. Wounded by such Prussian arrogance, Conrad withdrew several divisions from the Galician front facing Russia to use against Italy. He did not inform Falkenhayn of this, but then Falkenhayn had not troubled to tell him about the Verdun offensive. The Austro-Hungarian attack against Italy fell apart. Then, on 4 June 1916, the Russians by purest chance chose the very point on the Galician front which Conrad had weakened as the place to attack with forty divisions. Because Brusilov lacked enough guns to mount a preparatory barrage, he attacked without one and caught the Austro-Hungarians by surprise, rupturing the entire front. Conrad had to grovel for German reinforcements. Falkenhayn realized that Austria–Hungary was about to be knocked clean out of the war. To gain time to decide what to do, he ordered the Fifth Army to halt its advance towards Verdun. He then sent three divisions east to prop up the Austrians. By the time he allowed the Fifth Army to roll again, the French had gained a second wind. Knobelsdorf achieved the usual early successes but he could not break through to Verdun. The new Green Cross or phosgene gas shells used to take out French batteries were lethally effective but not used enough. The French had just enough reserves to hold the line, the Germans too few to break through. In both cases, the delay of a few days and the dispatch of the three German divisions east were crucial.

As at the Marne in 1914, a Russian attack saved France by distracting the Germans. In both cases, the Russian effort turned out to be suicidal. When the Germans counter-attacked against Brusilov, the Russian Army collapsed, setting off a crisis that was one of the causes of the first Russian Revolution in February 1917. At Verdun, however, the initiative had slipped from German hands. The Germans knew this by the evening of 23 June. So did Nivelle, for it was on that evening that he issued the famous order 'They shall not pass'. A counter-attack the next day took back all the ground lost.

Alistair Horne regards 23 June as the turning-point of the Battle of Verdun and therefore of the Great War. Not only did the Germans fail to break through to Verdun, but a week later the New Army of Britain made its debut in force at the Somme. By the strict logic of Falkenhayn's thinking, time had run out on German hopes of a victory [*Doc. 2*].

The battle may have been decided but momentum kept it going. Although Falkenhayn suspended the offensive in July, Knobelsdorf went behind his back and got approval for one more push. This time, he planned to use phosgene gas shells intensively, and sure enough, when the German infantry went over the top, the French guns were silent. But when the Germans moved into the open, the French opened fire. Their crews were wearing improved gas masks and had held their fire to trap the Germans in the open. A handful of Germans reached Fort Souville, from which they caught sight of Verdun, but no one was following their advance, and they were killed or captured. Finally, after a month of futile struggle, the Crown Prince was able to persuade his father the Kaiser to sack Knobelsdorf. At the same time, the sudden entry of Romania into the war on the side of the Entente gave Bethmann Hollweg a chance to persuade the Kaiser to relieve his arch-rival Falkenhayn. In came Hindenburg and Ludendorff from the east. Their first reaction on seeing the Verdun Front was disbelief that the German army should have been squandered in such a pointless way. When Falkenhayn departed, the 'limited' battle he started had consumed 315,000 French soldiers, but also 280,000 German.

There was one more act in the drama of Verdun. Despite Pétain's reputation for pessimism, he was not unwilling to attack. He objected to inadequate attacks, carried out with insufficient strength along too narrow a front. He wanted the grand, set-piece attack, prepared in meticulous detail and based on an overwhelming superiority in men and guns. The infantry and the gunners would have to work closely as a team. So, once the German pressure eased, Pétain prepared to retake Douamont, and indeed all the ground lost since February. For a change, the partnership with Nivelle worked smoothly. Nivelle's expertise in artillery was channelled into preparing a creeping barrage behind which shock troops would advance. He took the time to train both the gunners and the infantry in the complexities of the barrage. When the French attacked in October, almost everything went right for a change. When Fort Douamont fell to the French, it was almost as empty as it had been in March when the Germans had walked in. What was left of Fort Vaux also returned to France after an attack costing 47,000 casualties.

Together, both sides lost around 700,000 men in the battle of Verdun itself, and for the war as a whole, the Verdun sector claimed over one and a half million lives. For what? Falkenhayn did not want to take Verdun; he wanted the French to defend it. Pétain did not want to defend it, but did so when de Castelnau picked up Falkenhayn's challenge. Thousands died to take or defend Côte 304 or Mort Homme, not because either was the key to Verdun, but because each was thought to be the key to some other position, which was the key to a further position, and so on, *ad absurdum*.

Yet to say that Verdun was utterly pointless is not to say it was insignificant. On the contrary, it changed the world history that followed. One way to see this is to try what is called 'counter-factual history'; in other words, to ask 'what if?' Answers are of course arbitrary and unprovable, but they focus our attention on the importance of what actually happened. What if the Germans had taken Verdun in June? War weariness was already growing in France. Such a setback, coupled with a minimally intelligent German policy of concessions, might well have detached France from the Entente. Germany would not have had to fall back on her doomsday strategy, unlimited submarine warfare. America would not have been provoked into entering the war. If the Germans chose to bargain with Russia rather than crushing her, the Russian military disaster of 1916 would not have pulled the last supports from the Tsarist autocracy. Above all, had the Germans won in June, the last attempt to win the war with limited methods would have worked. The world would have been spared the full dose of total war it got. Much of the poison that the war injected into history came only after mid-1916: hateful propaganda; double-dealing diplomacy, much of it dedicated to fomenting revolution in enemy nations and dependencies; weapons and tactics always more brutal; million-men armies wearing each other down, going nowhere, younger and less trained with each passing month. Such measures were of course present before 1916 and had been employed fitfully or reluctantly. They were not summoned out of a vacuum. But summoned they were, by the stalemate at Verdun.

THE SOMME

When the Allied commanders had met at Chantilly in December 1915, the joint attack Joffre proposed for the Somme valley would see 40 French divisions supported by 29 British divisions. Haig preferred a Flanders attack, where the German defences were known to be less formidable. The Somme offered no strategic prize for the Allies to take or the Germans to defend. It was chosen because that was where the French and British lines met. Haig also hoped for more time to train and equip his forces, especially the divisions of the New Army. When Falkenhayn attacked first at Verdun, the French part in what had originally been a French plan dwindled, until finally the French were committing only five divisions to the first wave compared with 14 British.

By 1 March the French Tenth Army had moved from Vimy to Verdun while the British First and Third Armies marched to the Somme. A new army, the Fourth, was created under General Rawlinson, who took over the planning. By 1916, preparations for battle were so elaborate that one might compare them to building a city (or, more accurately, a slum) for a million people. New roads and railways were built to carry the guns, ammunition and men; telephone cable from the front to battalion and divisional headquarters was dug in to a depth of six feet; reserve dumps were created, clear of enemy fire. By the end of March, Rawlinson had this massive logistical work well in hand, but he still lacked any clear strategic* objective. Because this strategic vacuum originated with the now-preoccupied Joffre, Rawlinson and his staff had no choice but to stick to tactics.*

The tactical objective was clear enough. The pastoral Somme valley was dominated by the Pozières Ridge running obliquely across the Front. To the north, the ridge was in British hands, but where the Ancre river, a tributary of the Somme, cut across the Front, the ridge passed into German hands. From this point near the village of Thiepval, the ridge twisted along the low valley of the Ancre for fifteen miles, down to where the Ancre joined the Somme. The objective of the attack would be the ridge south of Thiepval. Upon reflection, the staff of the Fourth Army decided to be more modest, and limited the attack to the eleven miles of ridge that ran from the Somme to a small hill called the Serre. This reflected Rawlinson's preference for 'bite and hold' tactics, as he put it in a letter the previous year. 'Bite off a piece of the enemy's line . . . and hold it against counter-attack. The bite can be made without much loss, and, if we chose the right place and make every preparation to put it into a state of defence, there ought to be no difficulty in holding it against the enemy's counter-attacks, and inflicting on him at least twice the loss that we have suffered in making the bite' (Sheffield, 2003: 22).

Rawlinson sent his plan to Haig, with a covering letter arguing that the real purpose of the attack was to take the high ground of the ridges and thus to kill as many Germans as possible with the fewest losses. This would seem like simple attrition were it not for Rawlinson's hope of luring the enemy into making costly counter-attacks. In reply, Haig complained that the plan had no strategic purpose and ignored the need for surprise. The trouble was that any attack along the Somme, however cleverly managed, would lack strategic purpose, because the only target worth attacking there was the German army. If the purpose Haig had in mind was a breakthrough, Rawlinson's proposal was indeed too limited. Yet Haig was concerned about raising false hopes. In the end, he asked the Fourth Army to increase the front to 15 miles and draw up more ambitious objectives. His complaint about the absence of surprise was more pertinent, but apart from suggesting mildly that the preliminary bombardment be short, he had no suggestions. No wonder. With the Germans looking down from the high ground, how could the British have surprised them? As for Haig's preference for more time, when the Germans finally took Fort Vaux, Pétain and Joffre appealed for help so emphatically that they could no longer be put off. On 15 June, Haig finally decided that the great attack would come within a month, in the manner and place given in the Fourth Army's revised plan.

For the British, everything depended on the guns. The Fourth Army got over 1,300 guns for the 15 mile front. The gunners were to lay down a bombardment beforehand to cut wire, destroy trenches and take out the enemy artillery. Then they would maintain a barrage during the battle to pin down the enemy. The planning was keyed to the range of the guns, which was assumed to be a maximum of 4,000 yards for observed, accurate fire. The staff assumed that every element of the German defence within this range would be destroyed.

The assumption about the power of the guns was fatally wrong. British artillery might have coped with Rawlinson's original and limited plan, but not with the expanded and ambitious version. With only around 400 heavy guns, the British lacked the weight of guns the Germans and French were using at Verdun. Although the shell shortage of 1915 had been overcome, around a million of the shells fired in the ten-day bombardment were shrapnel, useless against massed wire and hardened defences. They were used because British industry was not yet producing enough high explosive shells for the heavy guns. In addition, a high proportion of the shells were duds, the gunners were as inexperienced as the infantry, and the heavy guns had a built-in aiming error of at least 25 yards.

Because the work of the guns was so elaborate, infantry tactics were left simple. Each attacking company in the front line would go over the top at 7.30 a.m. and form a line, each man two or three yards from the next. There would be four lines in all, fifty to a hundred yards apart. The men would walk slowly in straight lines, through prepared gaps in the British wire, across No Man's Land, through the obliterated German wire and into the German front line. The reserves would pass through and take the second line in the same fashion. Each man would be carrying at least sixty-five pounds on his back [*Doc. 15, Marching Order, Full*]. The average weight of the British soldier in 1916 was 125 pounds.

The German defenders were not all dead or buried. Of the sixty British battalions in the first wave, German machine and field guns destroyed twenty completely before they even reached their own front line. On 1 July, 993 officers and 18,247 other ranks of the British army died; 1,337 officers and

34,156 other ranks were wounded; and 96 officers and 2,056 other ranks were missing and presumed dead or captured. Of the 120,000 men who attacked, around 60,000, or half, were killed, wounded, missing or taken prisoner. It was the worst day in the history of the British army; indeed, the worst day for any army in the Great War.

The attacks in the northern part of the Somme front were to be diversions. In the attack of VII Corps around Gommecourt, the 56th (London) Territorial division found the wire cut and reached the German third line, but its advance was cut off by a German barrage. The 46th Midlanders could not budge from the start line and took 4,300 casualties, grim yet, as Gary Sheffield observes, the lowest for the 13 divisions that attacked. To the south, VII Corps was to attack Serre and then turn to support the flank of the Fourth Army. The 31st Division (Pals from the North) ran into a barrage and got nowhere; the 4th Division took its objective but had to withdraw without the support of the 31st.

The worst shambles took place at Beaumont Hamel. The 29th Division was Regular Army, and for its service in Gallipoli had earned the sobriquet 'Incomparable'. Although the first attack failed when the mine blowing up Hawthorn Redoubt went off early and gave the Germans a head's-up call, General de Lisle thought the attack had succeeded and sent in his reserve. The brigade included the 1st Newfoundland Regiment. Finding the communication trenches blocked, they attacked over open ground and were caught by German machine-gun fire before they reached No Man's Land. The battalion took 684 casualties, 91 per cent of its strength. The 10th West Yorkshires of the 17th (Northern) Division suffered even more, with 710 casualties. In all, the Incomparable 29th lost 5,240 men. Next to the 29th, 36th Division (Ulster) of X Corps started well thanks to effective artillery support, but when it ran out they were left isolated and exposed, and took 5,104 casualties. The only success for the 32nd Division, a New Army division drawn from Glasgow and the North, came when the 17th Highland Light Infantry, also known as the Glasgow Commercials, took Leipzig Redoubt through an adroit attack. Finally, on the left wing of the attack, III Corps attacked on both sides of the road from Albert to Bapaume. The hardest task fell to 8th Division (Regular) which had to move almost half a mile over No Man's Land with German resistance on both flanks. The 8th reached German lines but could not hold its position. Next to it, the attack of the 34th Division (New Army) on La Boiselle failed completely. Once again, kicking off an attack by exploding mines served only to alert the enemy, and the 34th incurred the highest casualties on the day, 6,380.

South of the Albert–Bapaume road, results were less bleak. General Henry Horne commanded XV Corps well. The 7th and 21st Divisions mixed New Army in with Regulars. They shifted the Germans out of Fricourt and Mametz. Even better was the work of XIII Corps. Under the inspired command of one of the best teachers in the British Army, General Sir Ivor Maxse, 18th Division, one of the original K or Kitchener divisions, was defining what an elite division could do. Together with 30th Division, the Corps took its objectives by early afternoon, including Montauban village. The attack of the French Sixth Army on the far right of the front went best of all. The three corps involved were well supported by French gunners, who also helped the British to their left.

The first day at the Somme went so badly for the British because their reach exceeded their grasp. They had to learn, and learning would only come through trial and error. Above all, the common understanding that it had become a gunner's war had to be modified. Guns alone could not conquer. They had to work closely with the infantry; the two had to be integrated into a proper team or system. Firing plans had to be made more flexible, and of course the power of the guns had to be increased exponentially – the number of guns, the weight of explosive, which only complicated the firing plans as the guns grew more specialized. Infantry also had to evolve. The centre of gravity of the battalion had to move lower, to the platoon, and the sections making up platoons had to become specialists with bombs* (grenades) and Lewis guns (light machine guns) and not just riflemen. Advancing in line was obviously suicidal, and the supposedly green soldiers of the New Army and the Dominions proved to be quick learners when it came to more sophisticated tactics such as fire and movement, using the lay of the ground to advantage.

Learning and flexibility were the order of the day, and yet sheer mass still mattered. Only after Verdun and the Somme started did those in charge realize the colossal volume of heavy guns and shells and the staggering toll of human life that would be needed to force a decision. With each battle after 1916, the weight of fire increased exponentially. There was one gun for every sixteen yards of Front at the Somme; for the attack on Messines Ridge in the spring of 1917, there was a gun for every seven yards, usually a heavy. The Great War was an industrial war because of the guns. Anything thwarting the appetite of the guns had to be swept aside. Take the big guns away and the Great War would have been a war of infantry and field artillery; key everything to the guns and it became a war of entire organized economies, fought by attrition. This, however, would only become clear in retrospect. The staff officers were thus living life forwards but understanding it backwards, and made a natural mistake when they concluded that the ten-day bombardment they had planned would demolish the German defences.

Yet the Battle of the Somme still had 139 days to run; 600,000 British would be casualties in it, and, thanks to the strict policy of counter-attacking to retake ground lost, almost an equal number of Germans. Haig's early hopes of a breakthrough gave way to Rawlinson's style of bite and hold, preferably south of the Bapaume Road; ironically Rawlinson leaned to Haig's earlier idea of chewing up German reserves. Both Haig and his subordinate commanders tended to keep things on a rolling boil, which seemed to Joffre and Foch to amount to a string of uncoordinated and ineffective pin-pricks. The high hopes before 1 July seemed to have given way to dithering. Yet under the surface men were learning to manage their novel tasks, new men were emerging with new ideas, and new devices were taking shape. That the pay-off for innovation would not have to wait until a distant future was clear as early as 14 July, when the Fourth Army took part of Delville Wood, Trônes Wood and Bazentin Ridge, in effect capturing the German Second Position north of the Bapaume Road. Haig had assigned the youngest Army commander, Gough, to take over X and VIII Corps from Rawlinson, who was freed to focus on the tasks of XV and XIII Corps, under Generals Horne and Congreve, who had proved their worth on 1 July. What they came up with would seem to belong to 1918: a surprise attack that went off at 3.30 in the morning after a five-minute bombardment. The gunners managed their counter-battery work and wire-cutting well, and the weight of shells the German positions received was much greater than it had been on 1 July, although Rawlinson had a third fewer guns. Although the British broke into the German Second Position, breaking through or breaking out was still a fond dream, and would remain so at least on the Western Front for the rest of the war. High and Delville Woods eventually fell, but only to a grinding set-piece attack.

What attracts attention at the Somme are the tribulations of the British Army. The Germans suffered too, in no small part from their own handling of the battle. The seven-day British bombardment before 1 July might have failed to meet its goals, but it was nonetheless an ordeal for the Germans huddled in their deep bunkers, and cost the Germans over a hundred guns. Falkenhayn then played into British hands, or would have had they respected 'bite and hold', by insisting on immediate counter-attacks to retake lost positions. To underscore the point, Col. Lossberg became the Chief of Staff of von Below's Second Army when Below wanted to pull back to shorten the line. Ironically, Lossberg subsequently became an undisputed genius at setting elastic defences in depth, the very opposite of what Falkenhayn was doing. To help the Second Army, Falkenhayn added seven divisions to reinforce as early as 2 July, seven more in the next week, and 42 over July and August, 35 of which opposed the Fourth and Reserve Armies. The units north of the Somme were reorganized into the First Army under Below; those to the south became the Second Army under General Max von Gallwitz, who also commanded the new Army Group the two armies formed. Pushing so many reserves to the Somme had the impact the Allies hoped. On 12 July Falkenhayn suspended major operations at Verdun. His cunning plan to achieve an unlimited victory through limited means had failed utterly. Gary Sheffield argues that from this time on, the Allies held the strategic initiative. The Germans were back on their heels because of the French resistance at Verdun and the British attack on the Somme.

Fighting continued in the Somme sector until mid-November. The British finally took Delville Wood and High Wood towards the end of July. Gough and his staff mismanaged the attacks of the Reserve Army, but the excellence of the Australian divisions bailed them out. The 5th Australian Division and the British 61st took Fromelles on 19–20 July, after which the 1st Australian Division took Pozières Village. The attack of the 2nd Australian Division was hustled along too quickly under pressure from on high, and after a better effort in August, the Australians had Pozières.

In subsequent attacks on Delville Wood, Thiepval, Guillemont, Courcelette, Morval and the Ancre river, a pattern can be seen in hindsight, the only sight historians have. When the attack was concentrated on a narrow and manageable front, supported by a proper artillery fire plan and carried out by well-trained divisions, it tended to meet its limited goals. The attack of Maxse's 18th Eastern Division that took Thiepval showed that he had indeed trained an elite division. The Australians and Canadians were close behind. On the other hand, when objectives were too ambitious or too vague, when co-ordination between units and between infantry and artillery was tenuous, then the attacks soon bogged down into attritional brawls. In addition, the resistance the British faced changed because of the pressure they exerted. Crown Prince Rupprecht of Bavaria was a very able field commander. After Falkenhayn was sacked, Hindenburg and Ludendorff gave him command of a new Group of Armies that included the First, Second, Sixth and Seventh. Its primary task was to wage a defensive battle using elastic defences in depth of the sort that Lossberg had been busy devising. Linear trenches were replaced with heavy machine guns sited in shell holes to provide interlocking fire. As with Pétain at Verdun, Hindenburg and Ludendorff intended to pit machines against men, bleeding the attacking side white. It was not just that attacks were more costly than defence. If defence involved counter-attacking, then the costs were equal. But if the defence were intelligent and supple, so that manpower could be spared, then the other side would attack itself to defeat. Or so the Germans hoped. There was a measure of second-best about the shift in German policy, a confirmation of Sheffield's view that the strategic initiative had passed from German hands. Rope a dope tactics worked for Muhammad Ali. They were not likely to save the weaker side in a *Materialkrieg*, a total war of industrial resources.

CHAPTER SEVEN

ORGANIZING FOR VICTORY

LUDENDORFF TAKES CHARGE IN GERMANY

Although Hindenburg and Ludendorff were given supreme command with a mandate to win the war, Ludendorff saw they would have to change the very nature of the war in order to win it. With German troops under heavy pressure both at Verdun and the Somme, attacking in the west was out of the question. Gradually, Ludendorff reverted to a defensive footing. He organized defences in depth, leaving the main line up to a mile or two behind battalion outposts. At its zenith a year later, the elastic defence featured three to four zones. The first zone was held lightly by interlocking outposts that acted as shock absorbers. The main battle zone was the trench system proper, while the rearward zone or zones served as a launching area for counter-attacks or a backstop if the enemy penetrated the main battle zone. The strategic equivalent of this came when Germany began the construction of an immense defensive line stretching south from the Somme area south-west to Soissons, where the Front turned east toward Verdun. This *Siegfried Stellung*, known in English as the Hindenburg Line, was more than a line or wall. Up to ten miles deep in places, it featured immense belts of heavy wire, machine-gun posts and concrete pillboxes. It was a main battle zone with an attitude. Behind it, the entire German nation was mobilized under the Hindenburg Programme, a war economy under military direction.

Ludendorff realized that going over to the defensive in the west might buy time but it would not bring victory. Unlimited submarine warfare was the only answer. When Ludendorff first took over, he supported the cautious approach, and for the next few months, sorting out the mess left by Verdun kept him from meddling in political matters. Then in September 1916, he forced the government to declare the creation of an independent Kingdom of Poland. Because the new state was carved out of Russian Poland, this declaration effectively destroyed any chances for a negotiated peace with Russia, which Ludendorff thought impossible in any case. Defence in the west meant attack in the east, his personal field of glory since 1914, and he wanted Polish aid.

UNLIMITED SUBMARINE WARFARE

The issue that brought the dispute over war aims into the open was the submarine. Those who favoured a moderate negotiated peace sided with Bethmann Hollweg, while the majority, who demanded sweeping annexations that would require a total victory, sided with the navy. When Tirpitz resigned in March 1916 after the submarines were restricted again, he led the creation of the Fatherland Party. It spread the message that only the ruthless use of the submarine would bring total victory and only total victory was worth considering. This upsurge in annexationism and war-fever mobilized radical pressure groups such as the Pan Germans outside the *Reichstag* and brought together a militant annexationist majority inside.

In October 1916, the *Reichstag* adopted a resolution presented by the Catholic Centre Party stating that the chancellor must bow to the expert military judgement of the High Command in deciding how to use submarines. The Centre Party moved towards support for total war because it had become convinced that a two-front war could not be won on land. Bethmann Hollweg also began to wonder whether his opposition to unlimited submarine warfare was wise. If unrestricted submarine warfare really would bring Britain to her knees in six months, how could he refuse to exploit the one weapon that could save Germany? America might come into the war as he had always argued, but how would she reach Europe if the submarine stood in the way? Faced outside with a growing alliance of politicians and generals, beset in his own mind by doubts about the virtues of caution, Bethmann Hollweg began to hedge. However, he resolved not to give way to his enemies until he had had one last try at ending the war diplomatically.

OFFERING PEACE

Bethmann Hollweg was not the only leader who tried to negotiate in 1916–17. In Britain, a former Foreign Secretary and die hard conservative, Lord Lansdowne, circulated a letter to the Cabinet in November 1916 calling for a negotiated peace. He made his appeal public a year later in a letter to the *Daily Telegraph*; *The Times* would not publish it. These peace feelers were not simply a product of war weariness. In late 1916, most people were still optimistic about the war, even those in uniform. War weariness did not come until 1917. Instead, the peace feelers served the double purpose of stopping the war before it became total if they succeeded, and of justifying total war if they failed. What doomed this last chance of negotiating peace before war became total were not the motives involved but the necessary ambivalence of even suggesting negotiations in the midst of war.

One rule of thumb in understanding coalitions in wartime is that allies usually end up distrusting each other. That being so, the first side to call for negotiations might be trying to weaken the other coalition by offering terms that favour one of the enemies, thus encouraging the contempt that familiarity breeds. If the favoured enemy expresses interest, the others will feel ill-used. The peacemaker might be appealing to enemy public opinion over the head of enemy governments. Or the peacemaker might be genuinely sick of war and interested in peace. The other side has to evaluate the motives behind the peace offer before responding. Peace was one more illusion that had to be exposed before the disenchanting reality of total war could be seen in all its horror.

As Bethmann Hollweg contemplated what to do about the submarine, he had one eye on the Social Democrats. A radical and pacifist section had split away from the SPD the previous March, and its contention that the government was waging an imperialist war of aggression was gaining credence among the working class. Bethmann Hollweg's other concern was Washington, where, in November 1916, Woodrow Wilson had been re-elected as the man who had kept America out of the war. Bethmann Hollweg knew that Wilson's commitment to neutrality was more than a trick to win votes. By November, British arrogance annoyed Washington more than German behaviour, because the British had started to seize American mail on neutral ships and to blacklist companies doing business with Germany. Moreover, the British treatment of Ireland since the Easter Rebellion in Dublin in 1916 had incensed Irish-Americans. Bethmann Hollweg knew that Wilson was preparing to offer himself as a mediator. If Germany could beat Wilson to the punch and announce the terms on which she would consider negotiations, then both the Social Democrats and the Americans would be appeased. If the Allies accepted these terms, then the gains Germany had made so far in the war would be consolidated in a peace treaty. If the enemy refused to concede a peace favouring Germany, the onus for prolonging the war would rest with them and the German conscience would be clear. On 12 December, Bethmann Hollweg declared that Germany and Austria–Hungary were ready to begin immediate peace negotiations for terms that would ensure their existence, honour and freedom.

Bethmann Hollweg's 'peace offer' coincided with Wilson's appeal to all the warring nations to state their war aims clearly. In the end, Britain and France rejected the German peace offer out of hand and managed to deflect Wilson's attempt to insert himself as a mediator. How this was done shows the ambiguities of the situation and the virtual impossibility of stopping the war diplomatically. All these threads crossed in London, where Lloyd George had just replaced Asquith as Prime Minister in December 1916.

LLOYD GEORGE KNOCKS OUT PEACE

David Lloyd George rose to power as the champion of a total war effort to deliver 'the knock-out blow'. When the German peace offer arrived just after he had replaced Asquith as Prime Minister, his concern over the weakness of Russia and the carnage on the Western Front inclined him to take the offer seriously. This was reinforced when Wilson's appeal to state terms arrived, because Britain could not afford to alienate Wilson by appearing to be inflexible. Lloyd George wanted to avoid creating the impression that he had slammed the door to a negotiated peace.

When Lloyd George addressed parliament, he began by saying that France and Russia, the main victims of German aggression, had already replied to Bethmann Hollweg. He was simply going to support what they had said. He weighed war and peace, arguing that it would be a crime to prolong the war for no good reason but just as wrong to give up a righteous struggle simply out of weariness or despair. He had to respect the American wish that Germany be invited to state her terms and the French reluctance to state any terms at all. He solved the puzzle by arguing that, while he would listen to any useful terms Germany might offer, he was convinced that the fact of Prussian aggression ensured that worthwhile terms would not arise in the first place. Any German concessions would be worthless because they would be German, coming from the nation that had already violated pledges and treaties in 1914. In the end, he squared the circle, finding a way to pledge Britain to a fight to final victory without offending America.

Once the option of negotiation was discarded, Germany and Britain were locked into a fight to the finish. There was no longer room between them for American neutrality. On the final day of 1916, Ludendorff decided to cash the blank cheque the *Reichstag* had given him and demand unlimited submarine warfare. At a Crown Council on 9 January, Bethmann Hollweg accepted defeat and agreed to unleash the submarines. The last straw for him had been the cold reception his peace offer had received in London.

Not knowing of the German decision, Wilson still believed there was a chance to be the honest broker for peace. On 26 January, the British accepted his mediation. Wilson then learned that Germany was adopting unlimited submarine warfare. He immediately broke off diplomatic relations. In March, the British intercepted and carefully circulated a bizarre telegram from the German Foreign Secretary, Arthur Zimmermann, to the German ambassador in Mexico. Zimmermann offered an alliance to Mexico and the return of parts of Texas and New Mexico if she declared war on America. When the telegram was published, Zimmermann blithely admitted sending it. German submarines compounded the offense by sinking seven American merchant ships. Wilson felt he had no choice but to summon Congress and, on 6 April, to declare war on the Central Powers. The war was not only total now; it was finally a world war.

THE RUSSIAN REVOLUTIONS

Just when there seemed no way out but straight ahead, the Russian people opened a door. In March 1917 women queuing for flour rioted in Petrograd (St. Petersburg). When the authorities used the army to put down the demonstrations, the soldiers joined the angry crowds. With no support left, the Tsar abdicated. The *Duma* or parliament chose a provisional government under Prince Lvov. The new government tried to interest France and Britain in peace, but when they replied that the arrival of democracy in Russia improved the chances of victory, Russia stuck to its promises and stayed in the war. At first patriotism balanced war weariness evenly, but when the Russian offensive in June turned into a shambles, the loyalty of the provisional government to its allies was its undoing. The Socialist lawyer Alexander Kerensky took over the government, but the Bolshevik Vladimir Lenin, spirited from Switzerland into Russia via a sealed train thanks to the Germans, out-manoeuvred him easily. In November 1917, Lenin's unqualified hostility to the provisional government and exploitation of the issues of 'land, bread and peace' enabled him to seize power from Kerensky.

THE FALL OF BETHMANN HOLLWEG: JULY 1917

Lenin's sealed train would prove to be an unsafe container for 'the bacillus of revolution'. When word of the Tsar's abdication reached Germany, Bethmann Hollweg persuaded the Kaiser to mention political reform in passing in his Easter message. The dormant *Reichstag* stirred into life, and the parties in the centre-left majority formed an inter-party committee to consider reform. The dynamic Centre (Catholic) Party leader, Matthias Erzberger, had private information showing the failure of the submarine campaign. When he spoke in the *Reichstag* in favour of a negotiated peace, the left-wing parties included peace along with reform in their agenda and passed a Peace Resolution, the only such resolution put forward by any legislature during the war [*Doc. 3*]. Ludendorff argued that Bethmann Hollweg had lost control of the situation and forced the Kaiser to replace him with a nonentity, Georg Michaelis, who promptly gutted the Peace Resolution. Count Hertling later replaced Michaelis; he was almost as spineless, as was his vice-chancellor, the veteran Progressive Friedrich von Payer. With Russia about to drop out of the war and victory again in sight, the mood of the patriotic classes swung back to a peace of victory, just as the working classes moved towards peace and revolution.

CHAPTER EIGHT

TECHNOLOGY AND TACTICS

A TECHNOLOGICAL SOLUTION? THE AIR WAR AND TANKS

The phrase 'total war' evokes not just the open-ended sacrifices the nations were making by 1917 but also the way the sense of urgent necessity mothered inventions of all kinds. Two of the new technologies the war hastened deserve special mention, aviation and tanks.

The Air War

The public fascination with fighter pilots and dog-fights still obscures the more prosaic but important work of the airmen. That was to serve as an eye in the sky for the ground forces through reconnaissance and artillery spotting. Fighter aircraft evolved as a way to deny the other side this aerial view. Initially pilots carried side-arms to shoot at each other. Machine guns would obviously be better, but apart from finding a gun light enough for aircraft with such a limited lifting capacity, the aircraft themselves posed a problem. There was no place to mount a machine gun that gave a clear field of fire.

The airmen themselves addressed the problem of aerial gunnery by think-ing things through. On 1 April 1915, Roland Garros, a French pilot, used a forward-firing machine gun to shoot down a German observation plane. The gun was crudely synchronized with the propellor, and to deflect bullets that were unsynchronized, Garros fitted metal collars to the blades. He ruled the skies for two weeks until the underlying logic of industrial warfare took effect. Both sides were technologically equal. What one could achieve, so could the other. When Garros crashed behind German lines, Anthony Fokker discovered the secret of his success. Fokker was a Dutchman whose aircraft designs inter-ested the German authorities before the war. They now gave him Garros's aircraft and asked him to go one better. He was not impressed with the deflector plates that Garros had improvised; bullets could weaken the propeller or deflect back at the plane or the pilot. For some time he had been thinking about an interrupter gear to ensure that bullets would pass through the arc of the propeller only when the blades were clear. He installed the interrupter on his monoplane, the *Eindecker*. It was as fast as anything the Allies flew, and now it had the best gun in the air, fitted so that the aircraft itself was virtually a flying gun. The leading German pilot by 1915, Oswald Boelcke, was the first airman to bring down an enemy plane with the new gun. Max Immelmann flew the second *Eindecker*. He was the first true fighter pilot, the first to devise methods to exploit the technology, for example the 'Immelmann turn' which used a half loop and then a half roll to enable a pilot to make a quick 180 degree turn.

By 1916, the Allies had copied the interrupter technology, brought their own true fighters like the Nieuport Scout into service and ended the Fokker scourge. The Germans achieved supremacy over Verdun. The British held a similar edge over the Somme. Unlike the Germans, however, the Royal Flying Corps was not aiming for a passing and local tactical advantage. General Hugh Trenchard, commanding the RFC, wanted to dominate the air-space over German front lines permanently. His nominal reason was the pressing need for observation patrols, which was logical considering the Germans usually had the advantage of the higher ground. His real aim was to win a moral advantage. Raiding in the air thus had the same purpose as the ground raids that Haig encouraged at the time, fostering an 'offensive spirit'. In contrast, German policy in the air reflected their defensive posture on the ground. They concentrated their air power in mobile units known as 'flying circuses' that could move quickly to sectors under attack and assist the defence or counter-attacks. Accordingly they held the advantage wherever they happened to be concentrated. This advantage swung to the Germans and their Albatros series of fighters through early 1917, culminating in 'Bloody April', when the RFC suffered losses of 30 per cent a week while covering the Arras offensive. With the introduction of the SE5, the two-seater Bristol Fighter, the Sopwith series of Pups, Camels and Snipes, and the French Spad, the Allies regained the edge. They kept it by producing more pilots and machines. With pilots, this involved a drastic improvement in training methods. Nevertheless, according to the official records of the RFC, of the 14,166 pilots who died, 8,000 died in training.

Most aerial combats were unequal affairs between veterans and new-comers, or between the agile fighters and the slow two-seaters used for observation. Fighters also went after observation balloons. The pilots themselves naturally recognized the more skilful and successful members of their fraternity, which could also include the other side. The notion of the aces began with this in-group recognition, spreading to the French media and then to Britain and Germany. By late 1917, the first aces – Boecke, Immelmann, Albert Ball of Britain (44 victories) and Georges Guynemer of France (54 victories) – were dead. In their stead came Germany's Manfred von Richthofen, the 'Red Baron' from the colour of his Fokker triplane, with 80 victories, and from the RFC, Edward 'Mick' Mannock with 73 and the Canadian Billy Bishop with 72. Of these, only Bishop survived the war.

Passing along new techniques by learning from trial and error was not easy when the penalty for error was death. The pilots, nevertheless, worked out the new tactics of aerial combat. Contrary to the popular notion of dog-fights, the key to success was not tight turns and evasion but speed. The best technique was to dive from above, make the kill in a blazing run and leave the scene. The French were the first to move away from freelancing and organize fighters into tactical formations of six aircraft, the *Cigognes*. The Germans replied with the *Jagdstaffeln* or *Jastas*, the British with formations called flights. These were in turn co-ordinated into larger squadrons. By 1918, each side could send up formations of over a hundred machines, layered according to type and function.

Applying air power directly to the battlefield arose out of an obvious need. Applying it indirectly through bombing began as pure idea. The Ger-mans sent their dirigibles or Zeppelins against Britain in May 1915. When the initial sensation died down and their success proved limited, Germany turned to heavier-than-air bombers. The campaign of the so-called Gotha bombers starting in May 1917 got the attention of the British press and parliament, and led the government to commission Field Marshal Jan Smuts to investigate the future of air power. Out of his report came the Royal Air Force, formed under Trenchard on 1 April 1918 with the amalgamation of the RFC and the Royal Naval Air Service. Trenchard quickly organized the Independent Air Force to bomb Germany. He achieved results as patchy as the Germans had had with their campaign against Britain. Between them, however, they had started on a path that led to Hiroshima.

Although strategic air power* remained an idea without much substance until the next world war, tactical air power,* the application of air power directly to the battlefield, was a reality by 1918. The Germans even devised an armoured fighter for ground attacks. The contact patrols the Allies flew during the German spring offensive in 1918 contributed to the gradual German loss of momentum. Ironically, strategic air power captured the interest of Britain and America after the war despite its marginal results. Even though tactical air power had worked for the British, the Germans were the ones who noticed and developed it. The same was true with tanks.

Tanks

If aviation is an example of competition accelerating change, the tank demon-strates something else: competition forcing change along different paths. Because the Germans chose to concentrate their scarce resources on other weapons, notably gas shells because of the clear superiority of the German chemical industry over the Allied, tanks were exclusive to the Allies. The idea of the tank – that is, of an armoured vehicle that could cross trenches and eliminate machine guns – occurred to several people once the war stiffened into stalemate in 1915. The most relentless advocate was Colonel Ernest Swinton, who was also the first 'Eyewitness' for the War Office. By February 1915, Churchill was interested enough to form a Landships Committee at the Admiralty. The committee found that caterpillar tracks were superior to wheels, and soon produced 'Little Willie', a rectangular box with tracks along the sides. To lower the profile, the box was changed to a rhomboid shape with the tracks running around it. From this model, 'Mother', came the first operating tank, the Mark I, which had 'male' versions, with six pounder guns mounted on outboard sponsons, and 'female' versions with machine guns. The Mark I had armour 12 mm thick, a weight of twenty-eight tons, a top speed of 3.7 mph and a crew of eight, four of whom took care of the steering, which was done by gears that varied the speed of each track. The later Marks IV and V were comparable. The name 'tank' was meant to conceal the function of the vehicles, as if they were mobile water tanks. Meanwhile, Colonel Jean Estienne, inspired by the Holt tractors the British used to move their artillery, persuaded the French high command to start a tank programme.

Although the pioneers devised vehicles that were remarkably similar, they differed over how the tanks ought to be used. Swinton wanted tanks to support the infantry; he proposed massing them together and using them by surprise to break open the front, as a sort of can-opener, after which the infantry and artillery would take over. Colonel Hugh Elles, the eventual commander of the Tank Corps, and his Chief of Staff, J.F.C. Fuller, thought tanks should have a role independent of infantry. Fuller indeed thought the entire army should be mechanized. More important than the advocates, however, was the opinion of the commanders, especially Haig. Legend has it that he ignored tanks. On the contrary, he showed a keen interest from the start, and his memorandum of October 1916, written after the first use of tanks a month before, has been called 'clear-sighted and intelligent'. It was his subordinate commanders, Rawlinson and Gough, who had reservations about tanks, which was reasonable given the exaggeration of the advocates and the mixed results tanks showed in action.

The first concerted tank attack came at Cambrai on 20 November 1917. Behind a thousand-gun surprise barrage and a screen of 300 fighters, the British sent 378 tanks forward with eight divisions of infantry. Fuller choreographed the tanks and the auxiliary supply-carriers to cross the German wire and trenches. The result was an advance of over five miles along a seven mile front, with only 1,500 casualties. Half the tanks then fell to German fire, broke down or got stuck and the attack bogged down until the Germans counterattacked. Using storm troops and tactical air power, the Germans regained the ground they had lost.

Despite their inauspicious start, tanks played a role in the Allied and American attacks that ended the war. The Australians in particular practised and virtually perfected the co-ordination of infantry and armour. The Americans used French and British tanks and took to armour instinctively. Yet the tanks of World War One were too slow, fragile and prone to breaking down to amount to more than a support for the infantry. They were still at the end what they had been at the start: a clever idea that needed work. They were not the solution to the stalemate.

A TACTICAL SOLUTION?

If strategy had been reduced to brute endurance, despite the application of new technologies, what about tactics? Was there a more intelligent and effective way to fight? By 1917, the German, French and British armies understood the problem they faced and were innovating with tactics and technology. The Germans used the Eastern Front as a laboratory for new methods. After Falkenhayn was sacked, he took command of the campaign against Romania, repeating Mackensen's earlier success against Russia with a lightning victory. The team of Lieutenant-Colonel Georg Bruchmüller and General Oskar von Hutier brought new ideas to artillery and infantry tactics respectively. Bruchmüller's notion of the rolling barrage was similar to the creeping barrage the French and British had developed, a curtain of shells which advancing infantry followed closely. He organized the guns for the assault of Hutier's Eighth Army on Riga in September 1917. Hutier planned a fluid encirclement campaign of the sort the Germans had used in the east since 1914. He surprised the Russians by bridging the Dvina River where they were weak. Bruchmüller used mortars of all sizes to keep the Russians away from the infantry crossing the river in boats, and then gas shells to disable the Russian artillery. After five days, the Germans took Riga and 25,000 Russian prisoners for relatively slight losses.

The French reformed their tactics in earnest when they moved to attack at Verdun in the autumn of 1916. These changes, and ones the British army were implementing, were reflected in an interesting report General Arthur Currie, then commander of the 1st Canadian Division, made after a visit to Verdun. As a part time soldier before the war, Currie's advantage was that he knew that he had a lot to learn. He kept his eyes and mind open. He isolated four essentials for a successful infantry attack. First, the need for reconnaissance and information: raids were the conventional way to keep up to date, but Currie preferred aerial photographs of German positions. Second, the need for suitable objectives: the French went after tactical features rather than trenches or lines on the map. Third, training. The British made a start at simulating the site of attacks in their training in 1915 but the French took the notion of preparation much further. They instituted small-group training in special manoeuvres like leap-frogging and in the use of specialized weapons. This tied in with the fourth feature Currie noticed, the importance of the platoon. Out of necessity, the platoon had been a primary unit of the small

Canadian militia before 1914, so that Currie saw nothing new when the centre of gravity of the British army moved from the larger formations down to the company and platoon, which in turn were subdivided into bombing, Lewis gun and rifle sections. Momentum could be restored to the attack only by focusing responsibility for real-time decisions at the lowest possible level and letting the assault troops flow around resistance, which could be mopped up later.

CHAPTER NINE

1917: 'MERE UNSPEAKABLE SUFFERING'

The new methods got their baptism when the British attacked at Arras in support of the main French offensive. Building on his limited success at Verdun, Nivelle promised to break through the German defences. In essence, his secret was to expand the formula he had used at Douamont – increase the front of attack, so that the Germans could not pinch in the flanks with reserves, increase the number of troops in the first wave of the attack, and protect the advance with a creeping barrage. More than just these tactical improvements, however, Nivelle promised to restore the offensive spirit that had permeated the army in the early days of the war. He spoke perfect English and captivated Lloyd George, so much so that in February Lloyd George secretly agreed to subordinate the British army to Nivelle's command. After the British generals protested, the arrangement was limited to the period of the joint offensive, but relations between the British politicians and generals only got more poisonous.

Shifting the French effort from the Somme to the Aisne meant postponing the main offensive from February until April, which gave the Germans time to complete the Hindenburg Line. The delay also allowed rumours of the attack to reach German ears. Meanwhile, criticism of Nivelle mounted. Pétain treated all grandiose plans sceptically; he dismissed Nivelle's as fantasy. General Joseph Micheler, who was to command the attack, shared Pétain's doubts. The Premier, Alexandre Ribot, had been Nivelle's greatest supporter. He fell in March, and the new ministry under Painlevé was more sceptical. Yet it did not get rid of Nivelle or shorten his leash even when he offered to resign.

The British began with a diversionary attack at Arras. The first stage embodied many of the new methods, so that the German second line fell within three days. The most successful of these set-piece battles came on 9 April, when the four divisions of the Canadian Corps took Vimy Ridge. Virtually everything important worked as planned: the counter-battery fire* took out 83 per cent of the German guns, the new 106 fuse detonated at ground level and finally gave the gunners a way of cutting massed barbed wire, the first waves of infantry were protected in underground tunnels before attacking and rehearsing beforehand gave the infantry a realistic sense of what would happen and alternative ways of reaching their objectives. Even so, the British paid a grim price: 32,000 casualties at Arras and 10,600 at Vimy. Moreover, there seemed to be no way to sustain the momentum of the attack, so that Arras fell into uncoordinated scuffles once the initial goals were met and the infantry moved beyond the cover of the artillery. Even so, some success was better than none, which was the French fate with the Nivelle offensive.

THE NIVELLE OFFENSIVE AND THE MUTINY: APRIL TO JUNE, 1917

The French attacked on 16 April along a thirty-mile front between Soissons and Reims. The ancient Roman road, the Chemin des Dames, gave the sector its name. Knowing that the attack was coming, the Germans had increased their divisions in the sector from nine to forty, but held them out of range of the 7,000 guns Nivelle assembled. A million French soldiers went over the top, convinced that this time the generals had got things right. They were wrong. West and north of Soissons, the French advanced into empty space and then ran into the Hindenburg Line. In the main attack between Soissons and Reims, every one of Nivelle's preparations miscarried. The brief preliminary bombardment did not cut the German wire; the creeping barrage fell most often in the middle of the French infantry; and the German pillboxes on the commanding heights of the Chemin des Dames were intact. By the second day of the attack, 120,000 French were dead or wounded and the medical stations and trains were overwhelmed. Knowing his career was at stake, Nivelle ignored the disastrous opening days and stuck to his plan. The French army did not appreciate his stubbornness. It mutinied.

To this day, we know less about the French mutiny of 1917 than about any other event in modern French history. The army covered up what it regarded as a disgrace. Yet from the fragmentary reports we have, including the record Pétain kept, the mutiny was essentially a spontaneous act of sanity, a mass strike against the way the war was being fought.

No units at the Front mutinied; it was front-line units in the rear returning to the Front that rebelled. They shouted against the war or bleated like sheep; units coming back to rest accused those going up of strike-breaking. Red flags and revolutionary songs broke out. The first mutiny occurred near Reims, where a battalion refused to parade when it was ordered back to the Front after only five days' rest. From 29 April to 10 June, 'collective indiscipline' was at its height. On 3 May, the 21st Division, which had been through the thick of Verdun, refused to return to battle. The leaders of the mutiny were summarily shot or sent to Devil's Island; two days later the division was decimated at the Front. On 4 May, infantry in the Chemin des Dames sector started to desert. The 120th Regiment refused to fight, and when the 128th was ordered to shame them by attacking, it too refused. By the third week in

May, violence against officers, hitherto absent, was reported in the Aisne region. By the end of May, then, eight entire divisions which had either fought at Chemin des Dames, or were being sent there, had mutinied.

As long as the Nivelle offensive continued, so did the mutinies. By early June, fifty-five divisions, half the French army, were affected. None of the outbursts, whether violent or not, lasted for long, but the very spontaneity of the uprisings meant that trouble appeared all over the central sector of the Front, especially at rest camps or railway stations in the rear. Although revolutionary slogans and symbols appeared when the rebellions were at their peak in early June, radical ideology was not a primary cause of the mutinies, despite what the generals thought. Pétain's private records, however, indicate he noticed the connection between the offensive and the mutinies. When Nivelle was sacked in mid-May, Pétain knew why the army had broken and therefore how to fix it. For the rest of his long life, he regarded his handling of the mutiny as his finest accomplishment.

First of all, Pétain visited over ninety divisions. To each, he explained patiently that there would be no more bold offensives. Lest anyone doubt his meaning, he expressed himself in the plain language of the soldiers, as when he remarked that 'we must wait for the Americans and the tanks'. There would be attacks, but they would be quick and limited, aimed at keeping the Germans on guard. He talked with individual soldiers, listening to complaints about the lack of any system for rest and leave, about the wretched food and bad wine, and above all about the way nobody seemed to care about the suffering of the army, a view expressed in a song that the army actually banned [*Doc. 4*]. Pétain cared. He set up a proper system of leaves, ordered the installation of lavatories, showers and sleeping accommodation, saw that cooks were actually trained to cook, and improved the wine ration while cracking down on the drunkenness that had accompanied the mutiny. Along with the carrot he applied a stick as well. French military justice, following along its regular path, handed out sentences to 3,427 men; of these, 554 were death sentences, of which 49 were actually carried out.

Pétain felt the home front needed purging too. The news of the Russian Revolution sparked wild hopes in France. There had been strikes in the munitions factories since mid-1916 and radical agitators were stirring up workers and soldiers home on leave. The Minister of the Interior, Malvy, refused to interfere with the agitation. By the end of June, there were almost 180 political strikes tying up the war factories. The police listed 2,500 troublemakers, but the civilian authorities, guided by Malvy, turned a blind eye on them, fearing that repression would only ignite the entire working class.

Malvy was finally driven from office, bringing down the Ribot government by his departure, but the new premier, Painlevé, was almost as defeatist as Malvy had been. By the autumn of 1917, French politics resembled Russia's before the fall of the Romanovs. The complaint of the Right about German influence in high places was not just paranoia, because war weariness had indeed led even conservative Frenchmen to long for an early and separate peace with Germany and an end to the unnatural alliance with the old enemy, England. The Painlevé ministry seemed to be riddled with such defeatism. It fell in November. To be the new Prime Minister, President Raymond Poincaré could choose between Caillaux, who had become a leader of the movement for a negotiated peace, and the great outsider of French politics, the Tiger, Georges Clemenceau. Even though he was seventy-six and had been active in politics since 1871, Clemenceau burned with an energy that made other politicians seem lethargic. Like his British counterpart, Lloyd George, he attacked the slip-shod way the war was being run and came to monopolize the cause of total war. As soon as he took over, he backed Pétain to the hilt and turned on the Chamber to smash the pro-German factions. Pétain had saved the army just before it fell apart; now Clemenceau saved the nation. He was at least as domineering as Lloyd George. He was nowhere as subtle. His roars about waging war, prefiguring Churchill in 1940, were, however, pure rhetoric. Pétain had calmed the army by promising the soldiers, often in person, that there would be no more costly offensives. Such a policy was wise and humane, but it was not a policy of waging war. Once Pétain took over the French army, the lead in waging the war passed to the British.

THIRD YPRES (PASSCHENDAELE)

On 1 May, Haig wrote to the War Cabinet to propose a massive breakout from the Ypres Salient. Coupled with an amphibious landing at Ostend and the full co-operation of the French, such an attack would capture the ports of Flanders from which German surface raiders and submarines were believed to be operating. It might even shake loose the entire northern German front. On 1 June, Pétain sent Haig a hint that discipline in the French army was not what it should be, and a week later, he reported to Haig in person about the mutiny. He added that he had the situation in hand. Haig treated Pétain's news as confidential and did not bother to inform Lloyd George. The prime minister could sense that something odd was going on, and so he was turning against the idea of a joint Anglo-French attack. Apart from his worries about the soundness of the French, he was alarmed at the news from Italy, where he wanted to send up to twelve divisions from the Western Front to save the situation. The prospect of supporting yet another sideshow would itself have been enough to make Haig redouble his preparations for a Flanders campaign. What worried Haig's friend and supporter back in London, the Chief of the Imperial General Staff General Sir William Robertson, was that Haig was talking about winning the war in one blow. Robertson preferred the sort of limited attacks with massive artillery support that had worked so well at Vimy. The army commanders agreed: Rawlinson had reverted to 'bite and hold' tactics after the Somme; Sir Herbert Plumer, commanding the Second Army, looked like a Colonel Blimp but was actually a shrewd field commander and a master of the careful attack; Sir Julian Byng, now commanding the Third Army, had commanded the Canadian Corps at Vimy; and Sir Henry Horne had seen the Vimy attack work. Only Gough with the Fifth Army preferred Haig's ambitious approach. Yet the alternative to Haig's grandiose offensive in Flanders was Lloyd George's idea of moving the British show to Italy, something no responsible soldier would countenance. At least Haig had a plan, however little it promised to succeed. Lloyd George had only his humane horror for the slaughter. As with Robertson and the field generals, the desire for final victory led Lloyd George to support Haig. The difference was that he was loath to admit it.

Haig launched the Third Battle of Ypres because he was certain that the Germans were running short of reserves and were close to collapse. This would not be another battle *of* attrition but the first battle to profit *from* attrition. Nor was this hope entirely groundless. The Third Battle of Ypres was not doomed before it began. It took hard work to turn the bright hopes of the spring of 1917 into the bleak despair of November. What made Passchendaele so tragic, apart from the appalling conditions, was the way it abridged hope. By the summer of 1917, the British no less than the Germans had acquired the experience and skill to make set-piece attacks work. Other factors, however, outweighed this experience.

The tragedy of the Third Battle of Ypres had three acts, with a spectacular preview before the curtain went up. The preview and the second act were successes; the first and third acts were unmitigated disasters. The preview was the capture of Messines Ridge by Plumer's Second Army. Almost a year and a half before, Plumer, the best senior British commander in the war, had figured out a way to take the Ridge, which anchored the German shoulder on the south of the Ypres Salient. He would blow it up. The Second Army began to drive mineshafts under the Ridge. By the spring of 1917, nineteen enormous mines had been laid at the end of the tunnels. They were set off on 7 June; all but two exploded and the bang not only reduced the Ridge to rubble and killed or dazed the Germans holding it, but set the ground in the Salient rolling like the ocean. The noise was heard in London. For once, the infantry got the walkover they were promised. The Second Army lost only a fifth of the men Plumer had expected. The key to Plumer's success, however, was the way his staff formed a close-knit team that could plan so that complexity did not mean rigidity. Because the plans of the Second Army were seen to be realistic and achievable, even the lowest private had faith in them. Thus, when Plumer's men took the Ridge, they stopped, just as the plan dictated. Headquarters preferred grand ambition and initiative and thought Plumer and his Second Army were stodgy. The leading role in the Big Push went instead to the youngest of the field generals, Sir Hubert Gough, and his Fifth Army. This was the first mistake.

The preliminary show was splendid. Yet the curtain did not go up on the first act for another fifty-three days. Why the delay, which meant the sacrifice of surprise? The War Cabinet still had doubts about the Flanders campaign and was debating whether to send British troops to Italy instead. Haig did not get the plan approved until 25 July. In any case, Haig himself had planned on a six-week hiatus between Messines and the Flanders attack.

The plan called for the Fifth Army to take a rail junction fifteen miles behind enemy lines in eight days. Rawlinson's Fourth Army, plus the French, would attack along the coast. Plumer's Second Army would move north-east from the Salient and take the long ridge running from Passchendaele village north to Staden. The first objective for the Fifth Army was Pilckem Ridge, a low hill just beyond British lines. By the day of attack on 31 July it was raining. To compound what nature had ordained, the two-week bombardment destroyed the drainage system. The battlefield had been turned into a swamp before the attack began. Finally, the Germans had been learning too. Lossberg improved his patented system of defence in depth. It now included concrete bunkers and specialized counter-attack units that struck when the British attackers were at their weakest. The Fifth Army took Pilckem Ridge after three days and 31,000 casualties. Not as bad as the Somme, but not the success of Vimy or Messines. The result was mixed enough to encourage Haig to push on, even after Gough advised against it. So the Fifth Army staggered on at Gheluvelt Plateau (10 August) and Langemarck (16 August). By the end of Act One, the British had lost 64,000 men and 3,000 officers in the mud and were nowhere near the objectives of the first day.

Act Two featured Plumer and his Second Army, with the Anzacs (Australian and New Zealand Corps) in the lead. The main objective was the series of ridges along the north-eastern side of the Salient. Plumer and his Chief of Staff Charles Harrington had three weeks to prepare attacks in the meticulous way they preferred: a careful advance behind a devastating barrage. Haig assigned 1,300 guns and howitzers, a gun for every five yards of Front. The weather turned warm and dry; bringing up the guns during the advance now became possible. The attacks would be restricted to a short front and shallow penetration. When the assault troops reached their targets, they were to stop, dig in against counter-attacks and wait for the guns to catch up. The Passchendaele–Staden Ridge was taken in three of these bite-and-hold hammer blows. First, Menin Road Ridge on 20 September in ideal weather, with the British and Anzacs advancing behind a creeping barrage and reaching their objective by midday. British pilots owned the skies and spotted targets for the artillery. The toughest critic of British generalship, Ludendorff, conceded that the British success proved the superiority of the attack over defence. The second blow fell on 26 September at Polygon Wood, in the southern part of the Salient. It was so dry by then that dust was hampering the aim of the guns.

Crown Prince Rupprecht, in overall command of the German defence, started to share Ludendorff's worries about the inferiority of even the most concerted defence against such hammer blows. Haig felt he had the upper hand, and on 28 September, he wrote that the enemy was tottering. If the railway junction which had been the original objective could now be taken, the Germans would have only one line left to supply themselves between Ghent and the sea, and would be routed. Plumer was left to carry on. Why not, given his record so far? For what such statistics are worth, under Gough, the British had lost 125,346 dead and wounded; the Germans, 111,500. Under Plumer, the British lost 40,312 men; the Germans, around 35,000. The third attack was at Broodseinde on 4 October, a great victory for the Anzacs and a black day for the Germans. But where was the victory? The Second Army had only a toe-hold on Passchendaele Ridge. The day after Broodseinde, Haig held a conference of senior commanders. The consensus was that the offensive should be stopped. The plan for an amphibious landing along the coast had already been dropped. Generals Birdwood, commanding the Anzacs, Gough, Plumer and even the chronically optimistic Chief of Intelligence, Charteris, all wanted to call a halt. Haig decided to press on. The good weather was holding, the glittering prize of a German collapse still beckoned, and Haig wanted the high ground for the winter.

Thus began Act Three, one of the grimmest moments in modern history. Ludendorff, ostensibly an unfeeling robot, caught its essence: 'It was no longer life at all. It was mere unspeakable suffering' (Ludendorff, 1919: 491). The whole battle had come down to the fight for the village of Passchendaele. The rain returned, turning the ground into a bottomless swamp. The British and Germans struggling and drowning for Passchendaele had no idea why they were fighting. Charles Carrington later decided he had become a 'zombie', although as such he won the Military Cross at Broodseinde. Guy Chapman rejoined his battalion after a spell on staff, and found that:

> The men, though docile, willing, and biddable, were tired beyond hope. Indeed, they knew now too well to hope, though despair had not overthrown them. They lived from hand to mouth, expecting nothing, and so disappointed nowhere. They were no longer decoyed by the vociferous patriotism of the newspapers. They no longer believed in the purity of the politicians or the sacrifices of profiteers. They were as fed up with England as they were with France and Belgium, 'fed up, f–d up, and far from home'. (Ludendorff, 1919: 79–80)

The three battles of Act Three – Poelcapelle on 9 October, the first battle of Passchendaele from 12 to 26 October, and the final taking of Passchendaele by Currie's Canadians on 6 November – can scarcely be distinguished from each other. Everything sinks into the mud. When the offensive finally stopped, the Ypres Salient had been enlarged entirely to the advantage of the Germans, and its tip at Passchendaele was still only six miles from Ypres.

Plate 4 Troops of the Canadian Machine Gun Company holding the line in shellholes near Passchendaele, November 1917. They are almost indistinguishable from the mud (Library and Archives Canada/Photo by William Rider-Rider/Department of National Defence Collection/PA-002162. Originally printed in *Relentless Verity: Canadian Military Photographers Since 1885* (Toronto, 1973)).

The British Official History puts the British dead and wounded at 245,000. In August 1918, the General Staff gave the War Cabinet a figure of 265,000, while Liddell Hart, the famous military historian, estimated 300,000. The German estimate of their losses ranged from 175,000 in the Official Medical History to 202,000 in the Military History. Even on the dubious grounds of attrition, Third Ypres was a failure, because Haig was losing three of his men for every two Germans lost. Passchendaele, however, cost the British more than lives alone. The final act, in particular, exacted a price in spirit which is still hard to assess but is palpably real. When the British folk memory henceforth assumed that generals were too stupid to check the weather, or that doomed men perished in degradation and anonymity, it was often referring to Passchendaele.

CHAPTER TEN

THE BITTER END: 1918

As the world staggered into 1918, war seemed to have become a permanent condition. War weariness manifested itself not just in revolution or pacifism but also in an obsessive commitment to a total war effort. As Lloyd George told the leaders of British trade unions in January, 'My own conviction is this, the people must go on or go under'. At the same time, however, he issued a statement of war aims more liberal than the better-known Fourteen Points President Wilson announced a few days later. He genuinely hoped for a positive German response, which might open the way to an alternative to going on or going under, a compromise peace. Ludendorff treated Lloyd George's gesture with contempt. He had his own ideas about an appropriate peace, and was demonstrating these to the shocked Bolsheviks at Brest-Litovsk. The ensuing treaty between Germany and Russia tore huge areas of Ukraine, the Baltic states and Poland from Russia. It is misleading to say that the Treaty of Brest-Litovsk showed what the war was all about. The Germany against which the Allies declared war in 1914 was not the same Germany Ludendorff now controlled. It would be more accurate to say that Brest-Litovsk showed what the war had created – in the case of Germany, a military dictatorship bent on creating an empire in the east on a scale that served Hitler as a precedent.

LUDENDORFF ROLLS THE IRON DICE IN THE WEST

With Russia out of the war, Italy reeling and peace feelers going nowhere, the Western Front was clearly where the final decision would take place. As the fighting closed down for the winter after the hellish ordeal of Passchendaele and Cambrai, 168 Allied divisions, including 98 French and 57 British divisions, faced 171 German divisions. The Allied totals did not change for the next three months.

On the German side, Ludendorff faced four choices as he contemplated the future. He could accept the stalemate on the Western Front and start to sound out the possibilities of a compromise peace, for example by giving Lloyd George a favourable response. The second choice, unconditional surrender, was even more out of the question. The third possibility was the most interesting. After shifting the forces freed by victory in the east to the west, Ludendorff could have deployed them defensively and then sent out a peace offer that only one of the enemy powers would find attractive. To attract Britain, Germany could make concessions over Belgium, or over Alsace-Lorraine to attract France. Faced with the impossibility of cracking the German defence and a public interested in the German concessions, the enemy coalition would either fall apart or let the fighting subside into a cold war. This option would require a mixture of military threat and political dexterity. What eliminated it from Ludendorff's mind was the American factor and the British blockade. In the long run, any attempt to go over to a defensive policy of Fortress Germany would run up against the Allied optimism that time was on their side, a view that Ludendorff shared with Falkenhayn [Doc. 2]. German superiority on the defence would not impress the enemy as long as the enemy believed that this superiority would eventually be overcome by American manpower and the starvation blockade. The threat alone of an attack in the west would not bring the enemy to the bargaining table. The attack could not be bluffed; it had to be made and it had to succeed, despite all the inherent obstacles to successful attack. So Ludendorff settled on the fourth option, using the forces freed by the collapse of the Russians to force a decision in the west.

What clinched Ludendorff's decision was his shrewd hunch that he now had the means of victory in hand. As a former commander in the east, he kept his eye on the innovations that had worked with such brilliant effect against Russia and Romania. Once he had decided to attack in the west, he brought in the innovators from the east to work their magic. General Hutier took over the 18th Army, while Geyer was put to work training carefully selected teams of infantry in methods of deep infiltration. Culled from the most aggressive troops in each regiment, these battle-teams, nick-named 'Storm Troops', were trained in special camps and equipped to move independently, without regard to flank support or artillery cover. Whenever they met resistance, they were to flow past it and carry on; mopping up would be the task of the regular line troops. The other edge Ludendorff thought he had was his artillery. Bruchmüller had worked out the use of phosgene and mustard gas shells and accurate, heavy and brief bombardments to paralyse and confuse the enemy at the very moment of attack. His techniques were not novel or unique; gunners in the French and British armies were working along similar lines. But they were novel for the German army on the Western Front, and would thus be a new experience for the victims on the other side. Rather than chewing up the ground, revealing the time and place of attack and getting in the way of the attacking infantry, Bruchmüller's barrage suppressed enemy fire; his sophisticated orchestration of the guns mcshcd smoothly with the new tactics of infiltration. With both Geyer and Bruchmüller, as with the innovations on the Allied side, one can see that the secret of successful attack was really not exotic but rather an intelligent application of the existing means of war. To be successful, an attack needed to co-ordinate infantry and artillery seamlessly. It needed the selective application of controllable force at just the right place.

The place Ludendorff chose was St. Quentin, where the tired British Fifth Army was scratching out a defensive line. From the Army Group under Crown Prince Rupprecht of Bavaria, the 17th Army was to head for Bapaume and Marwitz's Second Army for Peronne, after which both armies would wheel north to roll up the British lines. Hutier's 18th Army was to break through at St. Quentin and guard the flanks of the other two armies. By massing troops and guns along a fifty-mile front of attack, Ludendorff hoped to free the main thrust up the middle. When the Allied line was ruptured at the point where the British and French met, the British would have to pivot on their northern flank in Flanders and fold back to the coast, while the French would pull back in the other direction, on Paris. Ludendorff would be forcing open two swinging doors. There was no need to plan what would happen after the breakthrough in any detail; it would simply be a matter of exploiting success. 'In Russia,' Ludendorff told Rupprecht, 'we always merely set a near goal and then discovered where to go next' (Wilson, 1986: 556). Ludendorff had restored flexibility to grand strategy. It remained to be seen if he had brought too much flexibility and not enough strategy. In retrospect, his great offensive smacks of wishful thinking on a grand scale. If the British responded as he hoped, he might indeed win. But what if they hung on? Even if they broke, how did Ludendorff expect to move quickly to exploit his success? His cavalry remained in the east, garrisoning the conquered territories. He thought tanks were overrated, as perhaps they were at the time. So his flowing attack would depend upon foot-soldiers and artillery, and the need to keep the guns up would deprive the attack even of the mobility it had in 1914.

THE SPRING OFFENSIVE: WINNING THE WAY TO DEFEAT

The results of the first day of the great Kaiser's battle on 21 March seemed to confirm Ludendorff's genius. He restored movement to war, so that the fighting of 1918 is in many ways closer to the warfare of 1940 than of 1916. By 11 a.m., the British had lost 47 battalions, a fifth of their strength in the sector under attack. By midday, the second or Battle Zone was crumbling, especially in the southern sector of the attack where the Fifth Army was at its weakest. By the end of the day, the Germans had captured 98 square miles of British front and 19,500 prisoners. The British lost 7,500 dead and 10,000 wounded. The predictable cost of attacking had to be paid and the Germans lost 40,000 casualties, but they had hammered the Fifth Army almost out of existence. The British troops in the Forward Zone do not seem to have understood that they were supposed to pull back to the Battle Zone after an initial resistance, so that their function would be like a shock absorber rather than a speed bump. Instead, most thought they were supposed to fight to the death, and either did so or surrendered when honour was satisfied. Moreover, morning fog favoured the German attackers and would continue to do so until the end of July. At the Somme in 1916, 200 German machine guns had stopped the British attack. By 1918, the British defenders in the Forward Zone had 2,000 machine guns and 4,000 in the Battle Zone, but they could not repeat the German effort at the Somme because of the gas bombardment and the fog, which let the German Storm Troopers slip past the machine-gun nests.

Despite the apparent total success on 21 March, in retrospect we can see a few ominous flaws. Although the Germans captured the entire Forward Zone they were attacking, they broke into the British Battle Zone only in the south, where Hutier's Eighteenth Army performed superbly. Tactically Ludendorff was committed to flowing around resistance, but strategically he could not afford to be as opportunistic. His strategic goal was to break through, drive west and pinch the British between his army and the Channel. When the bulk of the British Third Army stood its ground, this created a strong shoulder to the north of the rupture, which slowed down the advance of the German Seventeenth and Second Armies. When Ludendorff decided to exploit Hutier's success, the net effect was to bring the French fully into the battle and relieve the pressure on the British. The Eighteenth Army indeed pushed a huge bulge to the south and west, eventually crossing the Marne, but the French and British lines held. When Ludendorff then restored the main thrust to Rupprecht's Army Group, and then later switched his attacks up to Flanders, he simply divided his strength and wasted it in improvised attacks. Even while the German army advanced, its spring offensive was fading, so that it was winning its way to defeat. Like the nation as a whole, it was starving; the advance was at times brought to a halt when even the elite Storm Troopers stopped to loot British supplies of food and liquor. As the Germans went forward, they were moving into the battlefields of 1916, devastated ground that favoured the defence and prevented supplies from keeping up with the advance. Moreover, the regular line troops were now moving in the open. After adapting to trench war, they felt vulnerable and often dug in out of habit. Just as often they had good reason to take cover, because moving out of the trenches exposed them to a danger they had hitherto been able to handle: attacks from the air. The Allied air forces flew strafing runs around the clock and, along with isolated gun batteries, slowed down the exposed Germans.

Throughout the late spring and early summer, Ludendorff kept launching fresh attacks in his desperate effort to bring the enemy to terms, but even though the goal of each new attack was defined more realistically, Ludendorff could not regain the initiative. With the Allied general reserves now under the command of Foch and the Allied troops gaining experience in defending, the Allies held their ground. All the Germans won were exposed flanks, diabolical supply problems and longer lines to defend. Ludendorff attacked the French at Reims to suck their reserves away from the British, so that the well-rested German Flanders Army Group would then be able to attack the British. Pétain, however, parried the Reims attack without calling for reserves. Confused about what to do next, Ludendorff decided to go ahead with the Flanders attack as a diversion.

THE ALLIES COUNTER-ATTACK

Before Ludendorff's latest improvisation could come off, the enemy clarified the situation. On 4 July, the Australians under General Sir John Monash achieved a brilliant success attacking with tanks at Hamel. Two weeks later, on 18 July, fifteen French and four American divisions, with 500 tanks, broke through the German line at Villers-Cotterets and pushed the Germans back ten kilometres.

The worst was yet to come. On 8 August, General Rawlinson, massing together ten Dominion divisions, four British and one American, three cavalry divisions and over 400 tanks, crashed through the depleted German Second Army near Amiens. The panic among German troops which had dismayed Ludendorff on 18 July was repeated on a more alarming scale, with retiring troops accusing reinforcements of strike-breaking and prolonging the war. In his memoirs, he called 8 August 'the black day of the German Army in the history of this war' (Ludendorff, 1919: 679).

THE COLLAPSE OF LUDENDORFF

When Ludendorff met the Kaiser on 13 August, he admitted that the war was lost and offered his resignation. The Kaiser coldly rejected the offer. Two days later, a colleague, Colonel Albrecht von Thaer, a staff officer recently posted to headquarters from the front, noted that Ludendorff was grave and depressed. 'He now sees clearly that our troops are more or less *kaput*. If one could gain some sort of rest for them, that would naturally be a great advantage' (Kaehler, 1961: 253).

Ludendorff was on a rack. Professionalism and success had brought him far beyond his modest bourgeois origins, but one slip, one sign of fallibility, would send him back to obscurity. He had staked everything on his spring offensive. When its tactical success did not translate into strategic advantage and the enemy was no closer to submission, he sensed that fortune had deserted him. Commanders are under intense stress at the best of times. Haig, for example, coped with the pressure by placing everything in the hands of God and keeping the obscenity of war well clear of his headquarters. What made Ludendorff's position intolerable to him was his personal and social vulnerability. Defeat does not come easily to anyone, but to an obsessive workaholic like Ludendorff it threatened personal humiliation. He had gambled everything to win the Great War and now he would be the greatest loser in history.

Rather than admit this, he kept up the habits that had brought him success: prodigious working hours, an obsession with detail and a rigid, impassive exterior. But with his energy focused on keeping up a bold front, he was unable to carry out his main duty. He could not face the situation he had created. The civilian government, and the new Foreign Secretary, Admiral Paul von Hintze in particular, waited for a straight report on the military situation. But how could Ludendorff tell mere civilians (or admirals) what he refused to admit to himself? At most, he would concede that the chance of military victory was now uncertain. That much was obvious to everyone. What the government needed to know was how well a defensive struggle might go, but that was the sort of loser's game Ludendorff would not play. So, as he stayed locked in the prison of his own head, Germany lost whatever slim chance there remained to organize a firm defence along the Hindenburg Line and put out careful feelers for a negotiated peace.

From the point when the twin disasters of 18 July and 8 August revealed both the chance of defeat and Ludendorff's nervous exhaustion, factions began to form among the staff officers at OHL. Ludendorff's protégé, Colonel Max Bauer, saw that his superior was cracking under the pressure and brought in a young officer to take over some of the paperwork. The new assistant, Colonel Wilhelm Heye, turned out to be more than a clerk. In fact, he soon became the key man in the effort to get rid of Ludendorff and put the Kaiser and the government fully in touch with the military situation.

On 25 September, Ludendorff ordered all Army Groups not to retreat an inch. Heye simply ignored the order. The next day, he and his colleagues decided to act. The representative of the Foreign Ministry at headquarters, Kurt von Lersner, telephoned the Foreign Secretary, Hintze, to tell him that the military situation was critical. Hintze did not fully accept the optimistic face Ludendorff was turning to him, but even so did not think the overall situation was critical. He was relying on his own sources and preparing the machinery for cautious peace feelers. Action waited upon the frank admission by the OHL that the military situation was grave. To act in advance of such an admission might shatter the morale of the army; to act too late, to wait until the chance of collapse became a reality, would open the way to anarchy and revolution. Hintze in fact believed that revolution was inevitable; the only question was whether it would come from below, as it had in Russia, or from above, as it had throughout Prussian and German history. He thus took from Lersner's message something other than what was intended. The staff officers thought he should know that a military collapse was possible. He knew what 8 August meant and assumed that the staff officers were hinting that a specific military reverse had just occurred or was about to. Hintze hurried along to see the chancellor and begged him to go to Spa to find out what was happening. When Hertling refused early on 28 September, Hintze decided to go himself to bring the situation to a head. Then Hertling told him that they would both go.

Hertling had changed his mind because the vice-chancellor, Friedrich von Payer, had told him that the co-ordinating committee of the left-wing majority in the *Reichstag* had decided that Hertling must be replaced by a chancellor enjoying the confidence of the *Reichstag* and pledged to peace and reform. Just when Hertling decided to bow to the *Reichstag* majority and resign, word arrived from Spa that the OHL wanted to talk to him about forming a new government. No one in Berlin realized that Ludendorff had decided that the game was over, and that the parliamentary politicians would be just the people to take the blame for losing.

What had happened on or about 28 September to force Ludendorff to admit openly what he had privately conceded for six weeks? A Franco-American attack had gone well in the Argonne on 26 September; on the 27th the Canadians forced the Canal du Nord which had blocked the path to Cambrai; and on the 28th, Bulgaria sued for peace, opening the way for the Allied forces in Salonika to move up the Danubian basin. The main attack came from the British, who were breeching the Hindenburg Line, and Ludendorff could stop them only by weakening his forces elsewhere, against the French in the centre or the increasingly effective Americans in the south. He faced a classic and total defeat. Even so, Germany still occupied more territory than she had the year before, and still had a solid and seasoned army of two and a half million men in powerful defensive positions. There was as yet no general Allied advance. Victory might have been out of the question, but the alternative to victory, even at this late hour, need not have been total defeat. A negotiated peace reflecting the stalemate in the west that had only just been broken was still possible. It required a defensive military strategy and very careful diplomacy. Both these requirements, however, depended on the mind and nerve of the Commander. On 28 September, Ludendorff collapsed. Realizing he was without supporters, feeling the panic of July and August return, he lashed out at his subordinates. He screamed that the Kaiser was a weakling, that the navy was to blame, that he was beset by treachery and deception. His voice shrill and hoarse, his fists clenched, he became hysterical; around 4.00 p.m., literally foaming at the mouth, he collapsed. Reports of his paralysis and collapse were later denied, but all the reports came from eye witnesses, the denials from his partisans who were not present.

By 6 o'clock, Ludendorff had recovered sufficiently to visit Hindenburg. He said that the collapse of the Balkan Front had convinced him that the defence of Germany was about to unravel. The government must therefore offer peace and request an armistice. Hindenburg agreed. The next day, 29 September, Hindenburg and Ludendorff met with Heye and Hintze. Hintze led off with a gloomy résumé and reviewed the preliminary steps he had taken to set up mediation through the Netherlands. Pessimistic though he was, he was not ready for what followed. Ludendorff described the military situation in bleak terms and insisted that an immediate armistice was necessary. To

Hintze, it seemed that Ludendorff was confirming what Lersner seemed to hint at earlier over the telephone, that there had been a catastrophe on the Western Front. Ludendorff later denied using the word 'catastrophe', and there does seem to have been a profound misunderstanding between the two men. Ludendorff thought that only an immediate armistice could prevent catastrophe; Hintze thought that an immediate armistice was the consequence of a catastrophe that had already occurred. He did not ask for details. Instead, Hintze, who had come to Spa to plead for an immediate change of government and then a peace offer as soon as possible, found that he would have to improvise an immediate peace offer *and* a change of government.

Hintze accompanied Hindenburg and Ludendorff to see the Kaiser, who had journeyed to Spa unaware of what was coming. Showing a composure rare in his tempestuous career but born of his intense dislike of Ludendorff, the Kaiser impassively absorbed the news that the High Command wanted peace. He approved Hintze's proposal that Hertling be replaced by a government including the Social Democrats, but felt that both the request for an armistice and the formation of the new government could wait a few days, lest haste create the wrong impression. When he started to leave with matters still up in the air, Hintze intercepted him and pointed out that the army was in a hurry. The Kaiser reluctantly signed an Imperial Decree announcing a new parliamentary government. When the decree was published the next day in Berlin, it was the first indication the *Reichstag* majority had that their demand for a share of power had been accepted.

Much of the confusion after the conference of 29 September and the Imperial Decree of 30 September arose from unclear language. Hindenburg and Ludendorff thought they had asked for an *immediate* appeal for an *eventual* armistice; almost everyone else, including the Kaiser, Hintze and the staff officers, thought they had asked for an *eventual* appeal for an *immediate* armistice. The more the two generals applied pressure on Berlin to send out the appeal as soon as possible, the more the people in Berlin were convinced that the appeal must be for an end to the fighting right away, at any price. To compound the confusion, the appeal had to come from the new, reformed government. To Ludendorff's primitive political mind, that posed no problem: hire some politicians. To Hintze and Payer, who were trying to put the new government together, the problem was monumental, because the *Reichstag* majority, not realizing it was about to take centre-stage, had no candidate lined up to become chancellor. Payer and his friend Conrad Haussmann inserted the moderately liberal Prince Max of Baden, a cousin of the Kaiser's, without informing their parliamentary colleagues. Prince Max then learned that his first task as chancellor would be to sue for a ceasefire on enemy terms. When he objected that this would bring on a collapse of the army, the Kaiser told him that he had not been made chancellor to make difficulties for the High Command.

With the exception of Hindenburg, those who learned of Ludendorff's decision of 28 September to call for an armistice reacted with shock and disbelief. This was true even of his closest associates at OHL. During the evening of 30 September, Thaer learned what had transpired at the meeting with the Kaiser. When he heard that Ludendorff had said that Germany was finished and needed an immediate armistice, he could not believe it. But later that evening, he learned of a staff meeting planned for the next morning, and wondered 'Will the terrible news be given out there?' It was. Ludendorff described the precarious situation. 'After he had come to the realization that continuing the war would be futile,' Thaer wrote, 'he took the view that an end to it must be made as quickly as possible, so as not to sacrifice brave men . . . uselessly.' He told the staff that Hertling had retired, and continued, 'I have however asked His Majesty to bring those circles into the government which we in the first place must thank for getting us into this position. We will thus put these gentlemen in the government. They should now make the peace which must now be made. Those who prepared the soup should eat it.' Thaer saw Ludendorff through a romantic mist as a Siegfried, nobly bearing all sorrow and calamities. 'While Ludendorff spoke, you could hear soft moans and sobs; many, indeed most, were in tears' (Kaehler, 1961: 237). When Payer learned of the decision, he too was shocked and wondered aloud to Hintze whether Ludendorff had taken leave of his senses – not a bad guess, as it happens.

By the time President Wilson replied to the German request with exactly the sort of onerous terms for an armistice that Prince Max and the new government had predicted, Ludendorff had recovered his nerve. He insisted that the terms must be rejected. The government asked him angrily what had changed in the previous week to make a continuation of the war feasible again. Ludendorff replied that the minister of war had found more men for his army. The truth was that Ludendorff had found scapegoats who would drink the soup that he had cooked. To see such off-loading of responsibility as Ludendorff's main goal might seem far-fetched until one reflects that his manoeuvre worked to perfection. Even though the *Reichstag* leaders knew that they were being set up, their sense of patriotism left them no choice but to play the role given them and hope for the best. In short, the Stab In the Back legend, the vicious lie that the Socialists, Catholics, Liberals and Jews had seized power at home and opened the gates to the enemy, did not begin after the war but was itself a vital part of the way the war ended. If the legend later exercised so much power over German minds and contributed significantly to Hitler's rise to power, that was in part because it was not entirely invented but rested on a grain of truth. The German Army *was* stabbed in the back in September 1918, not by the *Reichstag* or by the civilian government, but by its vengeful and unbalanced leader, Erich Ludendorff. That is how the Great War ended.

NUMBERS

The impact of the war was as complicated as its course and properly deserves a separate study. Sassoon tells us where to start: 'But they died, not one by one' [Doc. 14]. France lost 1.3 million dead, or thirty-four dead per thousand head of the pre-war population. Britain lost 723,000 dead, or sixteen per thousand people. Australia lost 60,000 dead, twelve per thousand people. New Zealand lost 16,000 dead, fifteen per thousand people. Italy lost 578,000 dead, sixteen per thousand people. Canada lost 66,066 dead, eight per thousand people. America lost 114,000 dead in just under a year of fighting, or one man per thousand people. Statistics about Russian losses are hopelessly vague, but one estimate is that Russia lost 1.8 million dead, or eleven men per thousand people. The Allied total was 5.4 million dead out of 45 million mobilized; from a total population of 204 million, that was 120 dead per thousand mobilized, or seven dead per thousand people. Austria–Hungary lost 1.1 million dead, or nineteen dead per thousand. Germany lost 2 million dead, or thirty dead per thousand people (Winter, 1986: 45).

SO WHAT?

Peace broke out in 1918 because, once again, the contending powers agreed on who was strong and who was not. Or rather, they seemed to agree, at least for the moment. Germany seemed to be admitting that she was weaker than the combination of France, Britain and America. However, from the very moment that this blood-drenched consensus was reached, it fell apart. Britain, France and America each believed that it was, in combination with the others, stronger than Germany, but each in turn saw itself as the decisive power in the victorious coalition. Germany, on the other hand, soon refused to admit that she was as weak as the enemy believed. Because the agreement about how power was shared out or balanced was so ephemeral, so was the peace.

Historians have recently revived a long-standing debate about the essential nature of the First World War [Doc. 19]. The debate is examined in 'Further reading', below. Some of the authors believe that to ask what the war accomplished is to ask a meaningless question. None of the warring nations could honestly claim that they had accomplished the aims for which they had gone to war, because none had any avowed aims other than self-defence and victory. Each power formulated predatory aims in private and noble aims in public. Yet these aims, noble and ignoble, were products of the war, not reasons for engaging in it in the first place. Quite apart from the appalling waste of 13 million lives, the war accomplished nothing because it could accomplish nothing except its own fulfilment. Accomplishment requires forethought and control; it needs some goal which is achieved because of controlled effort. Cancer 'accomplishes' nothing; it brings about only the weakening of the

Plate 5 'For What?' by Fred Varley (19710261-0770, Beaverbook Collection of War Art © Canadian War Museum (CWM)).

organism in which it lives, and to the extent that it succeeds, it brings on its own extinction.

Other historians see a clear purpose to the war, in some cases a purpose unnoticed at the time but in other cases one that corresponds to the more altruistic of the war aims of Britain, France and America. According to this view, Germany was the aggressor. Her unprovoked invasion not just of Belgium but of France required a forceful response from nations that valued freedom and justice. To trace the horrors of the Second World War back twenty years to the First World War is to commit the logical error of 'after this, therefore because of this'. If anything, the two world wars were similar: both were necessary struggles against militarist aggression.

There is less disagreement, however, about how the First World War changed history. When we pose such a question, or apply it to specific cases, we arrive at the paradoxical answer that the war altered modern history both far more than anyone realized at the time and far less. If nothing else, then, the study of the war illustrates the ironic complexity of historical change. One way to see this is to look briefly at the impact of the war on the major warring nations involved.

Ludendorff's cover-up was almost a total success in Germany. Try as the politicians might, they could not convince the nation that Ludendorff or the army had been defeated in the strict military sense of the word, in its will to carry on. In fact, the civilians did not try very hard to bring the truth to light, if only because they could not fully understand how the enemy had imposed its will on the Western Front and apparently snatched victory from the jaws of defeat. They knew that Ludendorff had called for a ceasefire to avoid the certainty of a total rout, but because the rout had been avoided, they came to believe that it would never have happened. Thus Friedrich Ebert, the Social Democrat who led the transitional government and then became President of the Republic, welcomed units of the army to Berlin by claiming they had been undefeated in the field.

Patriotic Germans soon convinced themselves that the war had been a draw and had ended with a bargain to build a new and better liberal world along the lines sketched in by President Wilson's Fourteen Points. As part of this new world order, Germany had reformed her internal affairs, creating a liberal and democratic republic which embodied not only the aspirations of the German reform movement as far back as 1848 but also the lofty ideals of President Wilson himself, or so the German reformers hoped. When the liberal dream failed at Versailles, it also failed in Germany. Western ideals seemed to be a Trojan horse that had taken Fortress Germany from within when all the world had failed to breach her walls.

Considering the German ordeal in the war, it might seem odd how little the Weimar Republic differed from the Kaiser's Empire. Once the steam went out of liberalism, the ambitious political and social reforms embodied in the new Constitution remained by and large a dead letter, at least federally. The state of Prussia became remarkably progressive, but few Germans cared. By 1925, the German Republic was close to what the Kaiser's Empire might have been by then had the war not intervened. Parliament had more authority in 1925 than it had in 1914, but it was still subordinate to the bureaucracy, which was virtually unchanged from the days of the old Empire. The Kaiser was gone, as were all the kings and princes, but the President of the Republic had more power in theory than the Hohenzollerns ever had in fact, and the president in 1925 was Field Marshal Hindenburg, who made a better Kaiser than the Kaiser had been. The army had shrunk to a tenth of its pre-war size, but even that did not displease those officers who had been alarmed by the growth of the mass army and the dilution of aristocratic privilege. The army of the Republic in fact had a larger proportion of aristocratic officers than had the Imperial army of 1914.

The war had changed very little permanently in Germany. Putting this another way, there was no revolution in Germany as there was in Russia. The vast majority of Germans, including the working class, preferred continuity. Revolution might have carried the day had it not been given an out-of-town preview in Russia. When the time came to play the revolutionary drama in Berlin, almost no one liked the ending. So they switched the parts of Kerensky and Lenin and had Kerensky win. The old elites did feel vulnerable for a while, and so they turned things over to the Social Democrats and adopted a low profile. The Social Democrats responded by begging the old elites to help out. By bringing on a momentary crisis of order, the war and defeat encouraged the Germans to seek continuity. Perhaps the Germans would have cleaned house had they known the way Ludendorff had driven their nation into the ground, aided in his witless imperialism by a supine civilian establishment. But Ludendorff had covered up, and the Social Democrats and Liberals covered up the cover-up. So the Great War did not discredit and destroy the old order in Germany. By 1930, the old elites were back in the saddle. All they needed was a popular following; they could use a pied piper to bring in the masses. Hitler was just the man, at least when his momentum began to flag in 1932 and the old elites thought he could serve as their puppet. In Hitler's fanatical dedication to returning history to the high tide of German success in the spring of 1918 and then making that fateful year turn out as it should have, he was, ironically, the man who would finally accomplish what the Great War did not, the destruction of the Imperial regime. Hitler, in so many ways a quintessential product of the Western Front, was a delayed time bomb in German history. Through him, the Great War finally had the destructive impact in Germany that it had in Russia.

The impact of the war was also delayed in France. Losing fewer men than Germany, but with a population only two-thirds as large, France hungered for security after the trauma of invasion. When the Treaty of Versailles proved to be hollow and the successor states to Austria–Hungary in Eastern Europe relied far more on France than France could rely on them, France turned inward. The Maginot Line and ultimately the collaborationist regime of Pétain after the defeat of 1940 were legacies not just of the First World War, but, even more importantly, of the aftermath of the war and the justified sense of insecurity that haunted the French.

Before the war, both the *avant garde* and the powerful small-town bourgeoisie of France had been critical of modernity, even though France was in many ways the least modern of the major Western nations. The destruction of so much French industrial equipment allowed the French to modernize their economy after the war. Yet the war had also magnified the conservative spirit of the intellectuals and bourgeoisie. The result was the unsettling collision of modernity and tradition, without the ingrained self-confidence that had hitherto calmed French fears. As the poet Paul Valéry wrote in 1922:

> Almost all the affairs of men remain in a terrible uncertainty. We think of what has disappeared, and we are almost destroyed by what has been destroyed; we do not know what will be born, and we fear the future, not without reason. We hope vaguely; we dread precisely . . . we confess that the charm of life is behind us, abundance is behind us, but doubt and disorder are in us and with us . . .
>
> One can say that all the fundamentals of our world have been affected by the war, or more exactly, by the circumstances of the war; something deeper has been worn away than the renewable parts of the machine . . . But among all these injured things is the Mind. The Mind has indeed been cruelly wounded; its complaint is heard in the hearts of intellectual men; it passes a mournful judgment on itself. It doubts itself profoundly. (Roth, 1967: 29)

This doubt was all that remained of progress, of the nineteenth-century faith in the perfectibility of humankind. France had embodied the liberal, bourgeois belief that history was controllable. It was a Frenchman, the socialist leader Jean Jaurès, who said that it was inconceivable that things would not turn out well. He said this just before he was assassinated in 1914. For the French, the future was no longer what it had been.

For America, the changes the war brought seemed ominous. By 1919 the Americans were consciously resisting what seemed to be the trend of history and were trying to turn the clock back to what the new President, Warren Harding, called 'normalcy'. For America as for Europe, the emergency of war not only opened the way to change but also heightened the desire for stability. The war gave President Wilson a chance to launch his liberal imperialist bid for world power but undermined the political base of that bid, which had to wait until Pearl Harbor in 1941. As with Germany and France, we see that for America the war tended not to start anything new. Nor did it sweep away the old, despite what many hoped or feared at the time. At most, it changed the agenda America faced; it altered priorities, as with, for example, the victory of prohibition and the post-war Communist scare. Above all, the war rarely altered history the way people thought it would, although it did alter the way people thought about history. Most often, the emergency of war tended to confirm pre-existing ideas. So in America, although both the reformers and the conservatives were surprised by the impact of the war, both camps reacted by digging in, almost as if they were front soldiers. Unlike Europeans, however, few Americans experienced anything in the war to shake their faith in progress or the exceptional destiny of America itself.

The British had not gone to war in 1914 to gain anything. That was just as well, because in the end they gained nothing. Indeed, they jeopardized the advantages that had kept them on top for so long, supremacy at sea and in international finance. Yet they had gone to war to defend something, their independence as a sovereign state and the liberal freedoms they associated with the parliamentary system. Ironically, the sovereignty of Britain herself was preserved at the cost of the wider Empire, although this would not become clear until after the Second World War. Ironically too, the liberal parliamentary system prevailed over German militarism and authoritarianism. The British did not have to copy the enemy to devise a system of centralized authority; on the contrary, by the end of the war the Germans were desperately trying to copy Britain. What the British had, they held, without becoming discernibly less British. To be sure, liberalism had to employ illiberal means to meet the emergency, but the severity of such aberrations as conscription, rationing, censorship and chauvinism should not be exaggerated. Except in the terrible final months of the war, the state led the people with relatively little coercion or manipulation, and the people followed stoically, keeping their sorrows to themselves and their emotions well in hand. The British did not comprehend how much France had suffered, and regarded the French obsession with security through alliances as precisely the sort of nonsense that had led the world down the path to war in 1914. The military victory of the British army, secured at the cost of 350,000 casualties in 1918 and 723,000 lives overall, meant as little to the British as it did to the Germans. Just as the Germans believed that their army had not been vanquished in the field, the British came to believe that their army had accomplished little. Hating Haig as he did, Lloyd George encouraged this view. So both Britain and Germany tended to ignore 1918 and think only of 1917, the Germans remembering how close they had been to victory, the British remembering how near they had been to defeat by submarines and to hell at Passchendaele. Appeasement was not born in 1938, when Neville Chamberlain abandoned Czechoslovakia to avoid untimely war with Hitler. He was only maintaining a trend that Lloyd George had established during the peace negotiations at Versailles. For the British, then, the war came to seem a colossal blunder, rooted in the evil of alliances and the narrow self-interest of foreigners. Only Hitler, with his naked barbarism and ultimately his miscalculations in policy, could have provoked the British to take up arms again.

The war had less impact on society than the British thought at the time or we might think now. For example, such wartime changes as the increased participation of women in the workforce and the recognition of labour as an equal partner with management were regarded as temporary and were rolled back in the twenties, along with many of the powers the central state had acquired. As elsewhere, the challenge to the old order that the war posed not only opened new paths but also led people in reaction to cling to or restore the past.

With the split and subsequent decline of the Liberal Party, it seemed that liberalism had died the death in the war, and yet it could be argued that both the Labour Party and the Conservatives moved into the middle ground the Liberals vacated. To be sure, neo-liberalism did not emerge right away, and in the ten years following the war, relics of the Edwardian Age dominated political life. But by the thirties, younger men were pushing their way up through the ranks of the two major parties, men who had learned to respect the working class while serving as junior officers in the trenches and who entered public life to bring about social reconciliation and state reform. They were often animated by a sense of obligation to dead comrades and a haunting sense that, as survivors, they were 'the runts of the litter'. Yet men like Harold Macmillan, Duff Cooper, Anthony Eden and Clement Attlee were anything but runts. The notion that the leadership of Britain between the wars was mediocre because the brightest and best had perished in the trenches has more of myth about it than reality. The younger generation was not too vitiated to lead; rather its challenge was vigorously resisted by an old guard that took as its credo the popular desire for peace and tranquillity [Doc. 18].

The new middle class, epitomized by the businessmen and the suburban-ites of the South, found its place in the sun between the wars. The older middle class declined, imprisoned by fixed incomes in an age of inflation. The aristo-cracy seemed to fade as well, with the slaughter of blue-bloods in the trenches counterpointing the memory of an Edwardian Golden Age. Obeying the myth, titled dandies danced on the grave of their class in the twenties. Yet once again, we can see now that the war had not turned everything upside-down. The aristocracy had been adapting to modern times before the war and continued to do so after, easily maintaining its presence in the corridors of power. If war hammered any class, it was the old Edwardian working class. Most of the dead came from its ranks, and all too often from its living human units, in part because of the tragedy of the Pals Battalions. Although the war brought a measure of equality to the unionized workers, the gains vanished after the war when the old industries like mining and ship-building were unable to revive. Even when the working class seemed to win, it lost, because the moderniza-tion that the war had stimulated tended to water down the compact and distinct culture of the old working class, making it more middle class while middle-class culture was proletarianized. Above all, a key element in the older proletarian culture, the deference to authority that had led the working class to accept the order of things and devise ways of adapting, took a heavy knock in the war. Exposure to incompetence in the army or profiteering at home led younger workers to ask 'what about us?' The miners of Britain had been among the most patriotic of the workers during the war; after, they led the angry campaign that culminated in the General Strike of 1926. But, before we see the war as a detonator for class conflict, we should notice that the upper class downed tools as well. Appeasement was also a form of job action; the upper classes simply refused to provide their sons to uphold the interests of the state. Enough was enough – at least until the danger to the state took the clear and present form it did when Hitler was poised to invade in 1940.

The Habsburg Empire broke apart in the last days of the war into the successor states: Austria, Hungary, Czechoslovakia, and, in part, Poland. Given the centrifugal forces long at work in the Empire, its disintegration might seem inevitable, yet the Empire stood up to the stress-test of war with remarkable resilience, and in the end succumbed not to obsolescence but to defeat, hunger, and the opportunism of the nationalists. Almost no one mourned the passing of Habsburg rule when it vanished, and yet Central Europe has missed the stability and civility of the Empire ever since. When Italy's jump to the winning side did not profit her in any obvious way, her prime minister walked out of the Peace Conference in a huff. The Italians felt like losers, and soon gave up on parliamentary democracy. The ex-socialist war veteran Benito Mussolini bluffed his way to power at the head of a Fascist ministry in 1922 and soon became a dictator. Under him, playing at war was much more entertaining than the real thing.

If, as the German historian Heinrich Treitschke said, it takes war to turn a people into a nation, the Great War made Canada and Australia. French Canadians were offended by conscription and turned against the war, but English Canadians retained their initial faith that they were fighting a just war for civilization and fair play. Indeed, as Jonathan Vance (1987, Chapter 1) has shown, the disenchantment with the war and the ensuing peace that swept through Britain and France evoked little echo in Canada. Both civilians and veterans in Canada remembered the war as an ennobling and successful crusade in which lives were not lost but willingly sacrificed to the cause. Australians were less dewy-eyed in remembering the war but no less convinced that it marked their coming of age as a nation.

In sum, we can see that the Great War ended in the worst possible way. The military triumph presided over by Foch and Haig was one of the strangest events in history. The Germans denied that it had happened. The Americans insisted that it was their doing. Although this was tactless, it was plausible, and yet, when Republican isolationists in the Senate defeated the treaty when it came up for ratification, the American presence in Europe was withdrawn, and the validity of the result thereby cancelled in American eyes. The French paid homage to the victory of 1918 and insisted that it was a purely French affair. Meanwhile, the British, whose army had actually hammered out the victory, ignored 1918 and soon decided that the whole business had been criminal and futile.

What then was great about the Great War? Why should we remember it? Was it the legacy of bitter irony and modernism, as Paul Fussell argues [6]? Was it the realization that life was little better than 'a cruel game, played without rules, culminating in a cheap funeral', as Sassoon lamented? Or was it that the war was a modernizing experience, as Eric Leed argues in his variation of Fussell's thesis (Leed, 1979), an experience in which people learned to be defensive in the face of industrial technology and Kafkaesque bureaucracy? Was it Black Adder's war after all? Both Fussell and Leed have caught the essence of the Great War, the way it embodied and clarified the essential features of modern civilization, while at the same time stripping those features of the myths, high diction and illusions that had made them tolerable. Yet the nature of history did not change because of the Great War. Rather our understanding of history changed, at least if we bothered to inquire into what people thought was happening and reflected over the ironic discrepancy between what was meant to happen and what did. As F. Scott Fitzgerald realized [*Doc. 10*] a 'lovely safe world' blew up after 1914.

One antidote to doubt was to will oneself to act or believe, what the Nazis called 'the triumph of the will'. Fascism* and Nazism* originated among war veterans; Hitler was almost a German version of the Unknown Soldier. As ideologies, Fascism and Nazism retained the front soldier's tribal sense of isolation from civilian society [*Doc. 16*], the acceptance of regimentation and above all brutalization resulting from the habituation with violence and death. The prophecy Wilfred Owen made in 'Strange Meeting', the last poem he wrote before he was machine-gunned within a week of the Armistice, came true:

Now men will go content with what we spoiled.
Or, discontent, boil bloody and be spilled.
They will be swift with swiftness of the tigress.
None will break ranks, though nations trek from progress.

After the war, a poet wrote of the 'heartbreak at the heart of things'. It is still there. It can be understood in the poetry of Owen and Sassoon [*Docs. 13 and 14*], relived in the novels of Manning or Remarque, seen in the art of Otto Dix or C.R.W. Nevinson, felt in the memorials tucked away in churches, village squares and cemeteries around the world or heard in Benjamin Britten's *War Requiem* or the first movement of Elgar's cello concerto. It is the most enduring legacy of the Great War.

PART SIX   DOCUMENTS

1.   BETHMANN HOLLWEG'S SEPTEMBER MEMORANDUM ABOUT WAR AIMS

2.   FALKENHAYN GIVES THE KAISER A CHRISTMAS PRESENT: VICTORY WITHOUT TOTAL WAR, DECEMBER 1915

3.   THE PEACE RESOLUTION OF THE REICHSTAG, 9 JULY 1917

4.   FRENCH ARMY SONG

5.   BRITISH SONGS

6.   FROM THE WIPERS TIMES NO. 2, VOL. 1, SATURDAY 26 FEBRUARY 1916

7.   A GERMAN VIEW OF TRENCH FIGHTING: EXCERPTS FROM THE DIARY OF RUDOLF BINDING

8.   PRIVATE FRASER SEES AN ATTACK FAIL AND THEN THE 'CREME DE MENTHE' MAKE HISTORY, COURCELLETTE, SEPTEMBER 1916

9.   DEFENDING BRITISH LIBERTIES: DORA (DEFENCE OF THE REALM ACT) 8 AUGUST 1914

10. TEN YEARS LATER: DICK DIVER LAMENTS

11. FINDING THE RIGHT WORDS ABOUT THE WAR

12. TELLING THE TRUTH ABOUT THE WAR: SASSOON

13. OWEN'S WARNING

14. AFTER SASSOON'S MUTINY

15. THE WORDS OF THE PBI: SOLDIERS' SLANG

16. US VERSUS THEM: THE GHOSTS SPEAK OUT

17. A NURSE'S FIRST ENCOUNTER WITH MUSTARD GAS

18. LAWRENCE OF ARABIA SHRUGS

19. THREE WAYS TO REMEMBER THE WAR

*Bethmann Hollweg's Memorandum of 9 September 1914 was described as
'provisional notes on the direction of our policy on the conclusion of peace',
which Bethmann Hollweg expected would come soon.*

The 'general aim of the war' was, for him, 'security for the German Reich in
west and east for all imaginable time. For this purpose France must be so
weakened as to make her revival as a great power impossible for all time.
Russia must be thrust back as far as possible from Germany's eastern frontier
and her domination over the non-Russian vassal peoples broken.

1. *France.* The military to decide whether we should demand cession of
Belford and western slopes of the Vosges, razing of fortresses and cession of
coastal strip form Dunkirk to Boulogne.

The ore-field of Briey, which is necessary for the supply of ore for our
industry, to be ceded in any case.

Further, a war indemnity, to be paid in instalments; it must be high enough
to prevent France from spending any considerable sums on armaments in the
next 15–20 years.

Furthermore: a commercial treaty which makes France economically dependent on Germany, secures the French market for our exports and makes it
possible to exclude British commerce from France. This treaty must secure for
us financial and industrial freedom of movement in France in such fashion
that German enterprises can no longer receive different treatment from French.

2. *Belgium.* Liège and Verviers to be attached to Prussia, a frontier strip of
the province of Luxemburg to Luxemburg.

Question whether Antwerp, with a corridor to Liège, should also be annexed
remains open.

At any rate Belgium, even if allowed to continue to exist as a state, must be
reduced to a vassal state, must allow us to occupy any militarily important
ports, must place her coast at our disposal in military respects, must become
economically a German province. Given such a solution, which offers the
advantages of annexation without its inescapable domestic political disad-
vantages, French Flanders with Dunkirk, Calais and Boulogne, where most of
the population is Flemish, can without danger be attached to this unaltered
Belgium. The competent quarters will have to judge the military value of this
position against England.

3. *Luxemburg.* Will become a German federal state and will receive a strip of
the present Belgian province of Luxemburg and perhaps the corner of Longwy.

4. We must create a *central European economic association* through common customs treaties, to include France, Belgium, Holland, Denmark, Austria-
Hungary, Poland [*sic*], and perhaps Italy, Sweden and Norway. This association

will not have any common constitutional supreme authority and all its members will be formally equal, but in practice it will be under German leadership and must stabilise Germany's economic dominance over Mitteleuropa.

5. *The question of colonial acquisitions*, where the first aim is the creation of a continuous Central African colonial empire, will be considered later, as will that of the aims to be realised *vis-à-vis* Russia.

6. A short provisional formula suitable for a possible preliminary peace to be found for a basis for the economic agreements to be concluded with France and Belgium.

7. *Holland*. It will have to be considered by what means and methods Holland can be brought into closer relationship with the German Empire.

In view of the Dutch character, this closer relationship must leave them free of any feeling of compulsion, must alter nothing in the Dutch way of life, and must also subject them to no new military obligations. Holland, then, must be left independent in externals, but be made internally dependent on us. Possibly one might consider an offensive and defensive alliance, to cover the colonies; in any case a close customs association, perhaps the cession of Antwerp to Holland in return for the right to keep a German garrison in the fortress of Antwerp and at the mouth of the Scheldt.

From Fischer, Fritz, *Germany's Aims in the First World War*, W. W. Norton, New York, 1967, pp. 103–5.

DOCUMENT 2   FALKENHAYN GIVES THE KAISER A CHRISTMAS PRESENT: VICTORY WITHOUT TOTAL WAR, DECEMBER 1915

France has been weakened almost to the limits of endurance, both in a military and economic sense – the latter by the permanent loss of the coalfields in the north-east of the country. The Russian armies have not been completely overthrown but their offensive powers have been so shattered that she can never revive in anything like her old strength. The arm of Serbia can be considered as destroyed. Italy has no doubt realized that she cannot reckon on the realization of her brigand's ambitions within measurable time and would therefore probably be only too glad to be able to liquidate her adventure in any way that would save her face.

If no deductions can be drawn from these facts, the reasons are to be sought in many circumstances, the details of which there is no need to discuss. But the chief among them cannot be passed over, for it is the enormous hold which England still has on her allies.

It is true that we have succeeded in shaking England severely – the best proof of that is her imminent adoption of universal military service. But that is

also a proof of the sacrifices England is prepared to make to attain her end –
the permanent elimination of what seems to her the most dangerous rival
... Germany can expect no mercy from this enemy, so long as he still retains
the slightest hope of achieving his object. Any attempt at an understanding
which Germany might make would only strengthen England's will to war as,
judging others by herself, she would take it as a sign that Germany's resolution was weakening.

England, a country in which men are accustomed to weigh up the chances
dispassionately, can scarcely hope to overthrow us by purely military means.
She is obviously staking everything on a war of exhaustion. We have not been
able to shatter her belief that it will bring Germany to her knees, and that
belief gives the enemy the strength to fight on and keep on whipping their
team together.

What we have to do is to dispel that illusion.

With that end in view, it will not in the long run be enough for us merely to
stand on the defensive, a course in itself quite worthy of consideration. Our
enemies, thanks to their superiority in men and material, are increasing their
resources much more than we are. If that process continues a moment must
come when the balance of numbers itself will deprive Germany of all remaining hope. The power of our allies to hold out is restricted, while our own is
not unlimited ... We must show England patently that her venture has no
prospects ...

The upshot of this discussion is that the attempt to seek a decision by an
attack on the English front in the West cannot be recommended, though an
opportunity of doing so may arrive in a counter-attack. In view of our feelings
for our arch enemy in this war that is certainly distressing, but it can be
endured if we realize that for England the campaign on the Continent of
Europe with her own troops is at bottom a side-show. Her real weapons here
are the French, Russian and Italian Armies.

If we put these armies out of the war England is left to face us alone, and it
is difficult to believe that in such circumstances her lust for our destruction
would not fail her. It is true there would be no certainty that she would give up,
but there is a strong probability. More than that can seldom be asked in war.

It is all the more necessary that we should ruthlessly employ every weapon
that is suitable for striking at England on her own ground ... The submarine
war ... is a weapon to itself. It is the duty of those who are conducting the
war to explain their attitude on this question.

Submarine warfare strikes at the enemy's most sensitive spot, because it
aims at severing his oversea communications. If the definite promises of the
naval authorities, that the unrestricted submarine war must force England to
yield in the course of the year 1916 are realized, we must face the fact that the
United States may take up a hostile attitude. She cannot intervene decisively in

the war in time to enable her to make England fight on when that country sees the spectre of hunger and many another famine rise up before her island. There is only one shadow on this encouraging picture of the future. We have to assume that the naval authorities are not making a mistake. We have no large store of experiences to draw on in this matter. Such as we have are not altogether reassuring. On the other hand, the basis of our calculations will be materially changed in our favour if we can increase the number of our submarines and make progress with the training of their crews. For all these reasons there can be no justification on military grounds for refusing any further to employ what promises to be our most effective weapon. Germany has every right to use it ruthlessly after England's unconscionable behaviour at sea. The Americans, England's secret allies, will not recognize that, but it is doubtful whether, in face of a determined diplomatic representation of Germany's standpoint, they will decide to intervene actively on the Continent of Europe. It is even more doubtful whether they could intervene in sufficient strength in time ...

As I have already insisted, the strain on France has almost reached the breaking-point – though it is certainly borne with the most remarkable devotion. If we succeeded in opening the eyes of her people to the fact that in a military sense they have nothing more to hope for, that breaking-point would be reached and England's best sword knocked out of her hand. To achieve that object the uncertain method of a mass break-through, in any case beyond our means, is unnecessary. We can probably do enough for our purposes with limited resources. Within our reach behind the French sector of the Western front there are objectives for the retention of which the French General Staff would be compelled to throw in every man they have. If they do so the forces of France will bleed to death – as there can be no question of a voluntary withdrawal – whether we reach our goal or not. If they do not do so, and we reach our objectives, the moral effect on France will be enormous. For an operation limited to a narrow front Germany will not be compelled to spend herself so completely that all other fronts are practically drained. She can face with confidence the relief attacks to be expected on those fronts, and indeed hope to have sufficient troops in hand to reply to them with counter-attacks. For she is perfectly free to accelerate or draw out her offensive, to intensify it or break it off from time to time, as suits her purpose.

The objectives of which I am speaking now are Belfort and Verdun.

The considerations urged above apply to both, yet the preference must be given to Verdun. The French lines at that point are barely twelve miles distant from the German railway communications. Verdun is therefore the most powerful *point d'appui* for an attempt, with a relatively small expenditure of effort, to make the whole German front in France and untenable ...

The memorandum is quoted in Erich von Falkenhayn, *General Headquarters 1914–1918 and its Critical Decisions*, Hutchinson, London, pp. 209–18.

DOCUMENT 3   THE PEACE RESOLUTION OF THE REICHSTAG, 9 JULY 1917

The Resolution was proposed by a leader of the Catholic Centre Party, Matthias Erzberger, and passed by an almost two to one majority of the Majority Social Democrats, Progressives and Centre parties . . . The High Command believed that its passage showed how weak Chancellor Bethmann Hollweg was, and when his erstwhile supporters held back, he succumbed to a backstairs plot and was replaced by Georg Michaelis. Michaelis then said he accepted the Resolution 'as I understand it', negating what little impact it held.

The Reichstag strives for a peace of understanding and the permanent reconciliation of peoples. Forced territorial acquisitions and political, economic, or financial oppressions are irreconcilable with such a peace. The Reichstag also rejects all plans which aim at economic isolation and hostility among nations after the war. The freedom of the seas must be made secure. Only an economic peace will prepare the ground for a friendly intercourse between the nations. The Reichstag will strongly promote the creation of international judicial organizations. However, as long as the enemy governments will not enter upon such a peace, as long as they threaten Germany and her allies with conquests and coercion, the German nation will stand together as a man and steadfastly hold out and fight until its own and its allies' right to life and development is secured. The German nation is invincible in its unity. The Reichstag knows that in this respect it is in harmony with the men who in heroic struggle are defending the Fatherland. The imperishable gratitude of the whole people is assured them.

From Lutz, Ralph, *Fall of the German Empire, 1914–1918*, Vol. II, Stanford University Press, 1932 (reprinted by Octagon Press, New York, 1969), pp. 282–3.

DOCUMENT 4   FRENCH ARMY SONG

This was widespread during the mutinies of 1917 despite an official ban on its singing. It was presented in the movie Oh What a Lovely War. *The French and English lyrics are given in Stephen O'Shea,* Back to the Front *(Toronto 1996) p. 127.*

> *Adieu la vie, adieu l'amour*
> *Adieu toutes les femmes*
> *C'est bien fini, c'est pour toujours*
> *De cette guerre infâme*
> *C'est à Craonne, sur le plateau*
> *Qu'on doit laissez sa peau*

Car nous sommes tous condamnés
Nous sommes les sacrificiés

Farewell to life, farewell to love
Farewell to all the women
It's all over now, finished for good,
Done by this awful war.
At Craonne, on the plateau
That's where we'll lose our lives
Because we are all doomed
We are sacrificed.

DOCUMENT 5   **BRITISH SONGS**

If you want the old battalion
I know where they are,
I know where they are,
I know where they are.
If you want the old battalion
I know where they are,
Hangin' on the old barbed wire.

I've seen them, I've seen them,
Hangin' on the old barbed wire.
I've seen them, I've seen them,
Hangin' on the old barbed wire.

* * * *

Bombed last night, bombed the night before,
Gonna get bombed tonight if we never get bombed no more.
When we're bombed we're scared as we can be,
Oh God damn the bombing planes from Germany.

They're over us, they're over us,
One shell hole for the four of us.
Glory be to God that three of us can run,
Cause one of us could fill it all alone.

Gassed last night, gassed the night before,
Gonna get gassed again if we never get gassed no more.
When we're gassed we're sick as we can be,
Cause phosgene and mustard gas are much too much for me.

They're warning us, they're warning us,
One respirator for the four of us.

Glory be to God that three of us can run,
Cause one of us can use it all alone.

* * * * * *

We're here
Because
We're here
Because
We're here.

Air: *Auld Lang Syne*

DOCUMENT 6 FROM THE WIPERS TIMES

NO. 2, VOL. 1, SATURDAY 26 FEBRUARY 1916

By Belary Helloc.

In this article, I wish to show plainly that under existing conditions, everything points to a speedy disintegration of the enemy. We will take first of all the effect of war on the male population of Germany. Firstly, let us take as our figures, 12,000,000 as the total fighting population of Germany. Of these 8,000,000 are killed or being killed; hence we have 4,000,000 remaining. Of these 1,000,000 are non-combatants, being in the Navy. Of the 3,000,000 remaining, we can write off 2,500,000 as tempermentally unsuitable for fighting, owing to obesity and other ailments engendered by a gross mode of living. This leaves us 500,000 as the full strength. Of these 497,250 are known to be suffering from incurable diseases. This leaves us 2,750. Of these 2,150 are on the Eastern Front, and of the remaining 600, 584 are Generals and Staff. Thus we find that there are 15 men on the Western Front. This number I maintain is not enough to give them even a fair chance of resisting four more big pushes, and hence the collapse of the Western Campaign. I will tell you next week about the others, and how to settle them.

The poet and essayist Hilaire Belloc contributed military articles to *The Times*.

NO. 4, VOL. 2, MONDAY 20 MARCH 1916

Military definitions.

Hooge	See Hell.
Quarter Master Or	
Master Quarter	A bird of strange habits: when attacked covers itself with indents [forms] and talks backwards.

Or	
Q. M.	
Rum	See Warrant Officer.
Dump	A collection of odds and ends, sometimes known as the Divisional Toyshop.
Hell	See Hooge.
Fokker	The name given by all infantry officers and men to any aeroplane that flies at a great height.
Adjutant	See grenades or birds.
Infantryman	An animal of weird habits, whose peculiarities have only just been discovered. It displays a strange aversion to light, and lives in holes in the earth during the day, coming out at night to seek whom it might devour.
	In colour it assimilates itself to the ground in which it lives.
Grenades	These are used to cause annoyance to any luckless person who happens to be near them.
Birds	Are of two kinds only – the Carrier Pigeon (a delicacy for front line trenches), and the nameless, untamed variety usually collected by junior officers.

The Wipers Times, later titled *The New Church Times, The Kemmel Times, The Somme Times, The B.E.F. Times* and, after the Armistice, *The Better Times*, was a trench newspaper published in Ypres. It was reprinted in its entirety in facsimile editions in 1930 and 1973, and is thus the most accessible of the many trench newspapers turned out by officers and men of all the armies in the war.

DOCUMENT 7   A GERMAN VIEW OF TRENCH FIGHTING:
EXCERPTS FROM THE DIARY OF RUDOLF BINDING

Vijfwege, April 24, 1915.

The effects of the successful gas attack were horrible. I am not pleased with the idea of poisoning men. Of course, the entire world will rage about it first and then imitate us. All the dead lie on their backs, with clenched fists; the whole field is yellow. They say that Ypres must fall now. One can see it burning – not without a pang for the beautiful city. Langemarck is a heap of rubbish, and all rubbish heaps look alike; there is no sense in describing one. All that remains of the church is the doorway with the date '1620' . . .

Last night I saved three captured guns that were lying in full view of the enemy's new line, not more than five hundred metres away. The moon was shining, and, apart from this, the enemy kept the battlefield continually lighted up with most damnably bright Very lights. We were all night on the job, constantly interrupted by furious bursts of fire and by the Very lights, which obliged us to lie flat on the ground as long as they were burning. Before dawn we got all three guns into safety, together with their limbers and ammunition. One of my men was shot through the heart because he tried to bring back a sucking-pig which he found squeaking in its lonely pen on one of the limbers. He sat on top, while his comrades put their shoulders to the wheels. Suddenly he fell lifeless between the wheels, still holding his little pig in the grip of death.

After fresh attacks a sleeping army lies in front of one of our brigades; they rest in good order, man by man, and will never wake again – Canadian divisions. [*sic*. Only one Canadian division was in France by April 1915.] The enemy's losses are enormous.

The battlefield is fearful. One is overcome by a peculiar sour, heavy, and penetrating smell of corpses. Rising over a plank bridge you find that its middle is supported only by the body of a long-dead horse. Men that were killed last October lie half in swamp and half in the yellow-sprouting beet-fields. The legs of an Englishman, still encased in puttees, stick out into a trench, the corpse being built into the parapet; a soldier hangs his rifle on them. A little brook runs through the trench, and everyone uses the water for drinking and washing; it is the only water they have. Nobody minds the pale Englishman who is rotting away a few steps farther up. In Langemarck cemetery a hecatomb had been piled up; for the dead must have lain above ground-level. German shells falling into it started a horrible resurrection. At one point I saw twenty-two dead horses, still harnessed, accompanied by a few dead drivers. Cattle and pigs lie about, half-rotten; broken trees, avenues razed to the ground; crater upon crater in the roads and in the fields. Such is a six months' old battlefield.

From Rudolf Binding, *A Fatalist at War*, Allen & Unwin, London, 1929, pp. 64–6.

DOCUMENT 8   PRIVATE FRASER SEES AN ATTACK FAIL AND THEN THE 'CREME DE MENTHE' MAKE HISTORY, COURCELLETTE, SEPTEMBER 1916

As zero hour approached I glanced around looking for signs to charge. The signal came like a bolt from the blue. Right on the second the barrage opened with a roar that seemed to split the heavens. Looking along the right, about forty yards away, I caught the first glimpse of a khaki-clad figure climbing over the parapet. It was the start of the first wave, the 27th Battalion. More Winnipeg men followed. Then glancing back over the parados I saw Sgt. Teddy Torrens rise up from a shell hole and wave his platoon forward. So quick, however, were the men of the 31st on the heels of the 27th that when I turned my head, those of my platoon beside Sgt. Hunter were actually up and over the parapet with a good five to ten yards start ahead of me. In a hurry to overtake them and carry the line as even as possible, I was up and over in a trice, running into shell holes, down and up for about twenty yards, until I found that if I continued this procedure and rate, loaded up as I was, I would be exhausted before I could get to grips with Fritz.

It was at this juncture that instinct told me to avoid the shell holes and move along the edges. I raised my head for the first time and looked at the Hun trench, and to my astonishment, saw Heiny after Heiny ranging along the line, up on the firing step, blazing wildly into us, to all appearances unmolested . . . Strange to say they all seemed to be pointing at me, an illusion but nevertheless that is how it appeared . . .

My wits sharpened when it burnt deeply into me that death was in the offing. At this stage an everchanging panorama of events passed quickly before my gaze, and my mind was vividly impressed. The air was seething with shells. Immediately above, the atmosphere was cracking with a myriad of machine-gun bullets, startling and disconcerting in the extreme. Bullets from the enemy rifles were whistling and swishing around my ears in hundreds, that to this day I cannot understand how anyone could have crossed that inferno alive. As I pressed forward with eyes strained, to the extent of being half closed, I expected and almost felt being shot in the stomach. All around our men were falling, their rifles loosening from their grasp. The wounded, writhing in their agonies, struggled and toppled into shell holes for safety from rifle and machine-gun fire, though in my path the latter must have been negligible, for a slow or even quick traverse would have brought us down before we reached many yards into No Man's Land. Rifle fire, however, was taking its toll, and on my front and flanks, soldier after soldier was tumbling to disablement or death, and I expected my turn every moment. The transition from life to death was terribly swift . . .

As the attack subsided and not a soul moved in No Man's Land save the wounded twisting and moaning in their agony, it dawned upon me that the assault was a failure and now we were at the mercy of the enemy. It was suicide to venture back and our only hope lay in waiting until darkness set in and then trying to win our way back. During this period of waiting, I expected we would be deluged by bombs, shrapnel and shell fire, and when darkness set in, ravaged by machine-gun fire, altogether a hopeless outlook, especially for our lot, who were lying up against his trench. The situation seemed critical and the chances of withdrawal to safety nigh impossible. So many things had happened, so many lives were snuffed out since I left the comparative safety of our front line, that I lost completely all idea of time.

Lying low in the shell hole contemplating events with now and then a side glance at my sandy moustached comrade, lying dead beside me, his mess tin shining and scintillating on his back, a strange and curious sight appeared. Away to my left rear, a huge gray object reared itself into view, and slowly, very slowly, it crawled along like a gigantic toad, feeling its way across the shell-stricken field. It was a tank, the 'Creme de Menthe', the latest invention of destruction and the first of its kind to be employed in the Great War. I watched it coming towards our direction. How painfully slow it travelled. Down and up the shell holes it clambered, a weird, ungainly monster, moving relentlessly forward. Suddenly men from the ground looked up, rose as if from the dead, and running from the flanks to behind it, followed in the rear as if to be in on the kill. The last I saw of it, it was wending its way to the Sugar Refinery. It crossed Fritz's trenches, a few yards from me, with hardly a jolt.

When first observed it gave new life and vigour to our men. Seeing away behind men getting up, and no one falling, I looked up and there met the gaze of some of my comrades in the shell holes. Instinctively I jumped up and quickly, though warily, ran to where I could see into Fritz's trench, with bayonet pointing and finger on the trigger. Running my eyes up and down his trench, ready to shoot if I saw any signs of hostility, and equally on the alert to jump out of view if I saw a rifle pointing at me, it was a tense and exciting moment but I felt marvellously fit and wits extremely acute, for any encounter. I expected opposition and was ready for danger, but a swift glance, and to my amazement, not a German was staring at me, far less being defiant. Down the trench about a hundred yards, several Huns, minus rifles and equipment, got out of their trench and were beating it back over the open, terrified at the approach of the tank. Only a moment sufficed to show that it was safer in the German trench than being up in the open, where one may be sniped, so with a leap I jumped into the trench, almost transfixing myself with [my] bayonet in the effort.

In several seconds a few more of the Company were into the trench. With two others, I proceeded south to clean up the line. Going about fifty yards without encountering any opposition, and meeting some more of our fellows, we retraced our steps and ran back forty yards or so beyond where we entered the trench when we connected up with some more of our men. There was not a single German capable of offering fight. To the south in the open, I saw Sgt. George West driving about ten prisoners towards our line . . . Further away on the flanks more Germans were seen hurrying back to our lines, apparently quite anxious to be taken captive. Finding the trench completely in our possession, we started shaking hands and telling each other who was killed and wounded. Young Hayden arrived on the scene and overhearing that his brother was killed commenced sobbing, but controlled himself when his brother suddenly appeared in our midst. The latter complained of being hurt in the eye and beat it out shortly afterwards. The danger of being shot by the front line Germans being now over, several of us set about collecting souvenirs.

From Reginald Roy (ed.) *The Journal of Private Fraser*, Sono Nis Press, Victoria BC, 1985, pp. 201–9.

DOCUMENT 9 DEFENDING BRITISH LIBERTIES: DORA (DEFENCE OF THE REALM ACT), 8 AUGUST 1914

An Act to confer on His Majesty in Council power to during the present War for the Defence of the Realm Be it enacted by the King's most Excellent Majesty advice and consent of the Lords Spiritual and Temporal, in this present Parliament assembled, and by the authority of the same, as follows:

1. His Majesty in Council has power during the continuation of the present war to issue regulations as to the powers an Admiralty and Army Council, and of the members of His Majesty's forces, and other persons acting on His behalf, for securing the public safety and the defence of the realm; and may by such regulation authorize the trial by courts martial and punishment of persons contravening any of the provisions of such regulations designed –

(a) to prevent persons communicating with the enemy or obtaining information for that purpose or any purpose calculated to jeopardize the success of the operations of any of His Majesty's forces or to assist the enemy; or

(b) to secure the safety of any means of communication, or of railways, docks or harbours;

in a like manner as if such persons were subject to military law and had on active service committed an offence under section five of the Army Act.

From Arthur Marwick, *The Deluge: British Society and the First World War*,
Macmillan, London, 1975, pp. 36–7.

DOCUMENT 10 TEN YEARS LATER: DICK DIVER LAMENTS

See that little stream – we could walk to it in two minutes. It took the British a month to walk to it – a whole empire walking very slowly, dying in front and pushing forward behind. And another empire walked very slowly backward a few inches a day, leaving the dead like a million bloody rugs. No Europeans will ever do that again in this generation . . .

This western front business couldn't be done again, not for a long time. The young men think they could do it but they couldn't. They could fight the first Marne again but not this. This took religion and years of plenty and tremendous sureties and the exact relation between the classes . . . You had to have a whole-souled sentimental equipment going back further than you could remember. You had to remember Christmas, and postcards of the Crown Prince and his fiancee, and little cafes in Valence and beer gardens in Unter den Linden and weddings at the mairie, and going to the Derby, and your grandfather's whiskers . . . This kind of battle was invented by Lewis Carroll and Jules Verne and whoever wrote *Undine*, and country deacons bowling and marraines and Marseilles and girls seduced in the back lanes of Württemburg and

Westphalia. Why this was a love battle – there was a century of middle-class love spent here . . . all my beautiful lovely safe world blew itself up here with a great gust of high-explosive love.

> Dick Diver at Beaumont Hamel a decade after the war, in F. Scott Fitzgerald's novel
> *Tender is the Night*, Longman, Harlow, Essex, 1993, pp. 57–8.

DOCUMENT 11   FINDING THE RIGHT WORDS ABOUT THE WAR

Before he returned to France, Owen drafted a brief preface for the book of poems that he hoped to publish. He left it unfinished, and it was not published until after his death; nevertheless, it belongs here, as a document in the wartime history of imagining the war, and one that is important enough to quote in full, familiar though it is.

> 'This book is not about heroes. English poetry is not yet fit to speak of them.
>   Nor is it about deeds, or lands, nor anything about glory, honour, might, majesty, dominion, or power, except War.
>
>   Above all I am not concerned with Poetry.
>   My subject is War, and the pity of War.
>   The Poetry is in the pity.
>   Yet these elegies are to this generation in no sense consolatory.
>
> They may be to the next. All a poet can do today is warn. That is why the true Poets must be truthful . . .'

Here, near the end of the war, is a war poet's manifesto, which is not about war but about language – a terse statement that simply prohibits the old high rhetoric without even bothering to say why, as though by now that was self-evident. And so it was, to poets like Owen and Sassoon and Graves. It was self-evident, too, to many prose-writers . . . and an army of other soldiers, and some civilians. What Owen wrote was what they all knew: the truth about the war was a matter of language – and especially of the words that you did *not* use.

> From Samuel Hynes, *A War Imagined: The First World War and English Culture*,
> Bodley Head, London, 1990, pp. 182–3.

DOCUMENT 12   TELLING THE TRUTH ABOUT THE WAR: SASSOON

A statement released to the press in July 1917. Because of his exemplary record, including the Military Cross, Sassoon was sent to Craiglockhart hospital to be treated for neurasthenia. There he met Wilfred Owen.

I am making this statement as an act of wilful defiance of military authority, because I believe that the War is being deliberately prolonged by those who have the power to end it. I am a soldier, convinced that I am acting on behalf of soldiers. I believe that this War, upon which I entered as a war of defence and liberation, has now become a war of aggression and conquest. I believe that the purposes for which I and my fellow-soldiers entered upon this War should have been so clearly stated as to have made it impossible for them to be changed without our knowledge, and that, had this been done, the objects which actuated us would not be attainable by negotiation.

I have seen and endured the sufferings of the troops, and I can no longer be a party to prolonging those sufferings for ends which I believe to be evil and unjust.

I am not protesting against the military conduct of the War, but against the political errors and insincerities for which the fighting men are being sacrificed.

On behalf of those who are suffering now, I make this protest against the deception which is being practiced on them. Also I believe that it may help to destroy the callous complacence with which the majority of those at home regard the continuance of agonies which they do not share, and which they have not sufficient imagination to realise.

From Siegfried Sassoon, *Diaries 1915–1918*, Faber & Faber, London, 1983, pp. 173–4.

DOCUMENT 13   OWEN'S WARNING

Bent double, like old beggars under sacks,
Knock-kneed, coughing like hags, we cursed through sludge,
Till on the haunting flares we turned our backs
And towards our distant rest began to trudge.
Men marched asleep. Many had lost their boots
But limped on, blood-shod. All went lame; all blind;
Drunk with fatigue; deaf even to the hoots
Of tired, outstripped Five-Nines that dropped behind.

Gas! Gas! Quick boys! – an ecstasy of fumbling,
Fitting the clumsy helmets just in time;
But someone still was yelling out and stumbling
And floundering like a man in fire or lime . . .
Dim, through the misty panes and thick green light,
As under a green sea, I saw him drowning.

In all my dreams, before my helpless sight,
He plunges at me, guttering, choking, drowning.

If in some smothering dreams you too could pace
Behind the wagon that we flung him in,
And watch the white eyes writhing in his face,

His hanging face, like a devil's sick of sin;
If you could hear, at every jolt, the blood
Come gargling from the froth-corrupted lungs,

Obscene as cancer, bitter as the cud
Of vile, incurable sores on innocent tongues –
My friend, you would not tell with such high zest
To children ardent for some desperate glory,
The old Lie: Dulce et decorum est
Pro patria mori.

DOCUMENT 14   AFTER SASSOON'S MUTINY

I am banished from the patient men who fight
They smote my heart to pity, built my pride.
Shoulder to shoulder, side by side,
They trudged away from life's broad wealds of light.
Their wrongs were mine; and ever in my sight
They went arrayed in honour. But they died,
Not one by one: and mutinous I cried
To those who sent them out into the night.
The darkness tells how vainly I have striven
To free them from the pit where they must dwell
In outcast gloom convulsed and jagged and riven
By grappling guns. Love drove me to rebel.
Love drives me back to grope with them through hell;
And in their tortured eyes I stand forgiven.

DOCUMENT 15   THE WORDS OF THE PBI [*POOR BLOODY INFANTRY*]: SOLDIERS' SLANG

ALLEY: Run away! Clear out! Or in full, *Alley toot sweet*.

ALLEYMAN: A German. French *Allemand*. Not much used after 1916.

ANNIE LAURIE: Lorry. Rhyming slang.

ARCHIE: Short for Archibald: facetious name for an anti-aircraft gun; also for its shell bursts . . .

BATTLE BOWLER: Officers' slang for steel helmet (cf. *Tin Hat*).

BENT: Spoiled, ruined, e.g. 'A good man bent' or even 'good tea bent'.

BITCH, TO: To spoil, ruin. From civilian slang.

BLIGHTY: England, in the sense of home. In this one word was gathered much of the soldier's home-sickness and affection and war-weariness. Far more than the actual distance separated him from England. He had entered another mode of existence, ugly, precarious, bearing hardly any resemblance to his normal life, which now had become to him abnormal and incredible.

Blighty to the soldier was a sort of faerie, a paradise which he could faintly remember, a never-never land. The word was further used as an adjective, not merely for things English and homelike, but as a general expression of approval. E.g. 'This is real Blighty butter' – meaning ideal, as good as English. It was also used of a wound (cf. *Blighty One*). The word is thought to be a corruption of the Hindustani *bilaik*: foreign country, especially England . . .

BLOWN TO BUGGERY: Destroyed by shellfire.

BOMBERS: Experts with hand grenades. Sometimes called *The Suicide Club*.

BOMB-PROOF JOB: Employment at the Base on the Lines of Communication.

BULL: Bullshit; not spit and polish but any kind of pretentiousness or incredible nonsense.

CAMEL CORPS: Infantry; from the heavy weights loaded on to their backs. [See Marching Order, Full.]

CHEERO: A salutation. Perhaps derived from the pre-1914 Cockney *what cheer*! The word was later developed, chiefly by officers, into *Cheerio*.

COAL-BOX: The shellburst of a 5.9 or heavier shell. From the black smoke. Sometimes used of the shell itself (cf. *Jack Johnson* and *crump*).

COMIC CUTS: An Intelligence summary or report. Officers' slang.

CRUCIFIX CORNER: On the Western Front almost any cross-roads or inter-section of roads with a Calvary.

CUSHY: Soft, comfortable, luxurious . . . Other people were always getting cushy jobs . . . From Hindustani.

DIRTY WORK AT THE CROSS-ROADS TONIGHT: A pre-1914 catch-phrase from melodrama. Used by the troops figuratively and sometimes for enemy shellfire on cross-roads.

DIXIE: A large iron pot, oval, with an iron lid and a thin white metal handle devised to bite into the hands carrying it . . . The word is not from the United States but India; *degshai*, a cooking-pot . . .

ESTAMINET: There is no equivalent in Great Britain. On the Western Front an *estaminet* was not a pub. Neither was it a café or a restaurant. It had some of the qualities of all three. It was never large and was found only in villages and very minor towns. It had low ceilings, an open iron stove; it was warm and fuggy; it had wooden benches and tables. It sold wine, cognac and thin beer, as well as coffee, eggs and chips and omelettes. The proprietress (a proprietor was unthinkable) had a daughter or two, or nieces, or younger sisters who served at table and made no objection to tobacco smoke and ribald choruses in English and pidgin French. No doubt some estaminets overcharged but in general they provided for the soldier off duty behind the line many and many a happy hour. The name had a magical quality in 1914–18 – and still has for those who survive . . .

F.A.: Sometimes lengthened into Sweet F.A. or bowdlerized into *Sweet Fanny Adams* (cf.). Used to mean 'nothing' when something was expected. E.g. 'Got any fags?' – 'Sweet F.A.'.

FRITZ: Diminutive of *Friedrich*. German soldiers, singly or collectively. After 1915 less frequent among private soldiers than *Jerry* (Also cf. *Boche, Hun, Heiny*).

FRONT: To people in Britain the Front meant Northern France and Belgium. Across the Channel it meant the forward area, not the front-line trenches especially. Used in the Boer (and perhaps earlier) wars, so probably derived from *frontier*.

GADGET: Naval, then Army technical, then general slang for any mechanical instrument or contrivance. The War brought it into general use.

GAME: 'It's a game!' meant 'It's ridiculous! There's no sense in it.' Frequently applied to the War as a whole and to the methods and outlook of the Army.

HANS WURST: The German equivalent of Tommy Atkins; variants: *Hans, Gemeine*, more commonly of the infantry private soldier. The commonest German slang equivalents of *footslogger* were *Dreckfresser*, mud-eater, *Kilometerfresser*, kilometer-eater; *Fusslatsche*, foot-shuffler; *Lakenpatscher*, rather like our *mud-crusher*; *Kilometerschwein*; *Sandhase*, sand-hare . . .

HOM FORTY: A goods wagon on the French railway, in which troops were transported at an average speed of $1\frac{1}{2}$ miles an hour. From an inscription on the outer walls: *Hommes 40, Chevaux 8*.

HUN: German: singular and plural, adjective and noun. Little used by the other ranks, but occasionally applied – 'You Hun!' – to an unpopular comrade.

JOY-STICK: The pilot's controlling lever in an aeroplane. So named because of the thrills the operation could produce. Also for the penis.

MARCHING ORDER, FULL: On the road the infantryman carried besides his rifle and webbing or leather equipment, 60 pounds of ammunition, haversack (full), waterbottle (full), valise or pack (containing overcoat), a spare pair of boots, his steel helmet, a blanket, a gas respirator, a rubber ground sheet, iron rations, bayonet, entrenching tool and handle and sundry other articles. Spare boots and blanket were often omitted. The rifle alone weighed nine pounds and the total weight at times was probably seventy or even eighty pounds . . .

MINNIE: Minenwerfer. German for Mine (i.e. Bomb) Thrower. Also the bomb itself, which was sometimes called *football, rum jar, Christmas pudding* . . .

MUCKING-IN: A method of sharing rations, sleeping quarters and certain duties. Quite informal and arranged by the men themselves. A set of *mucking-in pals*, two, three or four, formed the true social unit of the army. Such a set would receive rations in a lump for all its members and divide them out: it would 'brew' its own tea and do its own cooking, when the company cooks provided nothing. *Mucking-in pals* would defend each other's property against scroungers, receive letters and parcels for an absent member of the group and – out of the line – drink and feast together.

NAPOO: Finished; empty; gone; non-existent. Corrupted from the French *Il n'y en a plus* – there is no more, given in answer to inquiries for drink, when the estaminet keeper expected officers of highly paid troops. . . . From this the word came to be used for many of the destructions, obliterations and disappointments of war, e.g. 'The bread's napoo'; 'The old dug-out's napoo'; 'Napoo rum' . . .

NUMBER UP, TO HAVE ONE'S: Fatalistic for to be in trouble, or even to be doomed to die soon.

N.Y.D.: A medical term, sometimes written on labels. Technically, 'Not yet diagnosed'. Interpreted by the patient as 'Not Yet Dead'.

OFFENSIVE: To attack on a large scale. Also used by G.H.Q. in 1916–17 for a frame of mind it desired to encourage in front-line troops in order to weaken the enemy's confidence. Enquiries were sent to commanding officers: did they consider they had been 'sufficiently offensive' that day. The word became a joke and another grudge against brass hats.

OOJAH: Or, in full, oojah-cum-pivvy. A military equivalent for 'thingamybob'; a word substituted when the proper name cannot be remembered; or, for the mere fun of using the fantastic syllables, when it is perfectly well known, e.g. 'I saw the S.M. going into the oojah-cum-pivvy down the road' – an estaminet being implied and understood. The Canadians said *hooza-me-kloo*; an English variant was *ooojiboo*.

P.B.I.: Poor Bloody Infantry.

POILU: French for an infantryman – hairy . . . French soldiers seem to have liked 'poilu' as little as British soldiers liked 'Tommy'. The French preferred to call themselves 'les hommes' or 'les bonhommes'.

READ A SHIRT: Examine the seams of a shirt for lice. The phrase, belonging to 1917–18, became generic for *chatt* [delousing].

REST CAMPS: Camps behind the lines where troops returning weary from the line were harried with incessant parades and brass-polishing. Also used ironically for cemeteries.

SAN FAIRY ANN: An extremely popular phrase, approximated into English from the French *ça ne fait rien* – it doesn't matter, it makes no difference, why worry? Fatalistic, cynical, applicable to all kinds of situations, 1916 and later . . .

SHOOTING GALLERY: The front line.

SOMETHING TO HANG THINGS ON: An infantry soldier self-described.

TOASTING FORK: A bayonet, which was in fact often used for toasting bread or sausages.

TOUR OF TRENCH DUTY: The period of duty for infantry in the front line or the supports varied. In normal conditions (they rarely were normal), reliefs were made after a four- or six-day tour. On a very quiet sector, it might be better to be in the line than out, because there were fewer fatigues and inspections.

TRENCH FEVER: A mysterious, perhaps rheumatic fever induced by the conditions of trench life. Many suffered from it.

TRENCH FOOT: Feet frost-bitten in the trenches. A common winter ailment; at one period it was a crime to get trench foot, but no humane commander enforced the penalty. He might wake up next day to find that he himself had trench foot.

TRENCH MOUTH: Infectious Stomatitis was little known before the War. In 1914–15 many men caught it.

WEST: *To go west* was the most popular euphemism in the Army for 'to be killed'. Used in such phrases, as 'Bill went west at Givenchy'. One of the few expressions which revealed the suppressed emotions of the soldier, and his secret sense of the tragedy in which he was caught . . . The phrase was also used trivially of things lost, stolen or strayed, e.g. 'My razor's gone west again'.

Excerpted from John Brophy and Eric Partridge, *The Long Trail: Soldiers' Songs and Slang 1914–18*, Books for Libraries Press, Freeport NY, 1965 (1930), *passim*.

DOCUMENT 16   US VERSUS THEM: THE GHOSTS SPEAK OUT

It is very nice to be at home again. Yet am I at home? One sometimes doubts it. There are occasions when I feel like a visitor among strangers whose intentions are kindly, but whose modes of thought I neither altogether understand nor altogether approve. I find myself storing impressions, attempting hasty and unsatisfactory summaries to appease the insatiable curiosity of the people with whom I am really at home, the England that's not an island or an empire, but a wet, populous dyke stretching from Flanders to the Somme. And then, just when my pencil is on the paper, I realize how hopeless it is . . .

As we exchange views, one of you assumes as possible or probable something that seems to us preposterous, or dismisses as too trivial for comment what appears to us a fact of primary importance. You speak lightly, you assume that we shall speak lightly, of things, emotions, states of mind, human relationships and affairs that are to us solemn or terrible. You seem ashamed, as if they were a kind of weakness, of the ideas which sent us to France, and for which thousands of sons and lovers have died. You calculate the profits to be derived from 'War after the War', as though the unspeakable agonies of the Somme were an item in a commercial proposition. You make us feel that the country to which we've returned is not the country for which we went out to fight! And your reticence as to the obvious physical facts of war! And your ignorance as to the sentiments of your relations to it! . . . We used to blaspheme and laugh and say, 'Oh, it's only the papers. People at home can't really be like that'. But after some months in England I've come to the conclusion that your papers don't caricature you so mercilessly as we supposed. No, the fact is we've drifted apart . . .

We have drifted apart partly because we have changed and you have not; partly, and that in the most important matters, because we have not changed and you have . . . The contrast between the life which men have left and the unfamiliar duties imposed upon them creates a ferment, not the less powerful because often half-conscious, in all but the least reflective minds. In particular, when, as has happened in the present war, men have taken up arms under the influence of some emotion or principle, they tend to be ruled by the idea which compelled them to enlist long after it has yielded, among civilians, to some more fashionable novelty. Less exposed than the civilian to new intellectual influences, the soldier is apt to retain firmly, or even to deepen, the impressions which made him, often reluctantly, a soldier in the first instance. He is like a piece of stone which, in spite of constant friction, preserves the form originally struck out in the fires of a volcanic upheaval . . . We see things which you can only imagine. We are strengthened by reflections which you have abandoned. Our minds differ from yours, both because they are more exposed to change, and because they are less changeable. While you seem – forgive me if I am rude – to have been surrendering your creeds with the nervous facility of a Tudor official, our foreground may be different, but our background is the same. It is that of August to September 1914. We are your ghosts.

> Anonymous, *The Nation*, 21 October 1916. The author was later revealed to be R.H. Tawney, the socialist historian. He included the piece among his essays in *The Attack and Other Papers*, Allen & Unwin, London, 1953, pp. 21–3.

DOCUMENT 17   A NURSE'S FIRST ENCOUNTER WITH MUSTARD GAS

[Letter] No. 7 [undated, but the Germans introduced dichlorethylsulphide or mustard gas in 1917].

'MUSTARD GAS!'

I am remembering the first gassed soldier we saw in war-torn England during the First Great War.

The Lord Derby War Hospital stood in quiet English fields. . . . My ward, at the moment was on the main floor – a long, wide room with floors like polished yellow glass supporting many round, smooth pillars. One hundred black iron cots stood close together in one end of the vast ward. The bed sheets were white and soft, the pillows snowy, and the scarlet-flowered bed quilts were gay, and belied the misery they covered . . .

We were admitting a convoy and the floor was cluttered with haversacks, and canvas kits; army boots and an array of souvenirs, such as soldiers always brought from France . . . At one end of the ward, orderlies, close to an open window, were putting a young soldier to bed. He did not look more than eighteen. Raised high on pillows, his handsome young body unbroken, he was gasping for breath with strange rattling sobs. His face was blue, but with stiffening lips he tried to smile. An orderly opened the window more and the soft sweet wind stole across the bed. I stopped to read the file at the foot of the bed. Mustard Gas, it said. We had read about it in the papers, but this was the first case I had seen.

Red cotton screens were adjusted around his bed, on the war side. The boy's brow was wet with sweat, and struggling to speak, he asked if his mother had come. His words died away with a shattering cough, and he was lifted higher on his pillows. An orderly and his helper hurried in with a cylinder of oxygen.

The boy's mother was hurrying across England in a train that had been bombed in the London depot. She arrived at dusk . . . Escorted by a dignified sergeant, she came into the ward pulling at her black cotton gloves, her hat pushed back from her face. An orderly moved the screen so she could walk around it to where a nurse was sitting beside the boy. Falling on her knees beside the bed she quavered; 'Mother's here, Johnny lad,' and he reached for her hand.

His face was dark purple now, and the oxygen with which science sought to relieve his agony appeared to make little difference. Strong men in nearby beds drew the scarlet quilts over their heads when the strangled breathing stopped. The mother raised streaming eyes to the face of our young one-armed padre – 'And they told me it was only mustard gas', she said.

From *Cameos in Courage*, by Jessie Bryan, a Canadian nurse with the Queen Alexandra's Imperial Military Nursing Service Reserve. The manuscript is a carbon copy of typewritten transcripts of Bryan's letters. From the author's private collection, with thanks to Mrs R.J. Moir of West Vancouver.

DOCUMENT 18   LAWRENCE OF ARABIA SHRUGS

We were fond together, because of the sweep of the open places, the taste of wide winds, the sunlight, and the hopes in which we worked. The morning freshness of the world-to-be intoxicated us. We were wrought up with ideas inexpressible and vaporous, but to be fought for. We lived many lives in those whirling campaigns, never sparing ourselves: yet when we achieved and the new world dawned, the old men came out again and took our victory to remake in the likeness of the former world they knew. Youth could win, but had not learned to keep: and was pitiably weak against age. We stammered that we had worked for a new heaven and a new earth, and they thanked us kindly and made their peace.

From T.E. Lawrence, *Seven Pillars of Wisdom*, Jonathan Cape, London 1963 (1940), pp. 22–3.

DOCUMENT 19   THREE WAYS TO REMEMBER THE WAR

Theme	1. Sacrifice and Remembrance	2. The Vast Cock-up	3. The Great Betrayal
Propagated by	Governments, Church, veterans' groups, official historians	Well-educated, academics, journalists, artists	Revolutionaries, traumatized veterans and their families, modernists, avant garde
The war was	A call to duty and a great trial	Mega-mistake	Meaningless waste
The dead were	Fallen heroes	Slaughtered sheep	Victims of manifest evil
Survivors	Benefited from comradeship and doing duty	Lucky to get out alive	Suffered irreparable damage: emotional and psychic if not physical
Relationship of soldiers to society	Home front and trenches are one	Alienated from home front	Soldiers sacrificed by their society
War and tradition	Soldiers fought to uphold tradition	Tradition caused the war	Tradition rejected
Characteristic quote from the war poets	'In Flanders Fields the Poppies Blow' McCrae	'Now all roads lead to France where heavy is the tread of the living and the dead returning lightly dance' Thomas	'If any question why we died, tell them, because our fathers lied' Kipling
Representative classic films	*Dawn Patrol*; *Sgt. York*	*All Quiet on the Western Front*; *Oh What a Lovely War*	*J'Accuse*; *Paths of Glory*
Representative classic memoirs	*Storm of Steel* Jünger	*Memoirs of an Infantry Officer* Sassoon	*Testament of Youth* Brittain

From http://www.worldwar1.com/heritage/recall.htm.
By Michael E. Hanlon of the Great War Society.

GLOSSARY

Airplanes, tractor and pusher   A tractor airplane had the propeller pulling in front. The pusher had the propeller at the back, pushing. This gave a clearer field of fire for the pilot but made the aircraft slower and less nimble.

Air power, strategic   The application of air power to the enemy home front to achieve a strategic purpose. Strategic bombing killed noncombatants (women, children, politicians) and promised to make war on land and sea obsolete. Ineffective in 1914–18, but nevertheless elevated to a super weapon, at least by the democracies, by 1939.

Air power, tactical   The application of air power directly to the battle or battlefield to achieve a tactical purpose, analogous to flying artillery. 'Tac air' killed soldiers. Because it required low-level flights into stiff anti-aircraft fire, pilots were less than thrilled about tactical missions. Its apotheosis came in the Normandy campaign in 1944, although it first appeared effectively in 1918.

Army/division, etc.   The structures of the British and German armies differed slightly, and are sufficiently obscure to most modern readers to merit an outline description, proceeding from top to what Wellington called 'that article there', the individual rifleman who carried the army.
   Britain: Army – Corps (a provisional tactical formation with permanent staff and arms such as heavy artillery and air force; permanent for the Canadians and Australians) – Division (~12,000 infantry; largest permanent unit of all arms) – Brigade (tactical formation; cf. Corps) – Battalion (embodied regimental names and traditions; nominal strength of 1000 men) – Company – Platoon – Section – Private.
   Germany: Army – Corps – Division (~17,000) – Brigade – Regiment – Battalion – Company – Platoon – Section – Squad.

Artillery   At the time of the Napoleonic wars, artillery was identified by the weight of shot, light or field guns four to six pounders in the British army, heavy guns eight to twelve pounders. These guns had a flat trajectory. The howitzer used a high arc and plunging fire; the lighter version became the mortar. By 1914 most guns were breech-loading, rifled (that is, with grooves inside to impart a spin to the shell as it emerged and enhance its stability in flight) quick-firing and high velocity. By the height of the war, howitzers and heavy guns used high explosive against fixed defences; field artillery fired shrapnel (small projectiles inside shells that sprayed upon detonation; named after inventor, Henry Shrapnel) against men and, quite uselessly, wire. Field artillery remained primarily horse-drawn, although the British introduced the Holt tractor to move the guns. Heavy artillery was usually stationary and controlled at a higher level, usually the Corps.

Attrition   Translation of the French '*usure*', for 'wearing down'. General term for the Allied strategy once early hopes of victory through manouevre failed. The side with more survivors was supposed to win. Interesting to note that one derivation is from the Middle English 'attricioun', 'regret'.

Austria–Hungary   The name of the Habsburg Empire after the union of Austria and Hungary in 1867.

BEF   British Expeditionary Force. The official name of the British and Imperial forces serving on the Western Front.

Bombs   The commonly used name for Mills bombs or hand-grenades. The specialists in using them to clear trenches, the 'bombers', were thought to have the nastiest dispositions at the Front.

Blockade   To isolate or seal off. The Royal Navy blockaded Napoleon's France. Instead of implementing a similar type of blockade against Germany, close to enemy ports to ensure the maximum isolation, the Royal Navy opted for a 'distant' blockade that sealed off the North Sea and the Channel. Britain thus became the stopper in a bottle. Because the German High Seas fleet consisted of heavy ships with a short range (compared to cruisers) it could not readily reach the blockading ships. To counter-blockade, the Germans had to turn to the submarine (*Unterseeboot* or U-boat).

Breech   The back of a rifle or gun, where the projectile is inserted.

Burgfrieden   'Truce of the castle', or the moratorium on politics in Germany from 1914 to 1917. Similar to domestic truces in the other warring countries.

Counter-battery fire   Fire directed against enemy artillery batteries to suppress them before or during an attack. Effective counter-battery fire made a great difference to the infantry; thus getting the range on enemy batteries without letting them know they were targeted was important.

Cruiser rules   By international convention, submarines were supposed to follow the same procedures as surface cruisers when intercepting merchant ships. They were to hail, board and inspect vessels for contraband cargo; if action were taken, the safety of the merchant crew was to be respected. Unlimited submarine warfare dispensed with such niceties. It also meant sinking every vessel the submariner considered hostile in the war zone.

Detente   The easing of tension between states or a state of friendlier relations.

Dreadnoughts   The class of super battleships Britain introduced with HMS *Dreadnought* in 1906. All its main guns were the same caliber, with ten 12-inch guns in five turrets; it used steam turbines for a top speed of twenty-one knots and foot-thick armour for protection. When the Germans responded in kind, the next step was the class of super-Dreadnoughts. Britain had twenty-four Dreadnoughts to fourteen for Germany by 1914.

Entente   An agreement between states to co-operate. The Allies were sometimes called 'The Entente powers' after the agreements between France, Britain and Russia. The United States was not allied to the Entente powers.

Fascism   A post-war movement in which veterans were prominent, starting in Italy with Benito Mussolini. Named after the 'fascis' or bundle of twigs that, bound together, symbolized strength in unity in ancient Rome. Unlike Nazism, Fascism was not necessarily anti-Semitic, but it was similarly enthusiastic about war and anti-communism.

Holding attack The basis for successful infantry tactics. One unit advances and fires to pin down the enemy, another works around the flank or behind cover to advance and in turn provides covering fire. Used increasingly in the war as both sides simplified and improved their tactics. Similar to 'fire and movement'.

Live and let live The phrase referring to the behaviour of front soldiers first appeared in the memoirs of the poet Edmund Blunden. Tony Ashworth adopted it to describe a complex system of manners and mores that influenced front soldiers when they had a chance to sound out each other's intentions across the lines [7]. To increase their own chances of surviving, they kept aggression and lethal violence to a minimum. Live and let live interacted with the front soldier's keen sense of Us against Them. Us referred to fellow victims, Them to outsiders to the front, especially staff officers and one's own home front [*Doc. 16*].

Logistics The side of military management that concerns obtaining, distributing, maintaining and replacing material and personnel. A subject that has not attracted heroes, artists or film-makers but is nonetheless vital in modern wars, which are, as the Germans say, *Materialschlachten*, wars of material. 'I know why you won; you piled up all the equipment and let it fall on us,' a German officer said to his Canadian captor in 1944.

Magazine The storage compartment for ammunition, especially on a warship.

Muzzle The mouth of a gun, out of which the projectile emerges.

Nazism National Socialism, the post-war movement centred on Adolf Hitler, his German National Social Worker's Party (NSDAP) and its message of racial hatred.

New Army (Kitchener's Mob) The flood of volunteers in Britain went either into Territorial divisions, comparable to a home guard, or into Kitchener's New Army. The original BEF had six divisions. A seventh and eighth soon followed, made up in part of regulars who had been overseas. The next six divisions of volunteers made up the 'first hundred thousand or K1' of six divisions, nine to fourteen; K2 formed divisions fifteen to twenty; K3 twenty-one to twenty-six; and K4 thirty to thirty-five, with three more divisions (27 to 29) made up again mainly of overseas recruits. After reorganization, K5 was set up in 1915 with divisions thirty-six to forty-one. The Pals tended to form in K4 and K5.

OHL *Oberste HeeresLeitung* or General Headquarters of the German army.

Pals battalions Also known as Chums. To encourage voluntary enlistment in 1914–15, the British War Office promised men who joined together that they could serve together. In *The Face of Battle*, John Keegan sees the names of the Pals Battalions as evidence of the living cells into which working- and lower-middle-class men organized themselves – workplaces, sporting clubs, Sunday Schools and so on. When such a battalion was hit hard, these living cells could vanish from history. The practice was discontinued.

Pan Germans Conservative ultra-nationalists who mobilized German public opinion on behalf of imperialism, colonial expansion, military and naval strength and the suppression of radicalism at home.

Plan XVII The final plan worked out by the French General Staff. In the event of war, France would hold back the limited German attack she expected in Belgium and reconquer Alsace and Lorraine, thus avenging the defeat of 1870 and showing the offensive spirit that made French infantry unstoppable.

Schlieffen Plan   Count General Alfred von Schlieffen, Chief of the General Staff 1891–1906, planned to win a two-front war by placing the bulk of the German Army first against France, moving through the Lowlands through northern France and around Paris so as to entrap the French army moving east. He believed the plan depended upon keeping the right wing that was doing most of the work as strong as possible. Maybe he was right, but he seems to have assumed that the men on the right wing never ate, slept or grew tired. For another weakness in the plan, see also 'logistics'.

Strategy   Relating to the higher conduct and aims of a war; thus assumed to be more important than mere tactics. 'We want total victory' would be strategy; how we actually achieve this involves the boring details. In an office, the boss takes care of strategy. See 'tactics'.

Tactics   Short-term, everyday matters like manoeuvring in the presence of the enemy, avoiding defeat and taking defended positions. In an office, secretaries handle tactics. See 'strategy'.

Traverse   A bend or partition in a trench, meant to limit the effect of a shell explosion or enfilade fire (i.e. fire straight along a trench).

Trenches: Firestep   The step running along the forward side – the fire bay – of a trench on which soldiers stood to keep watch or to fire [*Doc. 15*]; *fire-trench*: usually the front trench. The parts which were manned on Stand To were *fire-bays* [*Doc. 15*]; *parapet*: the side (topped by sandbags) of a fire bay which faced towards the enemy; the *parados* was the rearward side. Both words are taken from early French works on fortification; they have changed somewhat from their first significations [*Doc. 15*]; *trench and sap*: the former represents a line of defence: *front trench, support trench, reserved trench*, for the most part running approximately parallel to the line held by the enemy. A sap was a line of communication, whether from the rear to the front or from a trench to an emplacement, kitchen, latrine, store, etc. The main links between the front line and the supports and reserves were called communication trenches. Technically and correctly, a trench was made by digging downwards, a sap by digging outwards from an existing trench. Almost always it was the infantry who dug both saps and trenches [*Doc. 15*].

WHO'S WHO

Asquith, Herbert Henry (1852–1928): 1st Earl of Oxford and Asquith, Liberal politician; Prime Minister of Great Britain, 1908–16. Policy of governing through consensus brought the country through upheaval before 1914 but was less effective for wartime.

Beatty, Admiral Sir David (1871–1936): British sailor; commanded Battle Cruiser Squadron of the Grand Fleet, 1913–16; commanded Grand Fleet, 1916–21. Popularly thought to be more dashing than Jellicoe but showed similar caution when he took command of the Grand Fleet after Jutland.

Bethmann Hollweg, Theobald von (1856–1921): German politician; Chancellor of Germany, 1909–17. Regretted that Britain went to war with Germany because of a 'scrap of paper', the treaty guaranteeing Belgian neutrality.

Bishop, William 'Billy' (1894–1956): Canadian aviator, highest victory total among the aces who survived (72).

Boelcke, Oswald (1891–1916): German aviator, colleague of Max Immelmann, with whom he shared the award of the Pour le Merite ('Blue Max') in January 1916; developed theory for fighter tactics; forty victories.

Bruchmüller, Lt.-Col. Georg (1863–1948): German soldier; expert in artillery known as 'the organist of the guns'.

Brusilov, General Alexei (1853–1926): Best of the Russian generals; commanded Eighth Army 1914, South-Western Front 1916. His offensive in 1916 relieved German pressure on Verdun.

Bülow, General Karl von (1846–1921): German soldier; commanded Second Army in 1914; less aggressive than his neighbouring general, Kluck, and tended to hang back.

Byng, Sir Julian (1862–1935): British soldier; commanded Canadian Corps when it took Vimy Ridge in 1917; commanded Third Army 1917–18; Governor-General of Canada 1921–26. The Canadians warmed to his imaginative tactics and geniality.

Castelnau, Noël Joseph Edouard de Curières de (1851–1944): French soldier; Chief of Staff to Joffre, 1915–16; decided to hold the Right Bank at Verdun and bring in Pétain to command.

Churchill, Winston Leonard Spencer (1874–1965): British politician; entered parliament in 1900; First Lord of Admiralty 1911–15; Minister of Munitions 1917–19; Secretary for Air and War 1919–21. Blamed for the Dardanelles fiasco and left politics briefly to serve on the Western Front. Should receive credit for the preparedness of the Royal Navy in 1914.

Clemenceau, Georges (1841–1929): French Radical politician; Premier 1917–20; active in politics since the Franco-Prussian War in 1870–71; despite his age, he bolstered French morale in 1917 much as Churchill did for Britain in 1940.

Conrad von Hötzendorf, General Franz (1852–1925): Austrian soldier; chief of staff of the Imperial Army 1906–17; favoured aggressive policy against Serbia; as a commander, his reach exceeded his grasp, thanks to shortcomings of the army and his tendency to dream in colour.

Currie, General Sir Arthur (1875–1933): Canadian soldier; a teacher and real estate agent before 1914; trained as a gunner in the militia; commanded 1st Division, then Canadian Corps, 1917–18; open-minded and creative about tactics (*See* Monash).

Erzberger, Matthias (1875–1921): German politician; rising star in the Centre (Catholic) party; supported unlimited submarine warfare until private sources convinced him it had failed; supported Peace Resolution in July 1917 [*Doc. 3*]; signed the Armistice; murdered by nationalist fanatics in 1921.

Falkenhayn, General Erich von (1861–1922): German soldier; War Minister 1913–16; Chief of General Staff 1914–16; enjoyed the favour of the Kaiser and thus suffered the ill-will of fellow generals, including Hindenburg and Ludendorff, who wanted him to give them more support in the east. Tried to win an unlimited victory through a limited attack on Verdun in 1916 [*Doc. 2*].

Fisher, Admiral Sir John Arbuthnot (1841–1920): British sailor; First Sea Lord 1904–10; pushed through reforms of the Royal Navy, including the introduction of the *Dreadnought* in 1906, an all big-gun battleship the name of which matched his own temperament. Churchill recalled him to the Admiralty on the outbreak of war; he resigned suddenly in 1915.

Foch, Ferdinand (1851–1929): French soldier; military writer and thinker before 1914, devoted to the doctrine of the offensive; commanded Ninth Army at the Marne; close to Joffre and thus affected by Joffre's fall until Pétain revived his career; shone on the Italian front in 1917; appointed Allied Commander-in-Chief in April 1918 to supervise the disposition of reserves rather than command directly. He compared himself, accurately, to an orchestra conductor; as such, he played a key role in co-ordinating the final victory.

Fokker, Anthony (1890–1939): Dutch aircraft designer working for the Germans; in 1915 perfected the interrupter gear which enabled a machine gun to fire through the arc of a propeller; when fitted to Fokker's E1 or Eindecker monoplane, this led to the first true fighter aircraft.

Franchet d'Esperey, General Louis (1856–1942): French soldier; commanded Fifth Army at the Marne. Ended the war commanding the successful Allied attack on Bulgaria out of the Salonika beachhead.

French, General Sir John (1852–1925): British soldier; commander BEF 1914–15. Wavered between Eeyore's pessimism early in the war and Pooh's optimism later, rarely showing balanced judgement or impressing subordinates.

Galliéni, General Joseph (1849–1916): French soldier; recalled from retirement to be Joffre's deputy against Joffre's will in 1914; deserved credit for the French counter-attack that stopped the Germans at the Marne; War Minister 1915–16 until forced out by ill health.

George, David Lloyd (1863–1945): British politician; Chancellor of the Exchequer 1908–15; Minister of Munitions 1915–16; Prime Minister 1916–22. His rise to prime minister split the Liberal Party but energized Britain for the final push in the war effort.

Gough, General Sir Hubert (1870–1963): British soldier; youngest of the Army commanders by 1917; Haig assumed he was also the boldest. He was not. Staff work in his Fifth Army was deficient and he had the bad luck to preside over its collapse in the face of the German offensive in March 1918.

Graves, Robert (1895–1985): British writer; *Goodbye To All That* (1929) among the best-known memoirs by a British junior officer; friend of Siegfried Sassoon, whom he saved from the consequences of the Soldier's Declaration [*Doc. 12*].

Haig, General (later Field Marshal) Sir Douglas (1861–1928): British soldier; Commander I Corps in 1914–15; succeeded French as Commander BEF in 1915. His competence is still under intense debate. Critics accuse him of being an unimaginative butcher, keen on wearing down the enemy through frontal attacks; defenders, notably John Terraine, point to the absence of realistic alternatives to his policy of fighting beside the French on the Western Front and see the final victory as a product of his single-mindedness.

Hamilton, General Sir Ian Standish Monteith (1853–1947): British soldier; gentle soul placed in hapless command of the Dardanelles Expedition of 1915.

Hankey, Sir Maurice (1877–1963): British civil servant, Secretary, Committee for Imperial Defence, 1912, War Council 1914–16, War Cabinet 1916–18.

Hertling, Georg, Count von (1843–1919): German politician; leader of the Centre (Catholic) Party, second-last Chancellor of Imperial Germany (1917–18).

Hindenburg, Field Marshal Paul Ludwig von Beneckendorff und von (1847–1934): German soldier; brought out of retirement in 1914 to team with Ludendorff in command of the German Eighth Army in the east and later in command of the Chief of General Staff, with Ludendorff as nominal deputy. Their string of victories, together with Hindenburg's imposing appearance (especially when duplicated in a huge wooden statue in Berlin), led the German public to idolize Hindenburg.

Hintze, Admiral Paul von (1864–1941): German diplomat; last Foreign Secretary of German Empire, June to October 1918.

Hipper, Vice Admiral Franz von (1863–1932): German sailor; commanded scouting groups of the High Seas fleet.

Hoffmann, Col. (later General) Max (1869–1927): German soldier; Chief of Staff, Eighth Army; original author of the plans that led to the sweeping German victories over Russia in 1914.

Hutier, General Oskar von (1857–1934): German soldier; innovative tactician in the east, stressing need for infiltration around resistance with less regard to flanks; Commander, Eighth Army 1916–17, Eighteenth Army in the German Spring Offensive, 1918.

Immelmann, Max (1890–1916): German aviator; colleague of Oswald Boelcke with whom he shared the award of the Pour le Merite or 'Blue Max' in January 1916; first true fighter pilot, using the Fokker Eindecker.

Jellicoe, Admiral Sir John Rushwood (1859–1935): British sailor; expert in gunnery; Director of Naval Ordnance 1905; appointed Commander of Grand Fleet in 1914. Criticized for caution at Jutland, but his concern to keep the Grand Fleet intact rather than destroy the German High Seas fleet has since found support; First Sea Lord 1916–17.

Joffre, Marshal Joseph (1852–1931): French soldier; background was military engineering; worked up Plan XVII with Castelnau; Chief of General Staff 1911–16; known for calmness under pressure, which could also have been unconsciousness; as his reputation declined with his peers, he remained popular with the French public and the British until his failures caught up with him.

Kerensky, Alexander (1881–1970): Russian politician; justice minister in the Provisional Government, 1917; War Minister in May, Premier in July; undermined by the failure of the army's spring offensive and subsequent revolt.

Kitchener, Field Marshal Lord Horatio Herbert, 1st Earl Kitchener of Khartoum (1850–1916): British soldier; made War Minister in August 1914 on insistence of press; foresaw that the war would be at least three years long and would require a new British army of volunteers. When raised, it sometimes went by the name of 'Kitchener's Mob'. His past as a colonial administrator led him to work on his own, and after the Dardanelles he was as discredited as Churchill. Drowned on his way to Russia when the cruiser *Hampshire* hit a mine in June 1916.

Kluck, General Alexander von (1846–1934): German soldier; Commander, First Army, the largest and most important in the German attack in the west in 1914.

Knoblesdorf, General Schmidt von (1859–1943): Chief of Staff to the German Fifth Army under the Crown Prince of Russia.

Law, Andrew Bonar (1858–1923): British Conservative politician; leader of the Unionist (Conservative) Party 1911–21, Prime Minister in 1922–23. Colonial Secretary in the coalition government, 1915–16; Chancellor of the Exchequer 1916–18.

Lenin, Vladimir (1870–1924): Russian revolutionary; the Germans brought him by sealed train from exile in Switzerland to Petrograd, where he immediately insisted that his followers ('Bolsheviks') have nothing to do with the new provisional government. Overthrew Kerensky in November 1917.

Lossberg, Col. (later General) Fritz von: German soldier; oversaw the disposition of the German defences on the Western Front after the Somme in 1916.

Ludendorff, General Erich (1865–1937): German soldier; from humble origins, became a rising star in the General Staff specializing in mobilization plans; led the capture of Liège in 1914; paired with Hindenburg to command in the East (1914–16) and then overall in Germany, becoming a virtual dictator. A workaholic whose innovative tactics could not bring the total victory his primitive territorial ambitions required.

Mackensen, General (later Field Marshal) August von (1849–1945): German soldier, quintessential Prussian; commanded on the Eastern Front exclusively, first over the Eighth Army, then the Ninth and then the Eleventh. Commanded Army Group Mackensen in 1915–16.

Mannock, Edward 'Mick' (1887–1918): British aviator; top victory total on Allied side (73).

Moltke, Field Marshal Count Helmuth Karl Bernhard, Count von (1800–1891): German soldier; chief of Prussian and later German general staff, 1858–88.

Moltke, General Helmuth Johannes Ludwig, Count von (1848–1916): German soldier; nephew of the 'Great' Moltke; Chief of General Staff, 1906–14. Whether he ruined the plan he inherited from Schlieffen or preserved it despite its implausibilities is still open to debate. One of several senior commanders with no business playing the role (*See* French, Sir John and Joffre, Joseph).

Monash, General Sir John (1865–1931): Australian soldier; engineer in civilian life; commanded Australian Corps; open-minded and creative about tactics (*See* Currie).

Nicholas II, Tsar (1868–1918): Russian autocrat; last of the Romanov emperors or Tsars; thoroughly incompetent ruler whose personal assumption of supreme military command in August 1915 proved fatal for the dynasty and country.

Nivelle, General Robert (1856–1924): French soldier; background in artillery; succeeded Joffre as Chief of Staff in December 1916; promised that his new methods would bring victory; dismissed after his offensive miscarried badly and led to widespread mutiny. Nivelle had some good ideas about co-ordinating artillery with infantry, but he confused tactics with strategy and command with politics.

Northcliffe, Lord (born Alfred Harmsworth) (1865–1922): British press lord; created the *Daily Mail* in 1896, bought *The Times* of London; became head of the Department of Enemy Propaganda in 1918.

Owen, Wilfred (1893–1918): British poet; met Siegfried Sassoon after being hospitalized for shell shock in May 1917.

Painlevé, Paul (1863–1933): French politician; war minister; Premier 1917; succeeded by Clemenceau.

Payer, Friedrich von (1847–1931): German Progressive politician; Vice-Chancellor 1917–18.

Pétain, General Philippe (1856–1951): French soldier; pre-war career blighted by his scepticism about the cult of the offensive; the war vindicated his view; organized a tenacious defence at Verdun; given overall command after Nivelle; rebuilt the army after the mutinies. Lived one war too long.

Plumer, Sir Herbert Charles Onslow (1857–1932): British soldier; Commander, Second Army; looked more like a resident of Fawlty Towers than a general, but was probably the best the British had, with common sense and the common touch. Instead of disliking positional warfare, he sought to understand it.

Poincaré, Raymond (1860–1934): French politician, President of France 1913–20; he overshadowed the lightweight premiers before Clemenceau.

Rawlinson, General Sir Henry Seymour (1864–1925): British soldier; commander of Fourth Army at the Somme and later in 1918; understood early the importance of 'bite and hold' limited attacks but visions of victory led him to a faith in immense attritional attacks until sanity returned in 1918. In this he is a reverse image of Plumer.

Richthofen, Baron Manfred von (1892–1918): German aviator; nicknamed 'Red Baron' from colour of his Fokker triplane; credited with eighty victories, the highest score among the aces.

Robertson, General Sir William (1860–1933): British soldier; rose from the ranks to become Chief of Imperial General Staff; supported Haig loyally against those (like Lloyd George) who did not put the Western Front first. He kept his working-class accent, notably when he told Horace Smith-Dorrien he had been sacked: "'op it, 'orace, you're for 'ome".

Rupprecht, Crown Prince of Bavaria (1869–1955): German soldier; commander of Army Group on Western Front bearing his name; more than a figurehead, showing real military talent and a marked dislike for the policies of Ludendorff.

Sassoon, Siegfried (1886–1967): British poet and memorist; author of 'A Soldier's Declaration' [*Doc. 12*]; mentor to Wilfred Owen.

Scheer, Vice-Admiral Reinhard (1863–1928): German sailor; Chief of Staff of German High Seas Fleet 1910–16; commanded German High Seas Fleet.

Schlieffen, General Count Alfred von (1833–1913): Prussian-German soldier; Chief of General Staff 1891–1906; author of plan to deal with a two-front war by defeating France quickly. One of the dead men who is said to have started the war.

Smith-Dorrien, General Sir Horace (1858–1930): British soldier; showed solid ability commanding II Corps in 1914 and then Second Army in 1915; Sir John French used him as a scapegoat and sacked him after Loos.

Tirpitz, Admiral Alfred von (1849–1930): German sailor; Secretary of State for the Ministry of the Navy, 1897–1916; architect of the German battle fleet.

Trenchard, General Sir Hugh Montagu (1873–1956): British soldier; commanded the Royal Flying Corps (RFC) and, in 1918, the Independent Air Force; Chief of Air Staff 1919–29; dubious about the power of aerial bombing during the war, but keen on it after when he used bombing to increase his share of the defence budget.

Wilhelm II, Kaiser (1859–1941): German Emperor 1888–1918; tried to be an autocrat early in his reign but lapsed into inertia punctuated by outbursts of bombast and occasional good sense. One biographer said he approached every problem with an open mouth.

Wilson, Woodrow (1856–1924): American politician, President 1912–20; academic background; reluctant to intervene in the war, but German behaviour and American ties to the Allies gave him little choice; author of Fourteen Points in 1918, expressing American liberal imperialism in rhetoric that made it seem fuzzier than it really was.

Zimmermann, Arthur (1854–1940): German bureaucrat, Secretary of State at the Foreign Office, author of notorious telegram the British publication of which helped bring the United States into the war.

PRIMARY SOURCES, WEBSITES AND FURTHER READING

The place of publication is London unless otherwise noted. In the case of reissued books, the most recent date of publication is cited. Where possible the paperback edition is cited.

PRIMARY SOURCES

Stone, Norman, *Europe Transformed, 1878–1919*, Fontana, 1983.

Leed, Eric, *No Man's Land: Combat and Identity in World War I*, Cambridge University Press, New York, 1979.

Strachan, Hew, *The First World War: To Arms*, Oxford University Press, New York, 2001.

Wilson, Trevor, *The Myriad Faces of War: Britain and the Great War, 1914–1918*, Polity Press, Cambridge, 1986.

Fischer, Fritz, *Germany's Aims in the First World War*, Norton, New York, 1967.

Fussell, Paul, *The Great War and Modern Memory*, Oxford University Press, London, New York, 1975.

Ashworth, Tony, *Trench Warfare 1914–1918: The Live and Let Live System*, Holmes & Meier, New York, 1980.

Winter, J.M., *The Great War and the British People*, Macmillan, 1986.

Sheffield, Gary, *The Somme*, Cassell, 2003.

Ludendorff, Erich, *My War Memories 1914–1918*, Hutchinson, 1919.

Chapman, Guy, *A Passionate Prodigality*, Holt, Rinehart & Winston, New York, 1965 (1933).

Kaehler, Siegfried, 'Zur Beurteilung Ludendorffs im Sommer 1918', *Studien zur deutschen Geschichte des 19. und 20. Jahrhunderts*, Vandenhoeck & Ruprecht, Göttingen, 1961.

Roth, Jack, *World War One: A Turning Point*, Knopf, New York, 1967.

WEBSITES

The recent proliferation of books about the First World War has been matched by useful websites. A good portal from which to start is Trenches on the Web (www.worldwar1.com). Other good general sites are The Great War (http://www.pitt.edu/~pugachev/greatwar/toc.htm); The First World War (http://www.firstworldwar.com/) and The Western Front Association (http://www.westernfrontassociation.com/). An extensive collection of primary documents can be found at http://www.lib.byu/~rdh/ww1/. Sites dealing with Britain and the British Army include http://www.1914-1918.net (The Long, Long Trail: The British Army in the Great War);

the Imperial War Museum (http://www.iwm.org.uk/). France and the War is covered in http://www.1914-18.org/, in French, and The Great War Society's 'France at War', in English: http://www.worldwar1.com/france/. Links to study the Italian Front can be found at http://www.worldwar1.com/itafront/itlinks.htm. Another site created by the Great War Society is 'Doughboy Center: The Story of the American Expeditionary Forces' (http://www.worldwar1.com/dbc/ghq1arm.htm). The Australian National Memorial is a monument, a museum and a memorial project ongoing since the War; its website is http://www.awm.gov.au. The equivalent for Canada is http://www.civilization.ca/cwm/. German History Sources, edited by Dr Richard Weikart, includes documents on the Great War: http://www.csustan.edu/History/Weikart/gerhist.htm. For aviation and aviators, Aerodrome is good (http://www.theaerodrome.com/). The Wilfred Owen Multimedia Digital Archive, part of the Virtual Seminars for Teaching Literature set up by Oxford University, includes e-texts of some of Owen's drafts. It can be found at http://www.hcu.ox.ac.uk/jtap/. The BBC has a website devoted to the Great War: http://www.bbc.co.uk/history/war/wwone/index.shtml. The Gallipoli Campaign is covered by http://www.iwm.org.uk/upload/package/2/gallipoli/navigate.htm, which combines material prepared by the Australian War Memorial and the Imperial War Museum.

In addition to dedicated sites, those wishing to use the Internet to research specific topics can of course search with Google or Yahoo. If one enters 'First World War' in the search box, bear in mind that American usage prefers 'World War One' or even 'WW1'. Google Scholar will help searches of scholarly sources. Above all, treat the results of searching sceptically, as with any historical source. Consider who is writing or providing the source; take bias and special pleading into account. This also applies to Wikipedia, the 'free' encyclopedia put together collaboratively. It can be very useful for specialized topics such as military units, weaponry or battles, but its contents are edited by its readers.

FURTHER READING

The Great Debate

In the decade following the war, historians tended to focus their attention on the origins of the war. The history of operations and strategy tended to be standard 'shot and shell' narrative, either in official histories (with the outstanding exception of the official history of the Australian Expeditionary Force by the journalist Charles Bean) or in regimental histories. The appearance of novels and memoirs ten years after the war that shed a grim light on the experience of the soldiers led not just to a vogue for depictions of 'the war of the sewers' but also to a reaction against it by some veterans who felt their tribulations and triumphs were being deprecated. As mentioned on p. 103, in recent years historians have both revived and sharpened the terms of the earlier controversy, and have been engaged in a lively debate over how best to consider the war. In a general sense, the controversy comes down to different ways of remembering or imagining the war [*Doc. 19*]. More specifically, it has focused on evaluating the military performance of the armies that fought in the war, and especially of the British Expeditionary Force. The commonly accepted view by the 1960s, at least among readers of English language sources, was that the British Army might have fought like lions but it was led by donkeys, to cite a remark which Max Hoffmann was alleged to have made to Erich Ludendorff. This apocryphal quotation provided the title for a classic statement of the critical view, Alan Clark's *The Donkeys* (1965). It also infused *The First World War: An Illustrated History*, by A.J.P. Taylor (1963).

The reaction against the accepted wisdom about the war was led by John Terraine. In his biography *Haig: The Educated Soldier* (1963) Terraine took exception to the notion that Haig was isolated from the realities facing the men he commanded and indifferent to new tactical methods and new technologies. In the books and collections of essays that followed, Terraine elaborated his central thesis. The First World War was the middle of three great modern wars, the American Civil War coming before and the Second World War after. All were by necessity wars of attrition; all began as wars of movement and then bogged down; all were protracted. The world wars were also coalition wars in which none of the partners had a completely free hand. This is his theme in *The Road to Passchendaele: The Flanders Offensive of 1917* (1977), *To Win a War: 1918, the Year of Victory* (1978); *The Smoke and the Fire: Myths and Anti-Myths of War, 1861–1945* (1980); *White Heat: The New Warfare 1914–1918* (1982); and his general history *The First World War* (1983). It even colours his history of the Royal Air Force in the Second World War in Europe, *A Time for Courage* (1985), when he argues that the British and Americans turned to strategic bombing because they wrongly assumed it to be a way of achieving victory that avoided the costly stalemate of the trenches.

Terraine died in 2003. His perspective, now often referred to as 'revisionist', was taken up by Paddy Griffith's *British Battle Tactics of the Western Front* (1994) and persuasively by Gary Sheffield, in *Forgotten Victory. The First World War: Myths and Realities* (2001); *The Somme* (2003); *Leadership in the Trenches: Officer-Man Relations, Morale and Discipline in the Era of the First World War* (2000) and, together with Gary Todman, *Command and Control on the Western Front: The British Army's Experience* (2005). Tim Travers has taken his own position between the camps, critical of the arduous 'learning curve' of the British Army but avoiding stereotypes about delusional incompetents in command. His works include *The Killing Ground: The British Army, the Western Front and the Emergence of Modern War 1900–1918* (2003) and *How the War was Won: Command and Technology in the British Army on the Western Front 1917–1918* (2005). Books jointly written by Trevor Wilson and Robin Prior also offer a balanced and carefully researched view of the strengths and weaknesses of the British Army: *Command on the Western Front: The Military Career of Sir Henry Rawlinson 1914–1918* (2004); *Passchendaele: The Untold Story* (2002); and *The Somme* (2005).

The strength of Sheffield's work lies in the overview of the war that he achieves. Niall Ferguson praised *Forgotten Victory* in a review, yet his own study of interlocking themes, *The Pity of War* (1999), presents a contrasting perspective in some of its chapters, reviving the earlier view that the Germans fought more effectively and efficiently than the British and French. J.M. Winter and Antoine Prost, in *The Great War in History* (Cambridge, 2005) provide an excellent introduction to the controversies and debates about the war.

Overviews of the War

Hew Strachan is writing a multi-volume overview of the war. The first volume, *The First World War: To Arms* (2001), blends up-to-date research and reading, a breadth of coverage that befits a study of a *world* war, and clear, readable prose into an indispensable masterpiece. Strachan has also distilled his longer study into *The First*

World War: A New Illustrated History (2003). Two recent single volumes synthesize a remarkable range of sources into lucid and original interpretations of the war: David Stevenson's *Cataclysm: The First World War as Political Tragedy* (New York, 2004) and John Morrow Jr, *The Great War: An Imperial History* (2004). Stevenson asks the reader to consider the choices that people made when they created what they usually did not want, so that the tragedy mentioned in the title is laced with irony. Morrow goes beyond the Western Front to focus as well on the role of imperialism and the global dimension of the war. One of the most prolific scholars on the war, J.M. Winter, has written two general texts: *Experience of World War 1* (New York, 1989) and, together with Blaine Baggett, *The Great War and the Shaping of the 20th Century* (New York, 1996). *The First World War* by Robin Prior and Trevor Wilson draws upon their expertise in military history and offers excellent graphics. In *The First World War* (2000) one of the best-known military historians, John Keegan, provided an eagle's eye view with wit and flair.

Older general books are well worth using. Martin Gilbert provides a narrative history of the war mainly in Europe in *The First World War: A Complete History* (New York, 1994). R.F.M. Cruttwell's *History of the Great War* (1934) is crisp and judicious; it allows a modern reader to see how the war was imagined twenty years after it ended. B.H. Liddell Hart's *The Real War* (1930) offers a critique of the conduct of the war that is not as persuasive as it once was but is still worth considering.

Command, Strategy, Tactics and Technology

Fire Power: British Army Weapons and Theories of War, 1904–1945 (1982) by Shelford Bidwell and Dominick Graham broke new ground as an operational study of the British Army. Roger Chickering's *Great War, Total War: Combat and Mobilization on the Western Front 1914–1918* (Cambridge UP, 2000) and Ian Brown's *British Logistics on the Western Front* (1998) also analyse the structural aspect of the war. Gerhard Ritter brought the Schlieffen Plan to light in *The Schlieffen Plan: Critique of a Myth* (1958). Terence Zuber's *Inventing the Schlieffen Plan: German War Planning 1871–1914* (2003) sought to shed new light on the Plan. He claimed that it was little more than a memorandum Schlieffen left for his successor intended to justify increases in the military budget. After the war German staff officers elevated it into a full-blown plan that would have guaranteed victory in 1914 if it had been followed. Zuber's thesis has been vigorously disputed by Terence Holmes; the exchange between the two historians can be found in the journal *War in History* between 1999 and 2001.

Corelli Barnett analysed the crucial decisions of Moltke Jr, Jellicoe, Pétain and Ludendorff in *The Swordbearers: Studies in Supreme Command in the First World War* (1986). Although first published in 1963, its analysis remains fresh. Robert Asprey examined *The German High Command at War: Hindenburg and Ludendorff Conduct World War I* (1991). The classic study of German militarism, *Sword and Sceptre* (1973) by Gerhard Ritter, remains important. Volumes 3 ('The Tragedy of Statesmanship – Bethmann Hollweg as War Chancellor 1914–1917') and 4 ('The Reign of Militarism and the Disaster of 1918') deal with the war. Useful books by or about individual commanders include Gerard De Groot, *Douglas Haig, 1861–1928* (1988); Brian Bond, *Haig: A Reappraisal 70 Years On* (1999); Roger Parkinson, *Tormented Warrior: Ludendorff and the Supreme Command* (1978); Erich Ludendorff, *My War Memories* (1919); Erich von Falkenhayn, *General Headquarters 1914–1916 and its Critical Decisions* (n.d.); Michael Neiberg, *Foch* (2003); John Pollock, *Kitchener* (2002); P.A.

Pederson, *Monash as Military Commander* (Melbourne, 1985); and A.M.J. Hyatt, *General Sir Arthur Currie, A Military Biography* (1987).

Recent studies of tactics include Bill Rawling, *Surviving Trench Warfare: Technology and the Canadian Corps, 1914–1918* (1992); Bruce I. Gudmundsson, *Stormtroop Tactics: Innovation in the German Army 1914–1918* (1989); and Hubert C. Johnson, *Breakthrough!: Tactics, Technology and the Search for Victory* (Novato CA, 1994). The closely related subject of technology and its impact on tactics is examined in Tim Cook, *No Place to Run: The Canadian Corps and Gas Warfare in the First World War* (UBC Press, 2000); Al Palazzo, *Seeking Victory on the Western Front: The British Army and Chemical Warfare in World War I* (U of Nebraska, 2002); William Moore, *Gas Attack: Chemical Warfare 1914–1918* (1987); William McElwee, *The Art of War from Waterloo to Mons* (Bloomington IN, 1974); and Anthony Saunders, *Weapons of the Trench War 1914–1918* (1999).

War at Sea

Robert Massie has once again shown how popular history should indeed be popular in his two-volume study of the Anglo-German naval rivalry, *Dreadnought: Britain, Germany and the Coming of the Great War* (1991) and *Castles of Steel: Britain, Germany and the Winning of the Great War at Sea* (2003). General histories of the war at sea include Richard Hough, *The Great War at Sea* (1983) and Peter Liddle, *The Sailor's War 1914–1918* (1985). Specialized studies include, above all for the Royal Navy, Arthur Marder, *From the Dreadnought to Scapa Flow: The Royal Navy in the Fisher Era* (1961); Thomas Bailey, *The 'Lusitania' Disaster: An Episode in Modern Warfare and Diplomacy* (New York, 1975); John Campbell, *Jutland, An Analysis of the Fighting* (1986); James Goldrick, *The King's Ships Were at Sea: War in the North Sea 1914–15* (Annapolis MD, 1984); Holger Herwig, 'The failure of Imperial Germany's undersea offensive against world shipping, February 1917–October 1918', *Historian*, vol. 33 (1970–1), pp. 611–36, and *'Luxury' Fleet: The Imperial German Navy, 1888–1918* (1980); Paul Halpern (ed.) *Royal Navy in the Mediterranean 1915–1918* (1987); R.H. Gibson and Maurice Prendergast, *The German Submarine War 1914–1918* (Annapolis MD, 2003); and C.P. Vincent, *The Politics of Hunger: The Allied Blockade of Germany 1915–1919* (Athens OH, 1985).

War in the Air

General overviews of the air war include Richard Bickers, *The First Great Air War* (1988); Lee Kennett, *The First Air War 1914–1918* (New York, 1991); Bruce Lewis, *A Few of the First: The Royal Flying Corps and the Royal Naval Air Service* (1996); and, despite the apparent limitation of its titled subject, S.F. Wise, *Canadian Airmen in the First World War* (Toronto, 1980). For fighter planes and pilots, see Richard Hallion, *Rise of the Fighter Aircraft: 1914–1918* (Annapolis MD, 1984); Ira Jones, *King of Air Fighters: Biography of Major Mick Mannock* (1989); Wayne Douglas Ralph, *Barker, VC: William Barker, Canada's Most Decorated War Hero* (Toronto, 1997); Peter Kilduff, *Richthofen: Beyond the Legend of the Red Baron* (New York, 1993); Denis Winter, *The First of the Few: Fighter Pilots of the First World War* (1982). For policy and organization, see John Morrow, *German Air Power in World War One* (Lincoln NE, 1982); Malcolm Cooper, *Birth of Independent Air Power: British Air Policy in the*

First World War (1986). For campaigns, see Andrew Hyde, *The First Blitz: The German Air Campaign Against Britain* (2001); Douglas H. Robinson, *The Zeppelin in Combat: German Naval Airship Division, 1912–1918* (Seattle WA, 1971); C.M. White, *Gotha Summer: The German Daytime Raids on England, May to August 1917* (1986); Frederick Cutlack, *The Australian Flying Corps in Western and Eastern Theatres of War* (Queensland, 1984); and Bert Frandsen, *Hat in the Ring: The Birth of American Air Power in the First World War* (Washington DC, 2003). For a fictional account of the war in the air based on meticulous research and the author's experience in the next war, see the trilogy by Derek Robinson: *Goshawk Squadron* (1971), *War Story* (1987) and *Hornet's Sting* (1999).

Armour

One of the liveliest specialized books about the war is *A New Excalibur: The Development of the Tank 1909–1939* (1986) by A.J. Smithers. See also Dale Wilson, *Treat 'Em Rough: The Birth of American Armor, 1917–1920* (Novato CA, 1989); Frank Mitchell, *Tank Warfare: The Tanks in the Great War* (1987); and Ernest Swinton, *Eyewitness: Being Personal Reminiscences of the Great War, Including the Genesis of the Tank* (1932).

Battles and Campaigns

One of the happiest results of the revived interest in the war, and arguably a cause of the revival as well, has been a transformation in the art of telling the history of battles. Mind-numbing drum and trumpet narrative has given way to analysis. This welcome trend began with Barbara Tuchman's *The Guns of August* (1962), which President Kennedy read during the Cuban Missile Crisis, and picked up pace with John Keegan's *The Face of Battle* (1976), which dissected what happened at Agincourt, Waterloo and the Somme. Often the writers are from outside academic circles, which might account for their clear writing and their appeal. For the first phase of trench war, see John Terraine, *Mons* (1972) and Ian Beckett, *Ypres: The First Battle, 1914* (2004). For the battles of 1915, see Daniel Dancocks, *Welcome to Flanders Fields* (1989) about the Canadian divisions in 1915; Tim Travers, *Gallipoli 1915* (2004); and Niall Cherry, *Most Unfavourable Ground: the Battle of Loos, 1915* (2005). For 1916, see Alistair Horne's classic *The Price of Victory: Verdun 1916* (1978), which is still the place to start for a look at the longest battle in the war; Malcolm Brown, *Verdun 1916* (2003); Ian Ousby, *The Road to Verdun* (2002); Christina Holstein, *Fort Douamont, Verdun* (2002); Jack Sheldon, *German Army on the Somme 1914–1916* (2005); N.H. Farrar-Hockley, *The Somme* (1964); Terry Norman, *The Hell They Called High Wood: The Somme, 1916* (1984); and Peter Charlton, *Australians on the Somme, Pozières 1916* (1986). For 1917, see Pierre Berton's deservedly popular book about the Canadian assault on Vimy Ridge in 1917 in *Vimy* (1986); Ian Passingham, *Pillars of Fire: Messines Ridge* (2000); Philip Warner, *Passchendaele* (2005); Nigel Steel and Peter Hart, *Passchendaele: The Sacrificial Ground* (2001); and Peter Liddle (ed.) *Passchendaele in Perspective: The Third Battle of Ypres* (1997). For 1918, see Barrie Pitt, *1918: The Last Act* (1962); C.E.W. Bean, *Australian Imperial Forces in France During the Allied Offensives, 1918* (Australian War Memorial, 1983) and *The Australian Imperial*

Forces in France During the Main German Offensive, 1918 (1983); Daniel Dancocks, *Spearhead to Victory, Canada and the Great War* about the Canadian Corps in the last hundred days (Edmonton AL, 1987); Shane B. Schreiber, *Shock Army of the British Empire: The Canadian Corps in the Last 100 Days of the Great War* (Westport CT, 1997); J.P. Harris, *Amiens to the Armistice: The BEF in the 100 Days Campaign, 1918* (1998); and James McWilliams and R. James Steel, *Amiens: Dawn of Victory* (Toronto, 2001). For the Eastern Front, see Winston Churchill, *The Unknown War: The Eastern Front* (1931); Dennis Showalter, *Tannenberg: Clash of Empires* (Hamden CT, 1991); Norman Stone, *The Eastern Front 1914–1917* (1975); and Vejas Liulevicius, *War Land on the Eastern Front: Culture, National Identity and German Occupation in World War 1* (2000).

Experiences of War

Along with the tactical complexities of the war, the experience of fighting in it and its impact both immediately and in the longer run have come to attract the most attention. One of the most original and thoughtful studies is *Trench Warfare 1914–1918: The Live and Let Live System* (London, 1980) by Tony Ashworth. Ashworth argues that the closeness of static front lines encouraged soldiers to exchange non-violence where possible, by direct truces, by inertia and, when high command prevented these ploys, by ritualizing aggression – for example, by ensuring that artillery rounds landed at a particular time and place. Reaching a different conclusion, in *No Man's Land: Combat and Identity in World War One* (Cambridge and NY, 1979) Eric Leed examined the way being trapped in an industrial war forced soldiers to adopt a defensive personality at odds with their hopes of being active warriors. In *Tommy: The British Soldier on the Western Front 1914–1918*, Richard Holmes has examined his subject from all angles and at all levels. In a series of 'vernacular' histories, Lyn Macdonald has organized first-hand accounts of the British and Commonwealth experience that now covers the entire war: *They Called it Passchendaele* (1978); *The Somme* (1983); *1914* (1987); *1914–1918: Voices and Images of the Great War* (1988); *1915: The Death of Innocence* (1993); and *To the Last Man: Spring 1918* (1998). Drawing heavily upon interviews while these were still possible, Martin Middlebrook wrote the invaluable *The First Day on the Somme: 1 July 1916* (1971) and *The Kaiser's Battle 21 March 1918: The First Day of the German Spring Offensive* (1978). Detailed studies of the day-to-day realities of the trenches include John Ellis, *Eye-Deep in Hell* (1976); Malcolm Brown, *Tommy Goes to War* (1978); Denis Winter, *Death's Men: Soldiers of the Great War* (1978); Desmond Morton, *When Your Number's Up: The Canadian Soldiers in the First World War* (Toronto, 1993); Leonard V. Smith, *Between Mutiny and Obedience: The Case of the French 5th Infantry Division* (Princeton NJ, 1994); John Brophy and Eric Partridge, *The Long Trail: Soldiers' Songs and Slang, 1914–1918* (1972); R.H. Haigh, *World War One and the Serving British Soldier*; Peter Liddle, *The Soldiers' War 1914–18* (1979); James Churchill Dunn, *The War the Infantry Knew 1914–1919: Chronicle of Service* (1987); and Bill Gammage, *An Australian in the First World War* (1976). Allen Frantzen, in *Bloody Good: Chivalry, Sacrifice and the Great War* (Chicago IL, 2003), Mark Girouard, in *The Return to Camelot: Chivalry and the English Gentleman* (1981) and Michael Adams, in *The Great Adventure: Male Desire and the Coming of World War I* (1990), link pre-war notions of chivalry and masculine assertion to the experience of war.

Inquiries into the physical and psychological damage soldiers suffered began during the war and have continued ever since. Anthony Babington, *Shell-shock: A History of the Changing Attitudes to War Neurosis* (1997) complements his earlier study on court-martials, *For the Sake of Example: Capital Courts-Martial, 1914–1920, Shell-shock: A History of the Changing Attitudes to War Neurosis* (1983). Peter Barham's *Forgotten Lunatics of the Great War* (2004) has a jolt in the title, but the author means the term 'lunatics' literally, using the contemporary term to cast light on soldiers who became psychotic. These were not the same as victims of 'shell shock' or what is now termed post-traumatic stress disorder. For a look at this affliction, see Peter Leese, *Shell Shock: Traumatic Neurosis and the British Soldiers of the First World War* (2002); Paul Lerner, *Hysterical Men: War, Psychiatry, and the Politics of Trauma in Germany, 1890–1930*; and E.E. Southard, *Shell-shock and Other Neuropsychiatric Problems Presented in 588 Case Histories From the War Literature, 1914–1918* (New York, 1973). For military medicine in general, see Denis Winter, *Death's Men: Soldiers of the Great War* (1978); Lyn Macdonald, *The Roses of No Man's Land* (1980); Ian Whitehead, *Doctors in the Great War* (1999); Frederick Albert Pottle, *Stretchers: The Story of a Hospital Unit on the Western Front* (New York, 1929); Janet Lee, *War Girls: The First Aid Nursing Yeomany in the First World War* (Manchester, 2005); and Ishobel Ross, *Little Grey Partridge: First World War Diary* (Aberdeen, 1988).

Because citizen armies fought the war, the sub-culture of the soldiers carried over much of the popular civilian culture from which they came. This proved to be a key to maintaining morale. The collapse of morale led quickly to mutiny, as with the French in 1917 and the Germans in 1918. For morale and the sub-culture of the soldiers, see J.G. Fuller, *Troop Morale and Popular Culture in the British and Dominion Armies 1914–1918* (Oxford, 1990); Stephane Audoin-Rouzeau, *Men at War, 1914–1918: National Sentiment and Trench Journalism in France During World War One* (Oxford, 1995); S.P. MacKenzie, 'Morale and the cause: the campaign to shape the outlook of soldiers in the British Expeditionary Force, 1914–1918', *Canadian Journal of History* (vol. 15, no. 2 (1990), pp. 215–32); Richard Schweitzer, *The Cross and the Trenches: Religious Faith and Doubt Among British and American Great War Soldiers* (New York, 2003); Duff Crerar, *Padres in No Man's Land: Canadian Chaplains and the Great War* (Montreal, 1995); Michael Moynihan, *God on Our Side: The British Padres in World War I* (1983). For mutiny and the maintenance of discipline, see John Hughes Wilson, *Blindfold and Alone: British Military Executions in the Great War* (2005); and Douglas Gill, *The Unknown Army: Mutinies in the British Army in World War One* (1985).

When used carefully, memoirs and collections of personal letters are a way for those of us who are necessarily outsiders to gain access to the experience of the front soldiers. Bear in mind that these first-person accounts usually reflect what the author thought at the time of writing. They can achieve the status of great literature. Among the finest are Guy Chapman, *A Passionate Prodigality* (1965), Robert Graves, *Goodbye To All That* (1929); Edmund Blunden, *Undertones of War* (1929); Charles Carrington, *A Subaltern's War* (1929); D.W.A. Hankey, *A Student in Arms* (1917); Ernst Jünger, *The Storm of Steel* (1929); Rudolf Binding, *A Fatalist at War* (1929); Marc Bloch, *Memoirs of War 1914–1915* (1980); Henri Desagneaux, *French Soldier's War Diary, 1914–1918* (1975); Henry Williamson, *The Wet Flanders Plain* (1988); Patrick Campbell, *The Ebb and Flow of Battle* (1979) and *In the Cannon's Mouth* (1979); Frank Hawkings, *From Ypres to Cambrai: the Diary of an Infantryman, 1914–1919* (1974);

Ernest Shepherd, *A Sergeant-Major's War: From Hill 60 to the Somme* (1987); Reginald Roy (ed.) *The Journal of Private Fraser* (Victoria BC, 1985) and John Laffin, *Letters from the Front 1914–1918* (1973).

Women and the War: Gender Studies

The benchmark study of British women and the war is by Gail Braybon, *Women Workers in the First World War: The British Experience* (1980). Contrary to the notion that the war opened the way for change, Braybon argues that the appearance of women in new roles in the workplace and society encountered fierce resistance. Another excellent study taking this line is by Angela Woollacott, *On Her Their Lives Depend: Munitions Workers in the Great War* (Berkeley CA, 1994). Arthur Marwick, in *The Deluge: British Society and the First World War* (1975) believes the cup of social progress was at least half full for women, as for other hitherto marginalized people. For a look at women and the vote, see Johanna Alberti, *Beyond Suffrage: Feminists in War and Peace, 1914–28* (1989). For women in America, see M.W. Greenwald, *Women, War and Work: Impact of World War 1 on Women Workers in the USA* (Westport CT, 1980). For the experience of women in Germany, see Ute Daniel, *The War from Within: German Working-Class Women in the First World War* (1997). Articles include Henriette Donner, 'Under the cross – why V.A.D.s performed the filthiest task in the dirtiest war: Red Cross women volunteers, 1914–1918', *Journal of Social History*, vol. 30, Spring 1997, pp. 687–704; Nicoletta F. Gullace, 'White feathers and wounded men: female patriotism and the memory of the Great War', *Journal of British Studies*, vol. 36, April 1997, pp. 178–206; and Susan Pycroft, 'British Working Women and the First World War, *Historian*, vol. 56, Summer 1994, pp. 669–710.

For the related fields of gender studies and notions of masculinity, see Margaret Higgonet (ed.) *Behind the Lines: Gender and the Two World Wars* (New Haven CT, 1987); Joanna Bourke, *Dismembering the Male: Men's Bodies, Britain, and the Great War* (1996); Michael Adams in *The Great Adventure: Male Desire and the Coming of World War I* (1990); Mark Girouard in *The Return to Camelot: Chivalry and the English Gentleman* (1981); and Nicoletta Gullace, *The Blood of our Sons: Men, Women and the Renegotiation of British Citizenship during the Great War* (2004).

Pacifism and Socialism

The schism that divided socialism between social democratic and communist camps began to appear before 1914 but was then driven by the war itself. The close affinity between socialism and pacifism that was evident in the meetings of the Second International vanished when the communists, led by Lenin of Russia, rejected pacifism as a bourgeois delusion that would cripple the impetus the war was imparting to history. These developments are explored in R.J.Q. Adams, *The Conscription Crisis in Great Britain, 1900–1918* (1987); F.L. Carsten's *War Against War: British and German Radical Movements in the First World War* (1982); Martin Ceadel's *Pacifism in Britain 1914–1945: The Defining of a Faith* (Oxford, 1980); Georges Haupt, *Socialism and the Great War: The Collapse of the Second International* (Oxford, 1972); Keith Robbins, *The Abolition of War: The Peace Movement in Britain 1914–1919* (Cardiff, 1976) and *The Abolition of War: The 'Peace Movement' in Britain 1914–1919* (1976); Carl

Schorske, *German Social Democracy 1905–1917: The Development of the Great Schism* (Cambridge MA, 1955); Marvin Schwartz, *The Union of Democratic Control in British Politics in the First World War* (Oxford, 1974); Jo Vellacott, *Bertrand Russell and the pacifists in the First World War* (New York, 1980); J.M. Winter, *Socialism and the Challenge of War: Ideas and Politics in Britain 1912–1918* (1974).

Propaganda

One legacy of the war was the widespread belief that it had been a war of words and images. When combined with the appearance of modern advertising and mass media, propaganda seemed a new way to disarm opponents bloodlessly. Earlier studies of propaganda in the war often accepted the propaganda about propaganda uncritically: for example, Harold Laswell's *Propaganda Technique in World War One* (Cambridge MA, 1971). A more recent study that stresses the autonomous power of propaganda is Peter Buitenhuis, *The Great War of Words: British, American and Canadian Propaganda and Fiction* (Vancouver, 1987). On the whole, studies of propaganda now tend to take a nuanced view about its impact, showing its limitations as well as its strengths. As Churchill observed in 1940, propaganda is all very well but it is events that make history. Among the best studies of propaganda and the war are the ones by Cate Haste, *Keep the Home Fires Burning: Propaganda in the First World War* (1977); Michael Sanders, *British Propaganda in the First World War, 1914–1918* (1983); Gary Messinger, *British Propaganda and the State in the First World War* (Manchester, 1992); Nicholas Reeves, *Official British Propaganda in the First World War 1914–1918* (1986); Martin Farar, *News from the Front: War Correspondents on the Western Front 1914–1918* (2003); Troy Paddock, *A Call to Arms: Propaganda, Public Opinion and Newspapers in the Great War* (New York, 2004); J. Lee Thompson, *Politicians, the Press and Propaganda: Lord Northcliffe and the Great War 1914–1919* (Kent State, OH, 2000); David Welch, *Germany, Propaganda and Total War, 1914–1918: The Sins of Omission* (Rutgers, 2000); Jeff Keshen, *Propaganda and Censorship During Canada's Great War* (Edmonton, 1996); P.J. Flood, *France 1914–1918: Public Opinion and the War Effort* (1990); and Martha Hanna, *The Mobilization of Intellect: French Scholars and Writers During the Great War* (Cambridge MA, 1996).

Culture: Novels, Poetry, Art

The most influential of the war novels appeared around a decade after the war. The exception is Henri Barbusse's *Under Fire* (New York, 1926), which appeared in English translation in 1916 and had an immediate impact on English writers such as Robert Graves. His memoir, *Goodbye To All That*, sits in the No Man's Land between memoir and fiction. So does Siegfried Sassoon's *Memoirs of George Sherston* (1937), although facing the other way, being a memoir pretending to be a novel. The most popular of the war novels was *All Quiet on the Western Front*, by Erich Maria Remarque (1929). However, *The Good Soldier Schweik*, by Jaroslav Hasek, which came out in Czech in 1922, was arguably the first anti-war novel and still one of the most compelling to read. It appeared in English in 1930. Some feel that *Her Privates We* by Frederic Manning (1926) is the novel that has best stood the test of time. More recent novels that rest on a thorough knowledge of the history of the war include the trilogy by Pat Barker: *Regeneration* (1993), *The Eye in the Door* (1993) and *The*

Ghost Road (1995). Worthwhile anthologies of the best of the war poetry include Brian Gardner's *Up the Line to Death* (1986); Jon Silkin's *The Penguin Book of First World War Poetry* (1981); and Jon Stallworthy's *Poets of the First World War* (1974). *The Great War and Modern Memory* by Paul Fussell (1975) continues to have a profound influence on our ideas about the impact of the war on culture. Samuel Hynes' *A War Imagined: The First World War and English Culture* (1990) is less sweeping than Fussell's work and thus more convincing. Other studies of the literature of the war include W.P. Bridgewater, *German Poets of the First World War* (1985); Frank Field, *British and French Writers of the First World War* (1975); Dorothy Goldman, *Women Writers and the Great War* (New York, 1995); and Arthur Lane, *An Adequate Response: The War Poetry of Wilfred Owen and Siegfried Sassoon* (Detroit MI, 1972). Two books cover high culture broadly in assessing the impact of the war: *Rites of Spring: The Great War and the Birth of the Modern Age* by Modris Eksteins (Toronto, 1989) and Richard Cork, *A Bitter Truth: Avant-Garde Art and the Great War* (New Haven CT, 1994).

Economic Aspects

Niall Ferguson devotes several chapters of *The Pity of War* (1999) to the economic side of the war – for example, 'Public Finance and National Security' (5), 'Economic Capability: The Advantage Squandered' (9), ' "Maximum Slaughter at Minimum Expense": War Finance' (11), and 'How (not) To Pay for the War' (14). For war financing and loans, see Kathleen Burk, *Britain, America and the Sinews of War, 1914–1918* (Boston MA, 1985). See also R.E. Bunselmeyer, *The Cost of the War 1914–1919: British Economic Aims and Origins of Reparations* (1975); John F. Godfrey, *Capitalism at War: Industrial Policy and Bureaucracy in France, 1914–18* (1987); Stephen Broadberry, *Economics of World War 1* (Cambridge, 2005); and Avner Offner, *The First World War: An Agrarian Interpretation* (Oxford, 1989).

Diplomacy

Most of the general studies of the war look at diplomacy both open and secret, but there are also specialized monographs worth a look. For the Allies and the United States, see E.M. Andrews, *The Anzac Illusion: Anglo-Australian Relations During World War I* (Cambridge, 1993); Richard Debo, *Revolution and Survival: The Foreign Policy of Soviet Russia 1917–1918* (Austin TX, 1979); Ludwig Dehio, *Germany and World Politics in the Twentieth Century* (1960); Reinhard Doerries, *Imperial Challenge: Ambassador Count Bernstorff and German-US Relations* (Durham NC, 1989); Ramparkash Dua, *Anglo-Japanese Relations During the First World War* (New Delhi, 1972); George W. Egerton, *Great Britain and the Creation of the League of Nations, 1914–1919* (Durham NC, 1978); L.L. Farrar, *Divide and Conquer: German Efforts to Conclude a Separate Peace, 1914–1918* (Boulder CO, 1978); Wilfried Fest, *Peace or Partition: The Habsburg Monarchy and British Policy 1914–1918* (New York, 1978); D.F. Fleming, *The United States and the League of Nations, 1918–1920* (New York, 1968); Michael Fry, *Lloyd George and Foreign Policy: The Education of a Statesman, 1890–1916* (Kingston, 1977); Elie Kedourie, *England and the Middle East: The Destruction of the Ottoman Empire 1914–21* (1956); Sterling Kernek, *Distractions of Peace During War: The Lloyd George Government's Reaction to Wilson* (Philadelphia PA,

1975); Walter McDougall, *France's Rhineland Diplomacy, 1914–1924* (Princeton NJ, 1978); H.I. Nelson, *Land and Power: British and Allied Policy on Germany's Frontiers 1916–1919* (1963); Jukka Nevakivi, *Britain, France and the Arab Middle East, 1914–20* (1969); Harry Rudin, *Armistice 1918* (Hamden CT, 1967 [1944]); David Stevenson, *French War Aims Against Germany 1914–1919* (1982) and *The First World War and International Politics* (Oxford, 1988); Ulrich Trumpener, *Germany and the Ottoman Empire 1914–1918* (Princeton NJ, 1968); A.C. Walworth, *America's Moment: 1918, American Diplomacy at the End of World War 1* (New York, 1977); Frank Weber, *Eagles or the Crescent: Austria and the Diplomacy of the Turkish Alliance 1914–18* (Ithica NY, 1970); Bruce Westrate, *The Arab Bureau: British policy in the Middle East, 1916–1920* (University Park PA, 1992); John Wheeler-Bennett, *Brest-Litovsk, the Forgotten Peace* (1963); David Woodward, *Trial by Friendship: Anglo-American Relations 1917–1918* (Lexington KY, 1993); and Z.A.B. Zeman, *The Gentlemen Negotiators: A Diplomatic History of the First World War* (1971).

Countries

Australia and New Zealand

Joan Beaumont edited a collection of essays, *Australia's War, 1914–18* (St. Leonard's NSW, 1995). See also Bobbie Oliver, *War And Peace In Western Australia: The Social and Political Impact of the Great War, 1914–1926* (1995); Alistair Thompson, *Anzac Memories: Living with the Legend* (New York, 1994); Michael McKernan, *The Australian People and the Great War* (Melbourne, 1980); Tony Matthews, *Crosses: Australian Soldiers in the Great War* (Brisbane, 1987); Bill Gammage, *The Broken Years: Australian Soldiers in the Great War* (Canberra, 1974); Brian Lewis, *Our War: Australia During World War I* (Melbourne, 1980); Paul Baker, *King and Country Call: New Zealanders, Conscription and the Great War* (Auckland, 1988); and Raymond Evans, *Loyalty and Disloyalty: Social Conflict on the Queensland Homefront* (Sydney, 1987).

Austria–Hungary

The best source on Austria–Hungary in the war is Holger Herwig, *Germany and Austria-Hungary 1914–1918* (1996). See also Robert Kann (ed.) *Habsburg Empire in World War One* (New York, 1977); Arthur May, *The Passing of the Habsburg Monarchy, 1914–1918* (Philadelphia PA, 1966); Mark Cornwall, *The Undermining of Austria-Hungary: The Battle for Hearts and Minds* (2000); Gary Shanafelt, *Secret Enemy: Austria-Hungary and the German Alliance, 1914–1918* (New York, 1985); and Z.A.B. Zeman, *The Breakup of the Habsburg Empire 1914–1918* (1961).

Britain

The Myriad Faces of War: Britain and the Great War, 1914–1918 (Cambridge, 1986) by Trevor Wilson is the classic big book about the war: wise, readable and indispensable. J.M. Winter has concentrated on Britain and the war. Apart from the studies cited elsewhere in this list, see his *The Great War and the British People* (1986) and *Capital Cities at War: Paris, London, Berlin, 1914–1919* (Cambridge, 1997). Surveys include

J.M. Bourne, *Britain and the Great War* (1989) and Andrew Thorpe, *The Longman Companion to Britain in the Era of the Two World Wars, 1914–45* (1994).

For politics and the state, see R.J.Q. Adams, *Arms and the Wizard: Lloyd George and the Ministry of Munitions, 1915–1916* (1978) and *The Conscription Crisis in Great Britain, 1900–1918* (1987); Kathleen Burk (ed.) *War and the State: The Transformation of British Government, 1914–1919* (1982); David French, *The Strategy of the Lloyd George Coalition 1916–1918* (Oxford, 1995) and *British Strategy and War Aims 1914–16* (1986); John Grigg, *Lloyd George: From Peace to War, 1912–1916* (Berkeley CA, 1985); Paul Guinn, *British Strategy and Politics 1914–1918* (Oxford, 1965); Cameron Hazlehurst, *Politicians at War: July 1914 to May 1915* (1971); David Lloyd George, *War Memoirs* (1936); Kenneth Morgan, *Lloyd George* (1974); Martin Pugh, *Lloyd George* (1988); John Turner, *British Politics and the Great War: Coalition and Conflict* (New Haven CT, 1992).

Social and local history have been well covered. See in particular Pamela Horn, *Rural Life in England in the First World War*, (Dublin, 1984); Bernard Lewis, *Swansea Pals* (2005); Helen McCartney, *Citizen Soldiers: The Liverpool Territorials in the First World War* (Cambridge, 2005); Martin Middlebrook, *North Midland Territorials Go to War: The First Six Months in Flanders Trenches* (2003); Christopher Martin, *English Life in the First World War* (1974); Arthur Marwick, *The Deluge: British Society and the First World War* (1975); Geoffrey Moorhouse, *Hell's Foundations: A Social History of the Town of Bury in the Aftermath of the Gallipoli Campaign* (1992); James Munson (ed.) *Echoes of the Great War: The Diary of Reverend Andrew Clark, 1914–1919* (New York, 1985); E.S Turner, *Dear Old Blighty* (1980); Jeanne MacKenzie, *Children of the Souls: A Tragedy of the First World War* (1986); and above all Bernard Waites, *A Class Society at War: England 1914–1918* (Leamington Spa, 1987).

Canada

Desmond Morton has written several important books about Canada and the war, including *Fight or Pay: Soldiers' Families in the Great War* (Sillert PQ, 1992); *Marching to Armageddon: Canadians and the Great War 1914–1919* (with J.L. Granatstein) (Toronto ON, 1989); *Peculiar Kind of Ministry: Canada's Overseas Ministry in the First World War* (Toronto ON, 1982); *When Your Number's Up: The Canadian Soldier in the First World War* (Toronto ON, 1993); *Silent Battle: Canadian Prisoners of War in Germany, 1914–1919* (Toronto ON, 1992); *Winning the Second Battle: Canadian Veterans and the Return to Civilian Life, 1915–1930* (Toronto ON, 1987) and *Supreme Penalty: Canadian Deaths by Firing Squad in the First World War* (Victoria BC, 1980). Writing popular rather than academic history, Dan Dancocks put together a series of books about the Canadian military experience: *Welcome to Flanders: The First Canadian Battle of the Great War* (Toronto ON, 1988); *Sir Arthur Currie, a Biography* (Toronto ON, 1985); *Legacy of Valour: The Canadians at Passchendaele* (Edmonton AB, 1986); *Spearhead to Victory: Canada and the Great War* (Edmonton AB, 1987) and *Gallant Canadians: The Story of the 10th Canadian Infantry Battalion 1914–1919* (Markham ON, 1990). *Surviving Trench Warfare: Technology and the Canadian Corps* (Toronto ON, 1992) must be studied by anyone interested in going beyond the stereotypes that still cloud our understanding of trench warfare. *The Road Past Vimy: The Canadian Corps 1914–1918* by D.J. Goodspeed (Toronto ON, 1969) is still useful as an overview. Jonathan Vance's *Death So Noble* (Vancouver BC, 1997) examines the unique way most Canadians remembered the war as a worthwhile crusade and has become a classic work.

France

Books in English about France and the war have been scarce, although this oversight is on its way to being corrected. Jean Jacques Becker's *The Great War and the French People* (1985) is a good book with which to start. Patrick Fridenson has edited a collection of essays on *The French Home Front 1914–1918* (1992). Useful biographies include Edgar Holt's *The Tiger: The Life of Clemenceau* (1976) and Michael Neiberg, *Foch* (2003). For the military dimension, see Anthony Clayton, *Paths of Glory: The French Army 1914–1918* (2003); Robert Doughty, *Pyrrhic Victory: French Strategy and Operations in the First World War* (2005); Leonard V. Smith, *Between Mutiny and Obedience: The Case of the French 5th Infantry Division* (Princeton NJ, 1994). For the home front, see P.J. Flood, *France 1914–1918: Public Opinion and the War Effort* (1990); Richard Cobb, *French and Germans, Germans and French: France under Two Occupations* (1983); Martha Hanna, *The Mobilization of Intellect: French Scholars and Writers During the Great War* (Cambridge MA, 1996); and Kenneth Silver, *Esprit de Corps: The Great War and French Art, 1914–1925* (Ann Arbor MI, 1982).

Germany

The go-to book on Germany and the war is Holger Herwig's *Germany and Austria-Hungary 1914–1918* (1994). The main strength of the book is its treatment of military affairs, but the analysis of the home fronts is excellent too. Another good general source is Roger Chickering's *Imperial Germany and the Great War* (Cambridge, 2004). For the military and naval dimensions, see Robert Asprey, *The German High Command at War: Hindenburg and Ludendorff Conduct World War I* (New York, 1991); Annika Mombauer, *Helmuth von Moltke and the Origins of the Great War* (Cambridge, 2001); John Horn, *German Atrocities 1914: A History of Denial* (New Haven CT, 2001); Erich von Falkenhayn, *General Headquarters 1914–1916 and its Critical Decisions* (1919); Bruce Gudmundsson, *Stormtroop Tactics: Innovation in the German Army, 1914–1918* (1989); Paul von Hindenburg, *Out of My Life* (1920); Martin Kitchen, *Silent Dictatorship: The Politics of the German High Command Under Hindenburg and Ludendorff, 1916–1918* (1976); Gerhard Ritter, *The Sword and the Sceptre* (1973). For politics and the home front, see Theobald Bethmann Hollweg, *Reflections on the World War* (1920); L.L. Farrar, *The Short War Illusion: German Policy, Strategy and Domestic Affairs* (Santa Barbara CA, 1973); Fritz Fischer, *Germany's Aims in the First World War* (1967); William A. Pelz, *The Spartakusbund and the German Working Class Movement, 1914–1919* (Lewiston ME, 1988); Lamar Cecil, *William II, Prince and Emperor, 1859–1900* (Chapel Hill NC, 1989) and *William II, Emperor and Exile 1900–1941* (1996); Marvin Edwards, *Stresemann and the Greater Germany 1914–1918* (New York, 1963); Klaus Epstein, *Matthias Erzberger and the Dilemma of German Democracy* (New York, 1971); Konrad Jarausch, *Enigmatic Chancellor: Bethmann Hollweg and the Hubris of Germany* (1973); Prince Max of Baden, *Memoirs* (1928); Alfred Tirpitz, *My Memoirs* (1919); Gerald Feldman, *Army, Industry and Labor in Germany, 1914–1918* (Princeton NJ, 1966); Jürgen

Kocka, *Facing Total War: German Society 1914–1918* (1984); Carl Schorske, *German Social Democracy 1905–1917: Development of the Great Schism* (New York, 1955). For culture and the arts, see Matthias Eberle, *World War One and the Weimar Artists* (New Haven CT, 1985); Peter Paret, *The Berlin Secession: Modernism and its Enemies in Imperial Germany* (Cambridge MA, 1980); Ann P. Linder, *Princes of the Trenches: Narrating the German Experience of the First World War* (Columbia SC, 1996); Jeffrey Verhey, *The Spirit of 1914: Militarism, Myth and Mobilization in Germany* (Cambridge, 2000); and W.P. Bridgwater, *German Poets of the First World War* (1985).

Italy

There are few books in English about Italy and the war. One is William Renzi's *In the Shadow of the Sword: Italy's Neutrality and Entrance into the Great War* (New York, 1987). See also M. James Burgwyn, *The Legend of the Mutilated Victory: Italy, the Great War and the Paris Peace Conference* (Westport CT, 1993); and Cyril Falls, *Caporetto 1917* (1965).

Middle East and Africa

The struggle in Gallipoli was marginal to the war but continues to fascinate readers. See Jenny Macleod, *Reconsidering Gallipoli* (Manchester, 2004); Tim Travers, *Gallipoli 1915* (2004); C.E.W. Bean, *Gallipoli Correspondent: The Frontline Diary of C.E.W. Bean* (Boston MA, 1983); Peter Liddle, *Men of Gallipoli: The Dardanelles and Gallipoli Experience, August 1914 to January 1916* (1976); Alan Moorehead, *Gallipoli* (1956); and Jeffry Wallin, *By Ships Alone: Churchill and the Dardanelles* (Durham NC, 1981). For the Middle East, see the classic *Revolt in the Desert* (1927) and *Seven Pillars of Wisdom* (1936); David Woodward, *Hell in the Holy Land: World War I in the Middle East* (Lexington KY, 2006); David Bullock, *Allenby's War: The Palestine-Arabian Campaigns* (1988); Mary Brugger, *Australians and Egypt, 1914–1919* (1980); A.J. Barker, *The Neglected War: Mesopotamia 1914–1918* (1967); Ronald Millar, *Kut: The Death of an Army* (1969); Cyril Falls, *Armageddon 1918: The Final Palestinian Campaign of 1918* (Philadelphia PA, 2003); and Edward Erickson, *Ordered to Die: A History of the Ottoman Army in the First World War* (Greenwood CT, 2000). For the war in Africa, see Brian Gardner, *German East: World War One in East Africa* (1963); and Byron Farwell, *The Great War in Africa, 1914–1918* (New York, 1986).

Russia

Bruce Lincoln's *Passage Through Armageddon: The Russians in War and Revolution 1914–1918* (New York, 1986) is a vivid narrative on the subject in the title. Peter Gatrell's *Russia's First World War* (2005) provides an overview. Orlando Figes' *A People's Tragedy: A History of the Russian Revolution* (New York, 1997) covers a broader period in great depth. The economic side of Russia's war is the subject of *The Politics of Industrial Mobilization in Russia, 1914–1917* (1983). For the war and revolution, see Sheila Fitzpatrick, *The Russian Revolution, 1917–1932* (Oxford, 1984); Marc Ferro, *October 1917: A Social History of the Russian Revolution* (1980); Alexander Kerensky, *The Kerensky Memoirs: Russia and History's Turning Point*

(New York, 1965); and Evan Mawdsley, *The Russian Revolution and the Baltic Fleet: War and Politics* (1978).

United States

Start with David Kennedy, *Over There: The First World War and American Society* (New York, 1980); Edward Coffman, *The War to End Wars: The American Military Experience in World War One* (New York, 1968); and Thomas Fleming, *The Illusion of Victory: America in World War I* (New York, 2004). In *Doughboys, the Great War and the Remaking of America* (Baltimore MD, 2003), Jennifer Keene examines the establishment and impact of the American Army. Gary Mead in *The Doughboys: America and the First World War* (2000) undertakes a similar project. For President Wilson and his foreign policy, see Robert Ferrell, *Woodrow Wilson and World War One, 1917–1921* (New York, 1985); Arthur Link, *Woodrow Wilson: Revolution, War and Peace* (Arlington Heights IL, 1979), *Wilson the Diplomatist* (Baltimore MD, 1957), and his five-volume biography, *Woodrow Wilson* (Princeton, 1957); and Patrick Devlin, *Too Proud to Fight: Wilson's Neutrality* (New York, 1975). Propaganda and popular culture have attracted a great deal of attention. See in particular W. Michael Isenberg, *War on Film: The American Cinema and World War 1, 1915–1941* (Rutherford NJ, 1981); Larry Ward, *The Motion Picture Goes to War* (Ann Arbor MI, 1985); Walton H. Rawls, *Wake Up America: World War One and the American Poster* (New York, 1988); and George T. Blakey, *Historians on the Home Front: American Propagandists for the Great War* (Lexington KY, 1970).

INDEX

Air war
  aces, 74
  birth of Royal Air Force, 75
  German defensive posture, 74
  Neuve Chapelle, 34
  Passchendaele, 84
  RFC offensive spirit, 74
  strafing against German spring offensive
    1918, 94
  strategic bombing, 75
  tactical air power, 75
  the Marne, 18
  Verdun, 53
  Zeppelins, 75
  'Bloody April', 74
Angell, Norman, 27
Anzacs, 37, 39, 84
Artillery, 5, 23, 45
  106 fuse, 79
  rolling or creeping barrage, 60, 77, 79, 80,
    84
  the Somme, 63, 65
  Verdun, 53
Ashworth, Tony, 32
Asquith, Herbert H., 15, 24, 42, 70
Atrocities, Belgian, 14
Australia, 27, 39, 42, 103, 110
Australians, 37, 42, 67, 76, 95, 110
Austria–Hungary, 24
  defeat in 1914, 21–2
  regain Przemyśl and Lemberg, 30
  Vittorio Veneto, 40
  war plans, 8

Ball, Albert, 74
Bauer, Col. Max, 96
Beatty, Admiral Sir David, 52
Below, General Otto von, 66
Bethmann Hollweg, Theobald von, 25, 60,
    56–60
  September Memorandum, 28
  submarine warfare, 45–48, 69–71
  fall of, 71
Bishop, Billy, 74
Boelcke, Oswald, 74
Brest–Litovsk (treaty), 91

Britain
  censorship, 44
  choices in 1915, 24–5
  conscription, 42
  German peace offer 1916, 70–1
  labour, 41–2
  New Army, 41, 62, 65
  Pals battalions, 41
  Royal Navy, 9–10, 24, 37–8, 45–7
  shell shortage, 44
  unity, 41
  volunteers in 1914, 41
  war plans, 9
  women in work force, 41–2
British Expeditionary Force (BEF), 15–20, 44
Bruchmüller, Lt.-Col. Georg, 77, 92
Brusilov, General Alexei, 16, 22, 48–9
Bülow, General Karl von, 14, 17–18
Byng, Sir Julian, 83

Canada, 27, 42, 103
Canadians, 67, 85, 97, 110
Carrington, Charles, 85
Castelnau, General Noel de, 56, 58, 61
Censorship, 44
Chapman, Guy, 85
Churchill, Winston, 24, 25, 27, 39, 52, 76,
    82
Clemenceau, Georges, 82
Conrad von Hoetzendorf, General Franz,
    21–2, 59
Crown Prince, Prussia, 57, 58
Currie, General Sir Arthur, 77–8, 85

Dead, approximate total, 3
Dead, by country, 103
Defence of the Realm Act (D.O.R.A), 40
Driant, Col, Émile, 54

Eastern Front
  Brest–Litovsk (place), 30
  Brusilov Offensive, 59
  Galicia, 21, 29, 59
  Kovno, 29
  Lemberg, 22, 30
  Masurian Lakes, 21

Eastern Front (*continued*)
　Przemyœl, 30
　Riga, 77
　Tannenberg, 20–1
　Warsaw, 30
Elles, Col. Hugh, 76
Erzberger, Matthias, 72

Falkenhayn, General Erich von, 19, 24, 29,
　30, 53, 54, 56–61, 66, 77, 92
Fatherland Party, 69
Fisher, Admiral Sir John, 10
Foch, General Ferdinand, 16, 18, 24, 65, 94,
　110
Fokker, Anthony, 73
France
　choices by 1915, 24
　and Italy, 40
　losses by end of 1915, 52
　mutiny of 1917, 80–1
　Russian provisional government, 72
　unity in 1914, 27
　war aims, 27
　war plans, 8–9
Franchet d'Esperey, General Louis, 17, 18
French, General Sir John, 16–19, 36, 44
Fuller, Lt.-Col. J. F. C., 76
　Cambrai, 76
Fussell, Paul, 31, 32, 111

Galliéni, General Joseph, 18, 19
Gallipoli, 37–9
　amphibious landings, 39
　Anzac Cove, 39
　bombardment, 37
　geography of, 37
　Cape Helles, 39
　evacuation, 39
　Kitchener, 37
　minefields, 37
　naval attack, 38
　Suvla Bay, 39
Gas, poison, 29, 34, 36, 59, 60, 75, 77, 92,
　94
Geddes, Sir Auckland, 42
Gentleman, myth of, 4
Germany
　Burgfrieden, 25, 28, 45, 48
　changes the war made, 91
　choices in 1915, 24
Great Transformation 1870–1914, 4
　domestic politics, 45–6, 72, 97–8
　strategic initiative, 29
　submarine warfare, 45–8, 68, 71
　the collapse of 1918, 95–9
　war aims, 27
　war aims majority, 45
　war aims movement, 45
Golden age, myth of, 3

Gough, General Sir Hubert, 66, 76, 83, 84
Guynemer, Georges, 74

Haig, General (later Field Marshal) Sir
　Douglas, 17, 34, 36, 37, 58, 61, 62, 63,
　65, 66, 74, 76, 82, 83, 84, 85, 88, 95,
　108
Hamilton, General Sir Ian, 38, 39
Hertling, Count, 72, 96, 97, 98
Heye, Col. Wilhelm, 96
Hindenburg Line, 68, 97
　Canal du Nord, 97
Hindenburg Programme, 68
Hindenburg, Field Marshal Paul von, 20, 24,
　29, 30, 60, 67, 68, 97, 98, 106
Hintze, Admiral Paul von, 96, 97, 98, 99
Hipper, Admiral Franz von, 52
Hitler, Adolf, 19, 91, 99, 106, 111
Hoffmann, Col. Max, 20
Horne, Alistair, 60
Horne, Sir Henry, 64, 66, 83
Hutier, General Oskar von, 77, 92, 93, 94

Immelmann, Max, 74
Ireland, 41, 70
Italy
　Caporetto, 40
　entry into war, 40
　Vittorio Veneto, 40

Jellicoe, Admiral Sir John, 52
Joffre, Marshal Joseph, 8, 9, 14, 15, 16, 17,
　18, 19, 36, 52, 53, 54, 56, 58, 61, 62,
　63, 65
Jutland, 51–2

Kerensky, Alexander, 72, 106
Kitchener, Field Marshal Lord Horatio, 17,
　37, 39, 41, 44
Kluck, General Alexander von, 14, 16, 17,
　18, 19
Knobelsdorf, General Schmidt von, 54, 57,
　58, 59, 60
Kunze, Sgt., 54

Lanrezac, General Charles, 15, 16, 17, 18
Lansdowne, Lord, 69
Law, Bonar, 27
Leed, Eric, 5, 111
Lenin, Vladimir, 72, 106
Liddell Hart, Sir Basil, 88
Live and let live, 32–4
Lloyd George, David, 24, 25, 42, 45, 70, 71,
　79, 82, 83, 91, 108
Long Peace, myth of, 3–4
Lossberg, Col. (later General) Fritz von, 66,
　67, 84
Ludendorff, General Erich, 20, 21, 29, 60,
　67, 68, 71, 72, 84, 85, 91–9, 105, 106

Lusitania, sinking of, 42
Lvov, Prince, 72

Mackensen, General August von, 29, 30, 77
Malvy, Louis, 81
Mannock, Edward 'Mick', 74
Marwitz, General George van der, 93
Masculinity, 3–4
Masterman, C. F. G., 42, 44
Maunoury, General Michel-Joseph, 18, 19
Michaelis, Georg, 72
Moltke, Field Marshal Count Helmuth von, 6
Moltke, General Helmuth von, 6, 7, 8, 13, 14, 16, 17, 18, 19, 20, 22

Naval Race, 9–10
New Zealand, 39, 103
New Zealanders, 37
Nicholas II, Tsar, 30, 72
Nivelle, General Robert, 58, 59, 60, 79, 80, 81

Painlevé, Paul, 79, 81, 82
Passchendaele (Third Ypres), 82–5
  Broodseinde, 85
  casualties, 85
  Haig's plans, 82–3
  Langemarck, 84
  Passchendaele village, 85
  Pilckem Ridge, 84
  Poelcapelle, 85
  Polygon Wood, 84
Payer, Friedrich von, 72, 97, 98, 99
Pétain, General Philippe, 56, 57, 58, 59, 60, 61, 63, 67, 79, 80, 81, 82, 95, 107
Plumer, Sir Herbert, 83, 84, 85
Poincaré, Raymond, 82
Poland, Germany proclaims independent kingdom of, 68
Prittwitz, General Max von, 20
Propaganda, 14, 42–4, 52

Rawlinson, General Sir Henry, 34, 36, 62, 63, 65, 66, 76, 82, 84, 95
Raynal, Major Sylvain, 58
Rennenkampf, General Pavel, 20, 21
Ribot, Alexandre, 79
Richthofen, Baron Manfred von, 74
Robeck, Admiral John de, 38
Robertson, General Sir William, 82, 83
Rumania, 60, 77, 92
Rupprecht, Crown Prince of Bavaria, 14, 67, 85, 93, 94
Russia
  February Revolution 1917, 71–2
  Germany, 7
  invasion of East Prussia, 20–2
  loss of Russian Poland, 29–30
  war plans, 9

Samsonov, General Alexander, 20, 21
Sassoon, Siegfried, 31, 103, 111
Scheer, Vice-Admiral Reinhard, 51–2
Schlieffen Plan, 4, 5, 7, 11–14, 22
Schlieffen, General Count Alfred von, 7, 8, 13, 16, 18
Seeckt, Hans von, 29
Serbia, 3, 8, 22
Shell shock, first appearance, 37
Smith-Dorrien, General Sir Horace, 17
Smuts, Field Marshal Jan, 75
Social Democratic Party of Germany (SPD), 25, 70
Soldiers, front
  behaviour, 30–4
  newspapers, 32
  slang, 32
  songs, 32
Stab In the Back legend, 99
Stopford, General Sir Frederick, 39
Swinton, Col. Ernest, 76

Tactical innovation, 77–8
Tanks, 75–7, 81, 93, 95
Thaer, Col. Albrecht von, 95
Tirpitz, Admiral Alfred von, 10, 45, 47, 69
Trench system, 19, 23, 30–1
Trenchard, General Hugh, 74
Turkey, 37

U-Boats, 45–7
United States of America
  a negotiated peace, 71
  Amiens, 95
  Argonne, 97
  British blockade, 47
  British propaganda, 44
  and Ireland, 70
  Ludendorff's thinking, 92
  Lusitania, 47
  strategic air power, 75
  submarine warfare, 46, 47, 48, 61, 69, 71
  tanks, 76–7
  war losses, 103
  Zimmermann Telegram, 71

Verdun, 52–61
  Avocourt, 57
  Bois de Caures, 54
  Côte 304, 57, 61
  Falkenhayn's plan, 53
  Fort Douaumont, 53, 54, 60
  Fort Moulainville, 53
  Fort Souville, 59, 60
  Fort Vaux, 53, 57, 58, 59
  French counter-attack, 60–1
  Mort Homme, 57
  the Bois Bourrus, 57
  the Voie Sacrée, 56

War
  distinct periods, 13
  restoring movement to, 23
  technology, 5–6
War fever and 'Spirit of August', 25–7
War-weariness, 51, 61, 69, 71, 72, 82, 91
Wellington House, 44
Wells, H. G., 28
Western Front, 18
  Aisne, 23, 67, 69
  Arras, 36, 74, 79, 80
  Artois, 36, 52
  Aubers Ridge, 36
  Battles of Frontiers 1914, 13–14
  Cambrai, 76, 91, 97
  Canal du Nord, 97
  Champagne region, 36
  First Ypres, 19–20
  German spring offensive, 93–5
  Guise, 17
  Hamel, 95
  Le Cateau, 17
  Lens, 36

Liège, 14, 20, 53
Loos, 36, 37, 44
Lorraine, 8, 9, 14, 17
Messines Ridge, 65, 83
Mons, 15–16
Neuve Chapelle, 34, 36, 44
Nivelle Offensive, 80
Reims, 80, 95
Second Ypres, 29
St. Quentin, 17, 93
the Marne, 12–13
the Somme, 61–7
the Somme: Courcelette, 67
the Somme: Beaumont-Hamel, 64
Villers-Cotterets, 95
Vimy Ridge, 36, 62, 79, 80, 83, 84
Wilhelm II, Kaiser, 10, 20, 25, 46, 47, 52, 53, 60, 72, 93, 95, 96, 97, 98, 106
Wilson, Trevor, 13, 23
Wilson, President Woodrow, 47, 70, 71, 91, 93, 99, 105, 107
Winter, J. W., 41, 103

Zimmermann, Arthur, 71

SEMINAR STUDIES   IN HISTORY

General Editors: Clive Emsley & Gordon Martel

The series was founded by Patrick Richardson in 1966. Between 1980 and 1996 Roger Lockyer edited the series before handing over to Clive Emsley (Professor of History at the Open University) and Gordon Martel (Professor of International History at the University of Northern British Columbia, Canada, and Senior Research Fellow at De Montfort University).

MEDIEVAL ENGLAND

The Pre-Reformation Church in England 1400–1530 (Second edition)
Christopher Harper-Bill

Lancastrians and Yorkists: The Wars of the Roses
David R. Cook

Family and Kinship in England 1450–1800
Will Coster

TUDOR ENGLAND

Henry VII (Third edition)
Roger Lockyer & Andrew Thrush

Tudor Rebellions (Fifth edition)
Anthony Fletcher & Diarmaid MacCulloch

The Reign of Mary I (Second edition)
Robert Tittler

Early Tudor Parliaments 1485–1558
Michael A.R. Graves

The English Reformation 1530–1570
W.J. Sheils

Elizabethan Parliaments 1559–1601 (Second edition)
Michael A.R. Graves

England and Europe 1485–1603 (Second edition)
Susan Doran

The Church of England 1570–1640
Andrew Foster

STUART BRITAIN

Social Change and Continuity: England 1550–1750 (Second edition)
Barry Coward

James I (Second edition)
S.J. Houston

The English Civil War 1640–1649
Martyn Bennett

Charles I, 1625–1640
Brian Quintrell

The English Republic 1649–1660 (Second edition)
Toby Barnard

Radical Puritans in England 1550–1660
R.J. Acheson

The Restoration and the England of Charles II (Second edition)
John Miller

The Glorious Revolution (Second edition)
John Miller

EARLY MODERN EUROPE

The Renaissance (Second edition)
Alison Brown

The Emperor Charles V
Martyn Rady

French Renaissance Monarchy: Francis I and Henry II (Second edition)
Robert Knecht

The Protestant Reformation in Europe
Andrew Johnston

The French Wars of Religion 1559–1598 (Second edition)
Robert Knecht

Phillip II
Geoffrey Woodward

Louis XIV
Peter Campbell

Spain in the Seventeenth Century
Graham Darby

The Origins of French Absolutism, 1598–1661
Alan James

EUROPE 1789–1918

Britain and the French Revolution
Clive Emsley

Revolution and Terror in France 1789–1795 (Second edition)
D.G. Wright

Napoleon and Europe
D.G. Wright

The Abolition of Serfdom in Russia 1762–1907
David Moon

Nineteenth-Century Russia: Opposition to Autocracy
Derek Offord

The Constitutional Monarchy in France 1814–48
Pamela Pilbeam

The 1848 Revolutions (Second edition)
Peter Jones

The Italian Risorgimento
M. Clark

Bismarck & Germany 1862–1890 (Second edition)
D.G. Williamson

Imperial Germany 1890–1918
Ian Porter, Ian Armour & Roger Lockyer

The Dissolution of the Austro-Hungarian Empire 1867–1918 (Second edition)
John W. Mason

France 1870–1914 (Second edition)
Robert Gildea

The Scramble for Africa (Second edition)
M.E. Chamberlain

Late Imperial Russia 1890–1917
John F. Hutchinson

The First World War (Second edition)
Stuart Robson

Austria, Prussia and Germany 1806–1871
John Breuilly

Napoleon: Conquest, Reform and Reorganisation
Clive Emsley

The French Revolution 1787–1804
Peter Jones

The Origins of the First World War (Third edition)
Gordon Martel

Women and the First World War
Susan R. Grayzel

The Birth of Industrial Britain
Kenneth Morgan

EUROPE SINCE 1918

The Russian Revolution (Second edition)
Anthony Wood

Lenin's Revolution: Russia 1917–1921
David Marples

Stalin and Stalinism (Third edition)
Martin McCauley

The Weimar Republic (Second edition)
John Hiden

The Inter-War Crisis 1919–1939
Richard Overy

Fascism and the Right in Europe 1919–1945
Martin Blinkhorn

Spain's Civil War (Second edition)
Harry Browne

The Third Reich (Third edition)
D.G. Williamson

The Origins of the Second World War (Second edition)
R.J. Overy

The Second World War in Europe
Paul MacKenzie

The French at War 1934–1944
Nicholas Atkin

Anti-Semitism before the Holocaust
Albert S. Lindemann

The Holocaust: The Third Reich and the Jews
David Engel

Germany from Defeat to Partition 1945–1963
D.G. Williamson

Britain and Europe since 1945
Alex May

Eastern Europe 1945–1969: From Stalinism to Stagnation
Ben Fowkes

Eastern Europe since 1970
Bülent Gökay

The Khrushchev Era 1953–1964
Martin McCauley

Hitler and the Rise of the Nazi Party
Frank McDonough

The Soviet Union Under Brezhnev
William Tompson

The European Union since 1945
Alasdair Blair

NINETEENTH-CENTURY BRITAIN

Britain before the Reform Acts: Politics and Society 1815–1832
Eric J. Evans

Parliamentary Reform in Britain c. 1770–1918
Eric J. Evans

Democracy and Reform 1815–1885
D.G. Wright

Poverty and Poor Law Reform in Nineteenth-Century Britain 1834–1914: From Chadwick to Booth
David Englander

The Birth of Industrial Britain: Economic Change 1750–1850
Kenneth Morgan

Chartism (Third edition)
Edward Royle

Peel and the Conservative Party 1830–1850
Paul Adelman

Gladstone, Disraeli and later Victorian Politics (Third edition)
Paul Adelman

Britain and Ireland: From Home Rule to Independence
Jeremy Smith

TWENTIETH-CENTURY BRITAIN

The Rise of the Labour Party 1880–1945 (Third edition)
Paul Adelman

The Conservative Party and British Politics 1902–1951
Stuart Ball

The Decline of the Liberal Party 1910–1931 (Second edition)
Paul Adelman

The British Women's Suffrage Campaign 1866–1928
Harold L. Smith

War & Society in Britain 1899–1948
Rex Pope

The British Economy since 1914: A Study in Decline?
Rex Pope

Unemployment in Britain between the Wars
Stephen Constantine

The Atlee Governments 1945–1951
Kevin Jefferys

Britain under Thatcher
Anthony Seldon & Daniel Collings

Britain and Empire 1880–1945
Dane Kennedy

INTERNATIONAL HISTORY

The Eastern Question 1774–1923 (Second edition)
A.L. Macfie

The United States and the First World War
Jennifer D. Keene

Anti-Semitism before the Holocaust
Albert S. Lindemann

The Origins of the Cold War 1941–1949 (Third edition)
Martin McCauley

Russia, America and the Cold War 1949–1991 (Second edition)
Martin McCauley

The Arab–Israeli Conflict
Kirsten E. Schulze

The United Nations since 1945: Peacekeeping and the Cold War
Norrie MacQueen

Decolonisation: The British Experience since 1945
Nicholas J. White

The Collapse of the Soviet Union
David R. Marples

WORLD HISTORY

China in Transformation 1900–1949
Colin Mackerras

Japan Faces the World 1925–1952
Mary L. Hanneman

Japan in Transformation 1952–2000
Jeff Kingston

China since 1949
Linda Benson

South Africa: The Rise and Fall of Apartheid
Nancy L. Clark & William H. Worger

Race and Empire
Jane Samson

India 1885–1947: The Unmaking of an Empire
Ian Copland

India under Colonial Rule: 1700–1885
Douglas M. Peers

US HISTORY

American Abolitionists
Stanley Harrold

The American Civil War 1861–1865
Reid Mitchell

America in the Progressive Era 1890–1914
Lewis L. Gould

The United States and the First World War
Jennifer D. Keene

The Truman Years 1945–1953
Mark S. Byrnes

The Korean War
Steven Hugh Lee

The Origins of the Vietnam War
Fredrik Logevall

The Vietnam War (Second edition)
Mitchell K. Hall

American Expansionism 1783–1860
Mark S. Joy

The United States and Europe in the Twentieth Century
David Ryan

The Civil Rights Movement
Bruce J. Dierenfield